THE CHURCH

De Ecclesia

THE CHURCH

BY

JOHN HUSS

TRANSLATED, WITH NOTES AND INTRODUCTION

BY

DAVID S. SCHAFF, D.D.

PROFESSOR OF CHURCH HISTORY, THE WESTERN THEOLOGICAL SEMINARY

Nemo tenetur quidquam credere nisi ad quod movet eum deus credere sed deus non movet hominem ad credendum falsum.

No one is held to believe anything except what he is moved by God to believe but God moves no man to believe what is false.

—John Huss, this treatise, p. 49.

GREENWOOD PRESS, PUBLISHERS
WESTPORT, CONNECTICUT

Library of Congress Cataloging in Publication Data

Hus, Jan, 1369?-1415.
  The church.

  Translation of De ecclesia.
  Reprint of the 1915 ed. published by Scribner, New
York.
  1. Church. I. Title.
BV600.A2H95 1974   260   72-109752
ISBN 0-8371-4242-3

Originally published in 1915 by Charles Scribner's Sons, New York

Reprinted from an original copy in the collections of the University
of Illinois Library

Reprinted in 1974 by Greenwood Press,
a division of Williamhouse-Regency Inc.

Library of Congress Catalogue Card Number 72-109752

ISBN 0-8371-4242-3

Printed in the United States of America

WYCLIF—

Vita et doctrina Christi sunt optimum speculum . . . cum manifestum sit quod omnis homo et solum talis qui est in vita et doctrina Christo contrarius est hereticus, et omnis christianus et solum talis qui est in vita et doctrina Christo conformis est ut sic ab heresi elongatus. —De Ecclesia, p. 41.

The life and teaching of Christ are the best mirror . . . for it is evident that every man who in life and teaching is contrary to Christ and only such a man is a heretic: and every Christian who in life and teaching is conformed to Christ and only such a Christian is removed from heresy.

HUSS—

Spero, ex Dei gratia, quod sum christianus ex integro, a fide non devians, et quod potius vellem pati diræ mortis supplicium, quam aliquid vellem præter fidem asserere, vel transgredi mandata Domini Jesu Christi. —Ad Palecz, Mon., 1 : 325.

I hope, by God's grace, that I am truly a Christian, not deviating from the faith, and that I would rather suffer the penalty of a terrible death than wish to affirm anything outside of the faith or transgress the commandments of our Lord Jesus Christ.

LUTHER—

Verum qui, in agone mortis, Jesum filium Dei passum pro nobis, invocat et ob talem causam tanta fiducia ac constantia in ignem conjicit sese, si is non magnanimum et fortem Christi martyrem sese præbet, haud facile quisquam salvus erit.—Preface to some of Huss's writings, 1527.

Truly he—Huss—who in the agony of death invoked Jesus Christ, the Son of God, who suffered for us, and for such a cause and with such faith and steadfastness threw himself into the fire, if he did not show himself a noble and brave martyr of Christ, then will scarcely any one be saved.

v

INTRODUCTION

Of the writings of John Huss of Bohemia, the *Treatise on the Church* is the most important.[1] From its pages the charges were drawn upon which the author was pronounced a heretic by the council of Constance and the same day, July 6, 1415, burned at the stake. It was written in Latin and the translation, here offered, is the first that has appeared in English and seems to be the first to be issued in any language. It is offered as a help in the appreciation of a memorable man who deserves well of Western Christendom and as a contribution to the study of ecclesiology.

I. THE AUTHOR. John Huss is the chief religious character of Bohemia, as Luther is of Germany, and John Knox of Scotland; and he is the one contribution his country has made to the progress of religious thought and of culture in Western Christendom. His fame it has been possible for several centuries to obscure through the semi-mythical personality of the Roman Catholic saint, John Nepomuk, but recently Huss's eminence as a notable preacher and an unselfish patriot has come to recognition among his people, and in Southern Bohemia, though it is loyal to the Roman Catholic church, his memory is yearly celebrated.[2]

Born in 1373, Huss studied at the university of Prague— then in the golden period of its history. In 1403, he was made its rector, holding the position six months and later,

---

[1] Loserth, who pronounces the same judgment, says that the treatise has inspired friends and foes alike with deep respect, *Wiclif and Hus*, p. 182. Huss's main treatise attacking John XXIII's bulls of indulgences and his *Reply to the Eight Doctors, Monumenta*, 1 : 215–237; 366–402, are more spirited and make the impression of being more direct, because they are less encumbered by quotations from the canon law and other sources.

[2] For details of Huss's life, see Schaff, *Life of John Huss*, N. Y., 1915.

vii

in 1409, for the term of a year. In 1403, he was also appointed preacher at Bethlehem chapel which had been founded ten years before to afford preaching in the native Czech tongue. Under Huss the chapel became the most conspicuous religious centre of the city next to the cathedral of St. Vite and the centre of a national movement. His sermons at once attracted attention by their Scriptural fervor and by their attacks upon the abuses of the clergy. As Æneas Sylvius bears witness,[1] he was forcible in speech; and his purity of character was such that no charge was ever made against it in Bohemia or during his trial in Constance. The hostility of the clergy, which his attacks aroused, followed him till his death.

There were three specific movements, which involved Huss in trouble and brought on violent dissension in Prague. ⚹The first was the spread of Wyclif's views. Soon after Wyclif's death, 1384, his writings were carried to Bohemia, where they made as deep an impression as in Wyclif's own country. His views had been pronounced heretical by Gregory XI and what was heresy in England was heresy in Bohemia. By some of the Prague clergy XLV Articles said to contain Wyclif's views were brought to the attention of the university, 1403, for its decision. In spite of Huss's protest and the protest of Palecz and Stanislaus of Znaim, Huss's intimate friends, and other members of the theological faculty, the writings were forbidden to be read or taught. Huss declined to accept the decision, and was charged with declaring for the remanence of the bread and wine after the words of institution and with publicly announcing the pious hope, that Wyclif's soul was among the saved. Vigilant for the interests of the orthodox faith, the clergy hostile to Huss appealed to Rome, and first Innocent VII and later the Pisan pontiff, Alexander V, instructed Zbynek, archbishop of Prague, to proceed against Wyclifite heresy, and Alexander ordered

[1] *Hist. of Bohemia*, chap. XXXV.

chapels, such as Huss preached in, to be closed. Against Huss's open protest the archbishop seized two hundred of Wyclif's writings and made a bonfire of them in the court-yard of his palace, 1410. After this event, Huss publicly defended one of Wyclif's writings, the tract on the Trinity.

⨂ A second movement which involved Huss in violent controversy and trouble was the change in the charter of the university, 1409. By this change the Czech element was given three votes, and the foreign nations reduced from three to one. Against Huss, the recognized leader of the movement, was aroused the bitter opposition of the German population which exercised an influence in the city out of all proportion to its numbers. · In this issue the court party was on Huss's side, but the hostility of the Germans, so Huss felt, thenceforth threatened even his very life.

⨂ The third cause of trouble for Huss was his attack, in 1412, upon the sale of indulgences authorized by John XXIII to enable him to carry on a crusade against Ladislaus, king of Naples. Deserted over this issue by most of his intimate friends at the university, Huss nevertheless spoke out as boldly as Luther did a hundred years later against the unholy traffic. He had already refused to obey a citation to Rome and was now placed under the ban of excommunication by the curia. This proving ineffective, the city of Prague was put under the interdict. In the meantime, Huss had appealed from the apostolic see to Christ himself, as the just judge and the supreme ruler of the church.[1]

The interdict meant moral and religious starvation. In part to avert the calamity of a cessation of divine ministries and heeding the friendly counsel of the king, Wenzel, Huss withdrew from Prague and spent the next two years, from the fall of 1412 to October, 1414, in the rural districts of Bohemia, protected by powerful members of the nobility,

---

[1] Palacky, *Documenta*, 192, 464-466, 726. See Schaff, *Life of Huss*, pp. 138, etc.

and preaching in the villages and on the fields and active with his pen.

The œcumenical council, which was appointed to meet at Constance in 1414, seemed to offer an opportunity for a fair hearing of Huss's case and the removal from Bohemia of the ill-fame of heresy which now attached to it. For Huss's name was spread all through Europe and was scarcely less notorious than Wyclif's. Provided with a safe-conduct by Sigismund, heir of his brother Wenzel and of the empire, Huss proceeded to the council but, soon after his arrival in Constance, was seized by the cardinals and consigned to prison, where he languished till death put an end to his trials.

Examined by one commission after another, including among its members such eminent men as d'Ailly and Cardinal Zabarella, he persistently refused to abjure, unwilling, as he professed, to offend against God and his conscience. On July 6, 1415, the council in full session charged him with thirty errors and turned him over to the civil authority to suffer the penalty appointed for heretics, death in the flames.

II. THE CIRCUMSTANCES under which the treatise was written. The immediate occasion of the writing of the Treatise on the Church was a document signed by eight doctors belonging to the theological faculty of the university, dated February 6, 1413. Its immediate occasion was the papal bulls calling for a crusade against that refractory Christian prince, Ladislaus of Naples, and the sale of indulgences on the streets of Prague. It asserted the duty of absolute submission to the commands of pope and other ecclesiastical superiors, condemned the XLV Wyclifite Articles as scandalous and heretical and demanded that the kingdom of Bohemia be cleared of heresy, if necessary by the severest ecclesiastical and also civil punishments.[1] The Bohemian clergy and nation, it affirmed, were in complete accord in all matters of belief and worship with the Roman

[1] For the text in Latin and Czech, *Doc.*, 475–485.

church—*tenet et credit fideliter sicut Romana ecclesia et non aliter*—the pope being the head of the Roman church and the college of cardinals its body. Of all names, so the doctors confessed, the name heretic is the most to be abhorred. As for the sentences pronounced by Rome upon Huss, it was not within the province of the clergy of Prague to sit in judgment upon them—*nec est cleri in Praga judicare si justa vel injusta est M. J. Hus excommunicatio et aggravatio a curia romana.*

These and other positions of the eight doctors the Treatise on the Church takes up one by one and discusses. Huss's work called forth replies from Palecz and Stanislaus of Znaim, two of the signers of the document, and to each Huss made a rejoinder as he also wrote a more elaborate and very vigorous rejoinder addressed to the eight doctors as a body.[1] In the first two of these rejoinders Huss cites his Treatise on the Church by name at least eleven times, and in the Reply to the Eight Doctors at least five times.[2] The Treatise on the Church grows in interest as it is read in connection with these three cognate works, which further elucidate some of its principles and add items of personal interest.

Intended as a reply to the document issued by the eight theological doctors, this treatise became Huss's *apologia pro sua vita*, the defense of the views which he had drawn from Wyclif and advocated. With Cajetan before Luther at Augsburg, the eight doctors knew of only one word applicable to Huss, the word recant. His case was not arguable. Unquestioning submission was imperative. Rome had spoken: "Yield and obey," they wrote—*obediendum et pariendum est.*[3] Huss's final reply was not recorded with pen or expressed by word of mouth. He sealed his convictions with his life at Constance.

[1] The text is given in *Mon.*, 1 : 318–331; 331–365; 365–408.

[2] *Mon.*, 1 : 320, 321, 323, 328, 329, 335, etc. In the rejoinder to the eight doctors the Reply to Stanislaus is quoted at least twice.

[3] *Doc.*, 1 : 480.

III. CONTENTS. Huss's line of thought runs as follows: First, the author defines the church and its headship. He proceeds by discussing the authority of the pope and the college of cardinals. The power of the keys is then taken up at length, and the limits in ecclesiastical matters of the authority of superiors over inferiors examined. Finally, the Scriptures are set forth as the sufficient standard of faith and conduct. The conclusions, thus reached, Huss then applies to his own case of alleged contumacy to the mandates of his ecclesiastical superiors with the result that a Christian's supreme duty is to the Scriptures and God, for, as he often repeats: "We ought to obey God rather than men."

Not only are these main principles also discussed in the three rejoinders referred to above, but they are taken up in other works such as his Six Errors,—*de sex Erroribus*—his Attack on the Bulls of Indulgence, his Reply to an Occult Adversary and in his letters written during the period of his semi-voluntary exile from Prague and his imprisonment at Constance, especially his letters to Christian Prachaticz, rector of the university of Prague.[1]

In the following fundamental positions the Treatise on the Church opposed the accredited ecclesiastical system which the fifteenth century had inherited from the age of the Schoolmen.

1. The Church.[2] The holy catholic—or universal—church is the body of the predestinate in heaven, earth and purgatory. The church is either general or particular. Wherever two or three are gathered together in Christ's name there is the church, whether in India, Greece, Spain, Rome or any other locality. The church is one throughout the world. The bond of unity is predestinating grace or, as Huss also put it, faith, hope and love.[3] The pope, as he affirmed dis-

[1] *Doc.*, 54–63. [2] Especially chaps. I–VII.
[3] Pp. 14, 49, 59 etc.

tinctly, is not the bond of Christiar unity, and nowhere does he represent the sacraments as the bond of unity.

Following Augustine, Huss proceeds to show that the church is a mixed body, made up of predestinate and *præsciti*, or reprobate, and he uses the parable of the net and other parables to prove it. Although according to the popular opinion—*vocationem vulgarem et reputationem ecclesiasticam*— all Christians are members of the church militant, yet it is one thing, Huss affirmed, to be in the church and another to be of the church. Judas was in the church for a season, but ultimately lost, and Paul by predestination was of it even during the period of his persecuting activity, when he was not in it.[1]

These definitions set aside the following views which prevailed in Huss's time.

The pope and the cardinals do not constitute the church. This was a wide-spread popular conception and Huss is at great pains to prove its fallacy. The document of the eight doctors had so defined the church. Wyclif, before Huss, had said that "the public understands by the Roman church the pope and the cardinals."[2]

The church is not confined to the body over which the apostolic see has jurisdiction. The particular Roman church is a company of the faithful living under the obedience of Rome, as the companies of the faithful living under the obedience of Antioch and Constantinople were called the church of Antioch and the church of Constantinople. In a notable passage in one of his letters to Prachaticz, Huss said succinctly: "The Roman church is not the catholic apostolic church, for no partial church can be the holy catholic church.

[1] Pp. 16 *sq.*, 21, 30 *sqq.*, 41 *sqq.*, 58, etc. Huss's word *præsciti*, or foreknown, does not contain all that the word reprobate means, although they are one in this that they both imply ultimate perdition. The first word does not involve an active decree of reprobation which the word reprobate is usually taken to involve.

[2] Pp. 58, etc., Wyclif's words are: *Communitas intelligit per Rom. eccles. papam et cardinales quibus est necessarium omnibus aliis obedire. de Eccles.*, 92.

However, among the militant churches the Roman church is the principal one." [1]

The church is not inerrant. One of the proofs given is that the church chose Agnes, a woman, pope and consented to be ruled over by her. Indeed, the Roman church with the pope and cardinals may be transformed into Sodom, but against the Church of Christ the gates of hell cannot prevail.[2]

Pope and prelates are not necessarily in authority by reason of appointment or election to office.[3] They only are true officials, and only the authority of those prelates is to be acknowledged, whose lives are in accordance with Christ's precepts. The standard of judgment is found in the words, "by their fruits ye shall know them," a passage Huss quoted again and again.[4]

All these assertions make straight in the direction of the rights of private judgment. On that principle Huss justified his refusal to obey the Roman pontiff and other ecclesiastical superiors.

2. The Papacy. The Roman pontiff is not the head of the church on earth. Christ is the head. Not by delegated authority does Christ's promise, "Lo, I am with you alway," become effective. Every predestinate person is immediately joined to him and receives from him grace and religious power even as the body receives sensation and guidance from the head. Were this not the case, the church would have many times been acephalous, without a head, as in the interims between the death of one pontiff and the election of his successor. The pope, so the doctors affirmed, is the head of the whole militant church, its heart, its navel, its unfailing fountain, and its all-sufficient refuge—*caput, cor,*

---

[1] Pp. 62, 63, etc., *Doc.*, 59.

[2] *Fallit et fallitur*, pp. 133 sq., etc.; *Doc.*, 59; also *ad Palecz, Mon.*, 1 : 323, 336; *Doc.*, 61, etc.; *tota militans eccles. errat in multis quæ concernunt div. judicium et statum, Mon.*, 1 : 227, 233, 358 sq.

[3] Especially chap. XIV.   [4] Pp. 136, 143, 145, 160, 182.

alveus, fons indeficiens et refugium sufficientissimum. In view
of such statements, Huss affirms that the doctors treated the
Roman pontiff as a fourth person in divine things and placed
him on an equality with the Holy Spirit.[1]

In the course of his discussion on the papal office, Huss
presents the following views:

The rock upon which the church is built, Matt. 16 : 18,
is Christ and not Peter.[2] The Apostles called Christ the
foundation. To Christ, not to Peter, did the patriarchs look
forward; and the early Christians did not base their faith
on the Apostle.

The Roman pontiff shares authority with other bishops
of the church, as Peter shared authority with the other
Apostles. Christ did not give the care of all the sheep to
Peter even as he did not exclusively give him the power to
preach and administer the sacraments.[3]

The word pope is not a Scriptural word and in the early
history of the church there were a number of popes.[4] Originally all bishops were called popes, and these were equally
the immediate vicars of Christ.

The pope is not infallible. In matters of faith popes
may err and have erred—*falli et fallere possunt.* They may
be led astray by avarice or be deceived by ignorance.[5]

The pope may also be a heretic and, as a matter of fact,
before the fifteenth century there had been both wicked
men and heretics on the papal chair. Here Huss drew for

[1] Especially chap. XIII. See *ad Palecz, ad Stanisl.,* and *ad octo doctt., Mon.,*
1 : 320 *sq.,* 326, 350, 353, 385, etc.; *Ponat doctor papam omnino sufficiens refugium omnibus filiis ecclesiæ sicut est Spiritus s. et dicam quod posuit quartam
personam in divinis,* 1 : 354.

[2] Pp. 59 *sq.,* etc., especially chap. IX. This formed the subject of the ninth
charge made against Huss at Constance. In his *Super IV. Sent.,* Huss did
not refer to the famous passage, Matt. 16 : 18. Comp. p. 559.

[3] Comp. *ad Palecz,* etc., *Mon.,* 1 : 320, 353, 356, etc.

[4] *Plures papæ, ad Palecz, Mon.,* 1 : 326, 342. Pope means father and was
first limited to the Roman pontiff by order of Gregory VII.

[5] Pp. 61, 66, 71. See also *Mon.,* 1 : 227, 233, 343, 359, etc.; *Doc.,*
58, etc.

historical data upon the Chronicles of Ranulph Higden, Martinus Polonus, and Rudolph Glaber.[1]

Repeatedly did Huss return to the list of popes heretical and popes flagitious. The rudest layman, a woman, a heretic, yea antichrist himself may be a pope.[2] But in none of these lists does the name of Honorius I appear, the pontiff on whose case Bishop Hefele, in 1870, rested the argument against the doctrine of papal infallibility.

Among the heretical popes Huss included Boniface VIII and Clement VII of the fourteenth century and, as more recent cases of papal errors, he cited the acts of Boniface IX setting aside Wenzel as king of the Romans and Sigismund as king of Hungary. During his trial Huss had another instance at hand of a disreputable pontiff in John XXIII, accepted by almost the whole of Western Christendom and then deposed for crimes and iniquities unspeakable. Huss also recalled that Gregory XII and Benedict XIII were pronounced heretics by the council of Pisa.[3]

But the case on which Huss laid most stress was the papissa Agnes who, according to the universal opinion of his time, occupied under the name of John VIII the papal office for more than two years. Gerson used her as a proof that it is possible for the church to err. It was monstrous, so Huss thought, for a female to rule Christendom, and such a female—a woman of unsavory repute before she was made pope and revealing her sex by the sudden birth of a child on one of the streets of the holy city.[4]

[1] Especially chap. XVII. Huss also presented these views from the pulpit. See *Life of Huss*, p. 38.

[2] *Mon.*, 1 : 342. In his *Theol. Symbolics*, p. 231, Doctor Briggs brushes aside the case of Honorius I as not pertinent, without even mentioning the names of Döllinger, Hefele, and other eminent Catholic historians who have taken the view that he was manifestly a heretic.

[3] *Mon.*, 1 : 232. Though the council of Pisa was treated as œcumenical by the council of Constance and was formerly accepted by accredited Roman Catholic historians, it is now universally disowned in the Catholic church.

[4] Some of the other references to Agnes outside this treatise are: *Mon.*, 1 : 324, 326, 336, 339, 343, 344, 347, etc.; *Doc.*, 58, 61, etc.

Huss went still further, in declaring that popes may be *præsciti*, reprobates, though legitimately elected to their office. Without definitely assigning by name this or that pontiff to hell, as did Dante, yet Huss declared that popes there have been who had conferred ample indulgences by word— *verbaliter*—and are damned. Christ chose a thief as an Apostle: so may the cardinals choose an antichrist as Roman pontiff. The only standard by which it can be judged whether a pope is a vicar of Christ or antichrist is by his conformity to the law of Christ in daily life and ministries.[1]

The outward display assumed by popes, the kissing of their feet, the name most holy—*sanctissimus*—by which they allowed themselves to be addressed, Huss stigmatized, as Luther did a hundred years later, as incompatible with their holy office.[2]

The origin of all this false pomp Huss found, as Wyclif did before him, in the donation of Constantine, the fictitious gift passed off upon credulous Europe by the pseudo-Isidorian Decretals in the ninth century and to which appeal continued to be made down to Alexander VI in his bull distributing America between Spain and Portugal "forever," and later. As a compensation for being healed of leprosy by Sylvester, Constantine bequeathed to that pontiff and his successors civil rule over Rome and all the regions of the West and conferred upon them the crown and the other insignia of temporal lordship and glory. This imperial gift, Wyclif and Huss contended, was the beginning of the decline of the church from its pristine purity, and modern— *moderni*—popes and cardinals who protruded their feet to be kissed and gloried in the address "most holy" did not possess a scintilla of sanctity and utterly lacked the power

[1] Pp. 62, 128, also *Mon.*, 1 : 229, 322, 328, 335, 339 *sqq.*, 343, etc.; *Doc.*, 58, 60, etc. The term antichrist Huss defined as "one who acts contrary to Christ."
[2] Chaps. XIII, XIV, etc.; *Mon.*, 322, 323, etc. Huss nowhere alluded to the divine titles assumed by Roman emperors such as "Lord God" by Domitian and our most holy lord—*sacratissimus dominus noster*—by Diocletian.

of the early rulers of the church, so that the demons could say of them: "Paul I know and Peter I know, but who are you?" With Gregory the Great, Huss affirmed that the name does not make the bishop but the life.[1]

One of the conclusions drawn in this treatise, as also in other treatises from Huss's hand, is that the church once got along very well without popes. And she might get along well without them again, Chapter XV.

A second conclusion was that papal decrees are not always to be obeyed. To rebel against an erring pope Huss boldly said was to obey God. So clear and emphatic were Huss's views on this subject that Luther declared that "Huss committed no more atrocious sin than to profess that a pope of an impious life is not the head of the church catholic. He conceded he was the head of a church, but not of the catholic church. Truly he ought to have said: 'No matter how criminal and wicked the pontifex maximus is yet ought he to be venerated for sanctity. He cannot err and all that he says and does is to be accepted and treated as an article of the faith.' The good men at Constance disposed of three wicked popes and would not allow them to be taken to the fire: but Huss was sentenced to death."[2]

3. The Power of the Keys. Huss's chief statements are as follows: The Apostles, as has already been said, were all the immediate vicars of Christ, Peter's authority not being universal and total but partial and particular. Without recourse to Peter the remaining Apostles ordained bishops and presbyters, taught and pastured.[3] Thomas, the Apostle to India, was not appointed by Peter, nor was Matthias.

---

[1] Pp. 143, 153, also *Mon.*, 1 : 320, 383, etc.; *Doc.*, 291, etc. In this connection we easily think of Thomas Aquinas who, visiting the pope, was shown the treasures of the Vatican with the words: "See, Thomas, Peter could no more say, 'Silver and gold have I none'"; to which Thomas replied: "Nor could he now say, 'Rise upon thy feet and walk.'"

[2] Preface to Huss's writings, 1537.

[3] Pp. 82, 110, also *Mon.*, 1 : 345, 353, 356, etc.

James presided as a superior over the conclave at Jerusalem and Paul required no human license—*sine licentia*—to preach and to rule.

Not only all bishops but all presbyters are successors of the Apostles, as originally the church was governed by presbyters. For this view Huss quoted Jerome's famous statement.[1]

It must be remembered that in the Middle Ages the episcopate was not looked upon as a distinct order. The three orders, according to Thomas Aquinas, were the subdeacon, deacon and priest.

The keys were conferred upon the church, Matt. 18 : 17, 18, and in binding and loosing, Peter acted as a representative of the church. The church is the final tribunal. In giving the power to Peter, Christ gave it in his person to every presbyter whatsoever.[2]

Priestly acts of all kinds are invalid except as the priest's life is conformed to Christ's law.[3] No one has ever more clearly laid stress on the necessity of purity of life to the clerical office than Huss.

The power of the keys, or of remitting sins and retaining them, is a declaratory power such as the priest under the old dispensation exercised in pronouncing the leper clean and as the disciples exercised in loosing Lazarus, John 11 : 44. The priest did not make the leper clean nor did the disciples release Lazarus from the bonds of death. Neither pope nor priest can absolve from sin except where God has before absolved. As Huss said in his attack against John XXIII's bulls, the pope's act in absolving is nothing more than the announcement of a herald—*factum papæ ad maximum non est nisi præconis Dei promulgatio.*[4] Peter bade Simon Magus

---

[1] P. 155.

[2] Chap. X, *Christus dicit Petro et in persona ejus cuicunque suo presbytero: quodcunque solveris,* etc., *ad octo doctores, Mon.,* 1 : 387.

[3] Pp. 47–50, also *Mon.,* 1 : 378, 383, 387 sq., 392, etc.

[4] *Mon.,* 1 : 227, also 228, 378, 392. This treatise, p. 101 sqq.

call upon the Lord for indulgence which he could not himself grant.

In his *Commentary on the Sentences of the Lombard* Huss presents substantially the same view that he presents in this treatise and the cognate writings, but not so boldly. There, he says, no one can be excommunicated unless he is first excommunicated by himself and except he offends against Christ's law.[1] In his treatise on The Six Errors, Huss quotes Peter the Lombard to show that the remission by a priest is a different thing from remission by God who remits of Himself, purifying the soul of guilt and loosing it from the debt of eternal death. Did the pope possess the power of the keys in the way generally supposed, as a thing of his own, then he might empty purgatory itself, and, if he neglected to do so, he would be guilty of ill-will or indifference. On the question of absolution Huss is most emphatic, and he restates his views again and again. No saint, he says, could be found who had the presumption to say: "I have forgiven thee thy sins," or "I have absolved thee."[2] With Wyclif, and upon the basis of the Lord's Prayer, Huss said that in a real sense every Christian has the right to absolve.

The two keys which are put into the hands of the church are knowledge and authority. The chief power given to the Apostles and their successors was to preach or evangelize. No prelatic authority has the right to inhibit one ordained from preaching the Gospel any more than it has the right to prohibit the giving of alms. As for the use of the prerogative to censure, Huss insisted that it should be exercised sparingly. Christ did not call down fire from heaven on the

---

[1] Pp., 607, 610.

[2] Pp. 103, 106, also *Mon.*, 1 : 229, 232, 239, etc. Wyclif declared that unjust excommunication was worse than the murder of the body, *de Eccles.*, p. 153. In the course of his treatment of this subject, Huss gives an exposition of Jer. 1 : 10, the famous passage which Gregory VII was wont to use for the supremacy of the papal power over the civil. *Ad octo doctores*, *Mon.*, 1 : 391. In this treatise Huss elaborated at greatest length the subject of the keys, *Mon.*, 1 : 385 *sqq.*

Samaritan city. By tears and prayers and Christian ministries should the supreme pontiff and priests fulfil their
office.[1]

Along the same line of curbing the assumptions of the
priesthood, Huss insists in this treatise upon the right of inferiors, including laymen, to examine the mandates of the
clergy and ecclesiastical superiors before giving them heed.
Even the civil realm has the right to punish priests and to
remove them from their offices as did, so Huss affirms,
Charles IV, king of Bohemia, and as Titus and Vespasian at
God's command had done in destroying Jerusalem and the
priests.[2]

4. The Scriptures. They are the supreme rule of faith
and conduct. This treatise and all Huss's writings abound
in Scripture quotations. A charge made against him by
Stephen Palecz was that more than any heretic before him,
he had fortified his heresies by appeals to the sacred volume.[3]
Huss expressed his hope to die in the faith, but also that at
the great judgment bar he might be found not to have denied
a single iota of their contents.[4] Charged with following
Wyclif, he replied that if he accepted Wyclif's statements,
it was because they were drawn from the Scriptures. The
holy volume, he maintained, is a book of life, an animate
thing. The priest's main duty is to set forth its truths and,
in being true to it, it is not possible to incur damnation

---

[1] Chap. XXI, also *Mon.*, 1 : 220, 389, etc.

[2] *Mon.*, 1 : 170, etc. So far as I know, Huss nowhere took up the case of
the emperor Trajan, a topic of constant discussion in the Middle Ages, in which
Wyclif also joined. According to the story, Trajan was prayed by Gregory the
Great out of hell into heaven, the only pagan to get to the abode of bliss. The
solemn question was whether he had gone direct to heaven as John of Damascus
claimed, or whether he first was brought back to the earth in order to be baptized, then dying over again before being taken up to the abode of the blessed
as Thomas Aquinas, Durandus, and others asserted. Wyclif, *de Eccles.*, 531
sqq., accepted the story but was concerned to show that Trajan's going to
heaven was by virtue of predestination. Bellarmine, *de Purg.*, 2 : 8, discusses
the subject.

[3] See Schaff, *Life of Huss*, p. 140.

[4] *Mon.*, 1 : 325, 330, 335; *Doc.*, 293, 319, etc.

through any prelatical command.[1] Huss's own following
was called the evangelical clergy—*clerus evangelicus*.[2]

In repeated discussions, Huss made the clear distinction
between apostolic commands, as contained in the Scriptures,
and papal mandates. No bidding is obligatory which is not
distinctly based on the Scripture—*præter expressam scrip-
turam*—and, where usage and Scripture disagree, usage is to
be set aside. In deciding what the Scriptures teach, reason
is to be employed. But the safest refuge of the church, Huss
declared, is no human authority but the Holy Spirit.[3]

In view of these positions on the supreme authority of
Scripture and the right of individual judgment, Bishop Hefele
rightly declares that Huss was fully out of accord with the
Catholic church and a true precursor of the Reformation.[4]

5. To these fundamental principles Huss, in this treatise,
adds another in which he also took solemn issue with the practice and the theory of the mediæval church,—the death
penalty for heresy. He calls it the "sanguinary corollary."
In repudiating it, Chapter XVI, he was setting himself against
Innocent III and the great pontiffs who came after him and
also against the theological statement of the Schoolmen. The
execution of religious dissenters was begun in 385 with the
death of the Priscillianists at Treves. Fathers of the ancient
church exhausted the dictionary for severe words to stigma-
tize heretics. Athanasius called them dogs, wolves and
worse. When ecclesiastical dissent reappeared in Western
Europe in the twelfth century, the words, "compel them to
come in," which St. Augustine used to justify physical measures to coerce the Donatists, were explained to justify the
putting of dissenters out of the world. They were likened
to scabby sheep and to the locusts of Joel hidden in the
dust. Heresy was a cancer to be cut out by the extermina-

---

[1] Especially chap. XVI, also *Mon.*, 1 : 326, 327, 331; *Doc.*, 297, etc.
[2] *Mon.*, 1 : 331.
[3] Pp., 71, 163; *Mon.*, 1 : 354 *sq.*
[4] Schaff, *Life of Huss*, 284, 297.

tion of the heretic. Innocent III set on foot the organized crusades for the extirpation of heresy with the sword in Southern France. Thomas Aquinas, d. 1274, made the solemn statement that as coin-clippers, who offend against the majesty of the state, are put to death, so heretics, who offend against the church, deserve to be put out of the world.

This principle was incorporated in the civil codes of the Schwabenspiegel and Sachsenspiegel and in the laws of Frederick II who proscribed death in the flames for heretics. In accordance with the old axiom that the church does not desire blood—*ecclesiam non sitit sanguinem*—it did not of itself execute the death sentence. However, it was participant in the execution, for it threatened civil magistrates with severest spiritual penalties who hesitated to execute it. Gregory IX demanded from the Roman senator a promise to search out heretics and to put them to death within eight days of their condemnation by the ecclesiastical tribunal. Louis IX, in France, and parliament by its act of 1401, in England, introduced the law of death. The horrors of the system of torture were authorized by Innocent IV, the successor of Gregory IX. Later, it remained for Sixtus IV in 1478 to open the second volume in the history of the horrors of the mediæval inquisition by sanctioning the holy office of Spain.[1]

Thus, by papal assumption and scholastic definition and state legislation, the claim was made to the awful power of shutting up dissenters eternally in hell and of depriving them of life on the earth.

In opposing this usage, Huss appealed to the example of Christ and the purpose of the Gospel. Christ did not assume civil authority. He refused the title of king. He did

[1] Lord Acton says of Pius V that "he held that it was sound Catholic doctrine that any man may stab a heretic condemned by Rome, and that every man is a heretic who attacks the papal prerogatives," *Letters of Lord Acton to Mary Gladstone*, p. 135.

not wish that men should be put to death—*nec voluit civiliter judicare nec morte corporis condemnare voluit.*[1] It is true that before d'Ailly and the commission at Constance Huss modified this statement, declaring that the suspected heretic should be labored with and instructed and only then, if necessary, punished corporally. As thus modified, the statement started a tumult among those present. And, when Huss went on to say that the priests and scribes who delivered Christ to Pilate had the greater sin, the tumult was repeated. It is possible that Huss was moved by the sufferings he was undergoing to make this modification, but exactly what he meant is not clear.[2]

In his attack against John XXIII's bulls calling for the crusade against Ladislaus, he repudiated the right of a pontiff to call for war against Christians in the absence of a special command from God. He denied the application of the cases of the Old Testament and Sapphira to Christian officials in the ordinary exercise of their authority. Only an express command from above would justify the use of the death penalty. Nor is torture to be applied to Christians. When Christ wished to defend himself against his enemies, he "meekly bore their attacks and did good to his detractors," an example priests should follow. By word and example Christ commended peace—*ad pacem ducit verbo et exemplo.*[3]

In dealing with Augustine's use of the passage "compel them to come in," Huss affirmed that it is one thing to compel and quite another to exterminate or kill. The death penalty for heretics was never expressly recommended by Augustine, and it is probable that Huss more nearly represented the views and spirit of the African Father than did the Schoolmen and the council of Constance. The armor of the church, Huss insisted, is not carnal but spiritual as set forth in the

[1] P. 170.   [2] *Doc.*, 294.
[3] *Mon.*, 1 : 395, also 393, 394, 397, etc., and chap. XXI of this treatise.

last chapter of the Ephesians, a passage he frequently expounded.[1]

Indeed, heresy has its uses, and heretics are to be reclaimed to Christ's sheepfold by methods of persuasion, so Huss affirmed. As for himself, he professed that excommunication and the harshest treatment are rather to be chosen than a pretended absolution from guilt and punishment, for he is more likely to be absolved from guilt and punishment who, in God's cause, suffers malediction and contumely even unto death, than he who prevaricates to himself or persecutes Christians.[2]

Thus, a hundred years before Luther wrote his famous words against the burning of heretics, Huss took the same position. But, so far as we know, there was not a single individual in the great council of Constance who had any sympathy with the views of the Bohemian heretic. Nay, the council went further than to burn Huss: it supplemented its verdict by a solemn declaration that faith is not to be kept with a heretic. The pity is that Bullinger—in the Second Helvetic Confession, John Calvin and other leaders of the emancipation of the sixteenth century did not fully conform to the principle set forth by Huss and Luther and shake themselves free from the method of the inquisition practised by our religious ancestors of the Middle Ages.

These fundamental principles, in regard to the church, the papal office, the keys and the Scriptures, for which Huss stood were adapted to shake the ecclesiastical organization of his day to its very foundations. The council of Constance when it stated them in its thirty charges fully appreciated the grave menace. Had that solemn assembly accepted Huss's principles it would have set aside the construction built up by the pride of the mediæval hierarchy and the laborious reasoning of the Schoolmen.

IV. Huss's DEBT TO WYCLIF. The leading principles

---

[1] *Mon.*, 1 : 405, etc.   [2] P. 25; *Mon.*, 1 : 234, 393.

set forth in his Treatise on the Church, Huss found in the
writings of Wyclif and particularly in Wyclif's treatise on
the same subject. Not only has he the main principles in
common with Wyclif, and also many of his quotations from
the Fathers and the canon law and his proofs from Scripture. Huss appropriated paragraph after paragraph from his
predecessor and transferred them often with little verbal
change to his own pages. The agreement has been convinc-
ingly shown by Loserth, who prints the corresponding paragraphs side by side. It is not necessary here to repeat what
he has done.[1]

Huss's reverend respect for Wyclif has already been indicated. Whereas Stephen Palecz, Stanislaus of Znáim and
other theological colleagues, who at first shared his admiration for the English teacher, came to regard his teaching as
honeyed poison—*mellatum venenum*—Huss continued to bow
before him as the "master of deep thoughts." And it was
for Wyclif's doctrines and, in a sense, in his stead he died at
Constance.[2]

The recent publication of Wyclif's works beginning with
1883, under the auspices of the Wyclif society, has made
possible a full estimate of the obligation which Huss owed
to his English predecessor. Up to that date only a comparatively small number of his writings, English as well as
Latin, were in print, and Wyclif's Treatise on the Church
appeared for the first time, 1886. In the light of Wyclif's
printed text, the theory advocated at length by Neander
that Huss was indebted to Matthias of Janow for his view
on the authority of Scripture and other topics is found to be
wholly without foundation. And, in fact, nowhere does Huss
express any debt to that writer of Prague who, by the way,
recanted his views which were pronounced erroneous. Never

[1] *Wiclif and Hus*, 181–225. The two sources upon which Huss drew were
Wyclif's *de Ecclesia* and his *de potestate Papæ*, ed. by Loserth, 1907.

[2] *Mon.*, 1 : 331, 334, 335, etc. For a larger statement of Huss's debt to Wyclif,
see Schaff, *Life of Huss*, chap. III.

did a man owe more to mortal teacher than Huss did to John Wyclif.[1] In the fundamental doctrines concerning the predestinate, the church, the papacy, the power of the keys and the authority of the Bible Huss agrees exactly with his predecessor.[2] They are one in their denunciation of Boniface VIII's bull, *Unam sanctam*, and of Constantine's donation. All the reformatory—and we may say revolutionary—principles affirmed by the former will be found in Wyclif.

However, Huss was not a servile imitator of Wyclif and it seems never to have occurred to his opponents in Prague to twit him on the use he made of Wyclif's writings. It must be borne in mind, that from no other source outside the pages of Scripture could Huss have learned what he came to believe as from the pages of Wyclif. Reading him was like taking clear water from a vessel filled at a spring rediscovered. And, it must be remembered, that Huss had no sooner left the university than he found himself in an atmosphere charged with the controversial spirit, himself the chief figure.

To these considerations the following must also be taken into account. Instead of transferring to his pages paragraphs from Wyclif bodily, Huss might easily have introduced into them words of his own or taken the meaning and re-expressed it in his own language. That he did not pursue this method is evidence that he had no intention of using the garments of his great teacher to make a reputation for himself. He was ready to die for his convictions and in this treatise the chief consideration was to give the most forcible expression possible to the views he and Wyclif were known to hold in

---

[1] A succinct and authoritative statement of the extent to which Wyclif's writings were put into print before 1883 may be found in Loserth's thorough article on Wyclif in the German Herzog, 21 : 225 *sq*. With that year the printing of the Latin writings was begun. The *Trialogus*, however, which gives Wyclif's distinctive views was published in Basel, 1525. The English writings had been gathered by two editors, Thomas Arnold, 1869–71, 3 vols., and F. D. Mathew, 1880, 1 vol.

[2] See Schaff, *Ch. Hist.*, V, part 2 : 325–349.

common. The chief weapon of attack against him was Wyclif's system as set forth in the XLV Articles, condemned by ecclesiastical authority and recently by the eight doctors to whom he was replying.

The materials, taken from Wyclif, are under Huss's hand subjected to altogether new collocations, and in matters of detail, where we would expect Huss to have drawn from his predecessor, he does not. For example, he does not repeat Wyclif's use of the ark and the seamless coat of Christ as figures for the unity of the church nor make reference to Solomon and the temple. Nor does he introduce David at the side of Peter as an example of one who is predestinate and yet is lacking for a time in righteousness. Huss omits many of the authors quoted by Wyclif such as Bradwardine, Henry of Gauda and, as already stated, Bonaventura. There is evidence, as Schwab long ago suggested, that Huss was well read in the canon law and used it independently. As for Augustine, Loserth has expressed the opinion that Huss knew his copy well. With Luther, at a later time, he felt profound respect for this father's theological learning and piety. In this treatise he designates Augustine now the "holy man" now the "great doctor" and pronounced him the foremost of biblical expositors, the man who was more profitable to the church than many popes.[1] As for materials from Scripture Huss's treatise contains much that Wyclif does not give as also fresh considerations from reason. His references to Christ, whom he frequently calls "the best of masters" will at times be found to be charged with true eloquence as well as piety.

If it were necessary to point to the custom of his age to justify Huss's procedure, the cases of John Gerson and Cardinal d'Ailly might be cited. Gerson, rector of the university of Paris, without making acknowledgment, appropriated a considerable part of one of Henry of Langenstein's

---

[1] Pp., 78, 149, 154, 201.

works and d'Ailly pursued the same method with Ockam's *Dialogus*.[1]

Huss's *Commentary on the Sentences of Peter the Lombard*, recently published in a volume of eight hundred pages, has re-established the author's claims to be a sane and well-balanced theological student. Here he expresses himself independently and shows himself conversant with those phases of theological thought which were a subject of special discussion in his day as well as with the fundamental catholic principles.[2]

Comparing the two treatises on the church along general lines this may be said:

Huss is the more clear and direct of the two writers. Much as he seems to repeat himself, he nevertheless pursues a definite aim. Wyclif, as was his custom, was drawn aside by the exuberance of his intellect into all sorts of discussions germane and not strictly germane. His treatise has extended paragraphs on canonization, mathematics, alms, relic worship, the evils of ecclesiastical endowments.[3] He shows his scholastic bent by that peculiar use of Latin terminology characteristic of mediæval scholasticism. Although Huss employs some of Wyclif's characteristic words, as antonomasia, yet he is comparatively free in this respect.[4]

---

[1] Schwab, *J. Gerson*, p. 121, says that Gerson's *Declaratio compendiosa*, etc., Du Pin, 2 : 314–318, is a literal copy—wörtlich—of chapters XVI–XX of Langenstein's *Consilium pacis de unione et reform. eccles.* Tschackert, *P. d'Ailli*, p. 43, says of d'Ailly that he copied Ockam almost literally—*fast wörtlich*.

[2] Flajshans, *Super IV. Sententiarum*, Prague, 1905. In his Introduction Flajshans, a liberal Catholic, pronounces Huss Bohemia's chief religious character. On the appearance of this work Loserth declared that his former judgment disparaging Huss's originality would have to be revised.

[3] *De Eccles.*, 44 *sqq.*, 97 *sqq.*, 162 *sqq.*, 274 *sqq.*, 465 *sqq.* In saying this, however, the occasion which led to the composition of Wyclif's work must be taken into account, that is the case of alleged sacrilege committed in Westminster Abbey. See Loserth's Introd. to his ed.

[4] See the glossary in Wyclif's *de dom. civ.*, ed. by Poole, pp. 479–483. Of the one hundred and fifty-nine words there given, Huss seems to use only seven in his *de Eccles.*

We come now to the temper in which the two works are written as indicated by particular statements as well as the general drift. Huss is much less severe in his judgments of individuals than is Wyclif. The latter called Gregory XI a terrible devil—*horrendus diabolus*—and blessed God for bringing him to his death when He did. The cardinals he stigmatized as the very synagogue and nest of Satan and a nest of heretics.[1]

At times, in his English writings, he calls the pope the vicar of the fiend—the devil. Huss joins with Wyclif in saying that it might be well to get along without a pope, though not in such strong language, but nowhere uses such an expression as Wyclif's, enormous pride of the Western church—*monstruosa superbia ecclesiæ occidentalis*—or plainly denounces the last clause of Boniface's bull as to be detested.[2] Nor did Huss in his treatise directly repudiate the authority of church teachers such as Thomas Aquinas and Bonaventura, as Wyclif did, although, as his pages show, he put strange interpretations on some of the statements of the canon law and seems to have been at times under the constraint of usage in clinging to those statements rather than of conviction.

Huss, in other words, was much less severe in his judgment of individuals and more moderate in his language than his predecessor. Wyclif used a sharp blade and sometimes the acrimony of the pamphleteer. The Bohemian carried to his desk the homiletic instinct of the preacher addressing an audience whose welfare he held in mind. The one was governed somewhat by the love of the truth as a matter of intellectual determination; the other altogether by the love of the truth as a practical force in daily life.

In his last months in prison, Huss definitely accepted the distribution of the cup to the laity and exclaimed against the impiety of the council's act when it threatened every priest with the ban who dared to distribute it. On the other

---

[1] *De Eccles.*, 88, 186, 358, 366.   [2] Wyclif, *de Eccles.*, 38, 362.

hand, he did not adopt Wyclif's doctrine of the eucharist but to the end insisted that he was wrongly charged with denying the church's dogma of transubstantiation.

V. IMPORTANCE. Huss's treatise has a place of first importance among works on the church. Its treatment is clear, elaborate and professedly based on Scripture. It is the best known work on the subject issued from Augustine to the Reformation period. It was the basis of charges in the most famous formal trial of a single individual in the history of the Christian church.[1] It was cherished and used by a large section of the Bohemian people. It has had a permanent influence upon the development of the idea of the church.

Upon the council assembled at Constance Huss's volume made a deep impression as a work calculated to be disastrous in its effects, unless counteracted by the severest measures within the church's reach. One of its foremost leaders, that eminent man Cardinal d'Ailly, who had probably more to do than any other man of the council with Huss, declared that by an abundance of proofs Huss's treatise combated the plenary authority of the church as much as the Koran combats Christ.[2]

Wyclif's Treatise on the Church was hidden away in manuscript until a generation ago. His followers at Oxford, soon after his death, repudiated his views. His name was a memory except as his English version of the Bible was read in narrowing groups of Lollards. That memory, indeed, was powerful, for the early Protestant Reformers looked back to him and Tyndale wrote: "They said it in Wyclif's day and the hypocrites say it now, that God's Word arouseth in-

---

[1] I do not forget the trials of Abælard, Savonarola, etc. Arius's views, rather than Arius himself, were on trial at the council of Nice, though Arius became personally involved, being restored, however, after he had been banished and his books burned. Of course, Savonarola's trial lacked the imposing element involved in the trial of Huss, an œcumenical council.

[2] Du Pin, *Works of Gerson*, 2 : 901.

surrection."[1]   And Bishop Tonstall, writing to Erasmus,
1524, said that the new views were "not a question of some
pernicious novelty, but only that new arms were being added
to the great band of Wyclifite heretics."

But what Wyclif's Bible was to the small company of
dissenters in England, Huss's Treatise on the Church was
to the large body of Bohemians who respected Huss's memory
and followed, in part or in whole, his views.

In Luther's time, Huss's name and also his treatise were
a live power. As for his treatise, a copy of it was sent by
Hussites to the German Reformer on the ground that he and
Huss were agreed and, in 1520, an edition was printed in
Mainz by Ulrich von Hutten.[2] Wyclif was not quoted by
the Reformers. They knew him through Huss.

The ancient church produced two writers on the specific topic of the church, Cyprian and Augustine. The Unity
of the Church written by the bishop of Carthage, though
small in compass, is of much importance for its view of the
episcopate. Augustine, in the controversy with the Donatist
dissenters, furnished material of great moment for the definition of the church without giving a succinct definition.[3]
The nearest approach to it were his statements that the
church is the holy body of all the faithful, to be saved—
sancta cong. omnium fidelium salvandorum—and the body of
the faithful who are elect and justified—*fidelium predestinatorum et justificatorum.*[4] The term catholic, or universal,
first used by Ignatius, was employed by these Fathers in conformity with the usage which had become general.

During the Middle Ages, the topic was not a matter of
special treatment. The ideas of Augustine were not questioned that baptism is essential to salvation and that all

[1] Preface to Exposition of St. John, Parker ed., p. 225.
[2] Under the title *de unitate Ecclesiæ cujus autor periit in concilio Constantiensi.*
For the influence of Huss's name and death upon Luther, see Schaff, *Life of
Huss*, pp. 291 *sqq.*
[3] See Loofs, *Dogmengesch.*, 4th ed., p. 370.   [4] P. 36, *Super IV. Sent.*, 616.

those, not in communion with the visible church, are lost.
The church was looked upon as a tangible, palpable institution, as much so as the duchy of Spoleto or the kingdom of
France. The Schoolman, who came nearest giving a definition, was Hugo of St. Victor who, in his work on the sacraments, called the holy catholic church the body of Christ
vivified by one Spirit, united in one faith and sanctified. It
is the number of the faithful, the totality of all Christians.[1]
Thomas Aquinas passed it by except as he discussed the
pope's absolute supremacy. The fourth Lateran indeed
spoke of the church as "the one universal church of the
faithful outside of which there cannot be any salvation"—
extra quam nullus omnino salvatur—a statement which nar-
rowed the church down to the limits of the Roman communion
in the profession demanded of the Waldenses, namely, "we
believe with the heart and confess that the one church is
not.of the heretics but the holy Roman catholic church outside of which no one can be saved." [2]

In his *Rule of Princes* and *Errors of the Greeks*, Thomas
Aquinas gave his assent to Innocent III's assumption claim-
ing for the Roman pontiff plenitude of power and declared
that obedience was due to the Roman church as to the Lord
Jesus himself—*cui obediendum est tanquam Domino Deo, Jesu*.
He used also the words: "subjection to the Roman pontiff
is of necessity to salvation"—*subesse romano pontifici est de
necessitate salutis*.[3]

A new period in the history of the conception of the
church opened with Boniface's bull, *Unam sanctam*, and was
forced by it, the text on which other writers as well as Wyclif and Huss comment frequently.[4] This notorious document
might have been relegated to the archives of innocuous legal

---

[1] *De Sacr.*, 1 : 2, Migne's ed., 176 : 416 : *eccles. s. corpus est Christi, uno spiritu
vivificata et unita fide una*, etc.

[2] See Schwane, *Dogmengesch. d. mittl. Zeit.*, p. 5c4.

[3] Reusch's ed., p. 9; also Mirbt, *Quellen*, 3d ed., p. 157.

[4] For Huss, see index of this vol. Wyclif, *de Eccles.*, 14, 26, 38, 112, 114, 314.
Wyclif speaks of Boniface as having entered the papacy as a fox, by craft, p. 34.

papers, had it not been for the fact that it confirmed Louis the Fair of France in his opposition to the temporal absolutism of the papal throne and united his kingdom around him in this interest. Groups of pamphleteers in Italy and France attacked now the claims of the papacy to secular authority, as Dante, and now its spiritual claims, as Peter Dubois and Marsiglius of Padua. These men agreed in repudiating Constantine's donation on the ground that Constantine had no right to bestow upon the Roman pontiff any such power; and Marsiglius went far along the line of making the claims which the Protestant Reformers afterwards united in making.[1] This keen critic, who was anathematized by John XXII for asserting that Peter was not the head of the church, also asserted that the distinction between bishops and priests is not founded in Scripture and that the church has no authority to coerce by physical measures. Contemporary with him, Ockam was also affirming that Christ did not appoint a primacy at Rome and that the pope is not essential to the church but is of human appointment—*ex ordinatione humana.*[2] This English Schoolman defined the church as "the community of the faithful comprehending clerics and laymen." It may be reduced to one person as it was to Mary when the disciples fled. A generation before, Philip the Fair had proudly reminded Boniface that the church was made up of laymen as well as priests.

The removal of the papacy to Avignon and the papal schism which followed, 1377–1415, were adapted to intensify the controversy over the nature and functions of the church,

---

[1] For this most interesting tract literature, see Riezler, *Die literarischen Widersacher der Päpste zur Zeit Ludwig des Baiers.* Finke, *Aus den Tagen Bonifaz VIII.* Haller, *Papstthum und Kirchenreform.* Scholz, *Die Publizistik zur Zeit Philipps des Schönen und Bonifaz VIII.* Schaff, *Ch. History* V., 1 : 674, 777.

[2] See David E. Culley, *Konrad von Gelnhausen, seine Lehre, seine Werke und seine Quellen.* Halle, 1913, p. 84 *sqq.* Hugo de St. Victor, as in the passage above quoted, also said that "the church is comprised of laymen and clerics, as it were the two sides of one body." To the laity, Hugo goes on to say, are committed terrestrial possessions, etc.

questions which had seemed to be forever settled before Boniface issued his bull. The discussions were participated in by a class of men of whom Konrad of Gelnhausen was one of the very first, and by Wyclif followed by Huss who constitute a much more advanced group. The opinions of the former group found expression in the Reformatory councils, notably the council of Constance. The opinions of the latter involved an ecclesiastical revolution and led straight forward to the Protestant Reformation.

The opening clause of Boniface's bull asserting the unity of the church, Wyclif and Huss both accepted, but they put upon it another interpretation from that intended by Boniface. The unity was not in the apostolic see but in predestinating grace as manifesting itself in the exercise of the Christian virtues. The other clauses they wholly repudiated, namely the clause that to the church is given both swords and the clause that it is altogether necessary for salvation that every creature be subject to the Roman pontiff. The latter repeats the very language of Thomas Aquinas. In renouncing these two propositions, Wyclif and Huss set themselves against the fabric of the mediæval system.

It was Huss's merit that he kept open the subject of the church by his death and this treatise. He passed Wyclif's views on to a later time, and his volume was the avenue for their transmission. Huss's tenets and his memory, embodied in the Christian dissenters known as "the Bohemians," were a constant source of interest and of controversy down to the age of Luther. At the close of the fifteenth century, Wessel exclaimed: "The church cannot err, but what is the church? It is the communion of the saints to which all true believers belong who are bound together by one faith, one love, one hope." The definition of the nature and the functions of the church was awaiting settlement, and the staggering blow to Boniface VIII's arrogance was given by the Reformation.

In view of our authorities, it would be false to say that

Luther learned directly from Huss, but Luther's assertions show that he not only took Huss under his protection, but that he was confirmed in his opposition to the pope by his regard for Huss and by his writings. Not to quote again what I have quoted in another place, Luther said: "I rejoice that Huss, a true martyr, is rising before this, our century, that is to be properly canonized even if the papists are broken to pieces. Oh! that my name were worthy to be associated with such a man.[1]

Luther's definition of the church is embodied in the Augsburg Confession. It was due to Luther and Zwingli that the terms visible and invisible were used to designate the true church from the body of the baptized.[2]

True to the mediæval conception and only six months before the nailing up of the XCV Theses, Leo X confirmed Boniface's *Unam sanctam*, and in reply to Luther Prierias declared the church to be in essence the community of believers but virtually the Roman church and the Roman pontiff—*ecclesia universalis essentialiter est convocatio credentium, virtualiter ecclesia Romana et pontifex maximus*. The catholic polemic of the seventeenth century, with Bellarmine at its head, made the rule of the papacy of the essence of the definition of the church. He expressly repudiated as heretical the definition of Wyclif, Huss and Calvin.[3] Still true to the mediæval idea, Pius IX, in 1873, in a communication addressed to the German emperor, William I, declared that all the baptized are in some sense subject to the Roman pontiff.[4]

Several matters in Huss's treatment call for passing note.

---

[1] Letter to Otto Brunfels, 1524, who edited some of Huss's writings, 1524. See *Mon.*, 1 : 423.

[2] In his Com. on Galatians, Luther spoke of the church invisible, *est invisibilis habitans in Spiritu*, etc., and Zwingli seems to have been the first to use both terms, in his *Expos. fidei*, 1531—*est autem eccles. aut visibilis aut invisibilis*. The XXXIX Articles use the term invisible. Schwane, *Dogmengesch.*, p. 510, says: "Huss rejected the definition that the church is a visible community of believers in Christ."

[3] *Lib. III de Eccles.*, chap. II.

[4] *Jeder welcher die Taufe empfangen hat, gehort in irgend einer Art und in irgend einer Weise . . . dem Papste an* Mirbt, *Quellen*, p. 371.

The first is that Huss, as also Wyclif before him, continued to call the church mother and holy mother. Although this designation has the prestige of high antiquity, it is to be used with great caution. The church is not a personality, giving birth to spiritual children. The designation is drawn from Paul's placing Christ and the church figuratively in the relation of bridegroom and bride. But nowhere in the New Testament is the church called mother or bringing forth ascribed to it. The term is bound up with the conception of the church as a saving institution and its use developed with the development of the sacramental system. From the Protestant standpoint it is fallacious. Wyclif and Huss, again and again, pronounce it a metaphor and so prepared the way for its rejection by the Reformers.[1]

Another remark is that Huss makes not a little of church history. He had the historical sense and less of the scholastic than we might expect. The age of criticism was dawning not only among the men of the Renaissance but in the church. It is interesting to compare Luther's conception of the use of history to do away with bad usages. In his Introduction to Dr. Barnes's *History of the Lives of the Popes*, issued in 1536, he said that, in the beginning, not being much versed in the lives of the popes, he attacked the papacy *a priori*, that is, from holy Scripture, but was wonderfully delighted that others were doing the same *a posteriori*, that is, from history.[2] Huss used history to prove the truth of Scripture.

A third remark is that nowhere in this treatise does Huss use the passage, John 17, "that they may be one as thou,

[1] In his *Super IV. Sent.*, p. 469, Huss speaks of the church as our most dear mother, the most worthy mother of predestination, etc. In his Com. on the Decalogue, Flajshans's ed., p. 19, he says of the fifth commandment: By some "thy spiritual father" is said to be the priest and truly "thy mother" is the church. He then went on to speak of another interpretation by which the Christian has three mothers, a mother after the flesh, a spiritual mother, the church, and a celestial mother, Mary. Cyprian presented the mediæval view when he said: "He cannot have God for his father who does not have the church for his mother." Schaff, *Ch. Hist.*, II, 173.

[2] See Jacobs, *Lutheranism in England*, p. 182.

Father, art in me and I in thee," so much quoted in this present age as if corporate union were the test of the fulfilment of the words. Huss's treatise presents an entirely different test of Christian unity. He must not be pressed too far. Nevertheless, it is plain that he laid stress on particular churches[1] and made the bond of union between them and between their members predestinating grace and an active life of Christian virtue.

VI. THE CANON LAW. The authorities used in this treatise are the Scriptures, accredited writers of the church, the canon law and Wyclif. Among the accredited writers frequently quoted are Augustine, Ambrose, Jerome, Gregory the Great, Bernard, and Peter the Lombard. It is noticeable that Bonaventura's name is not mentioned at all, whereas Wyclif's Treatise on the Church quotes him at least sixteen times, and, for some reason, Huss draws upon Thomas Aquinas much less than did his English precursor.

With few exceptions the places where these quotations are found in the volumes of Migne and the *Nicene Fathers* series have been noted, and also the references to the canon law as they are found in Friedberg's edition.[2] The verses of the Scripture texts, which in Huss's time had not yet been marked, have been supplied. All this matter, which the translator is responsible for, is enclosed in brackets, as also an occasional brief explanation.

Like the sacramental system, the universities and the cathedrals, the body of the canon law was one of the imposing constructions of the Middle Ages. It had as its first and chief compiler Gratian who, about 1150, was teaching church law in Bologna as Irnerius was teaching Roman law.

---

[1] The XXXIX Articles of Religion speak of "every particular or national church" as having authority, etc.

[2] A. Friedberg, *Corpus juris canonici*, 1879-1881, 2 vols., pp. 1468, 1340, is pronounced by the Catholic canonical writer, P. Hergenröther, *Lehrbuch d. kath. K.-rechts*, p. 192, "the best edition." A description of the canon law will be found in Friedberg's Introd. to vol. I and in Hergenröther, pp. 172-196. For a history of the subject of the treatment, see the elaborate work of J. F. von Schulte, *Die Gesch. der Quellen und Lit. des canon. Rechts*, Stutt., 3 vols., 1875-1880.

From the university of Bologna, which became the celebrated centre of the study of both laws, such eminent popes went out as Alexander III and Innocent III, and the advice of its jurisconsults was sought on questions of first import, as by Frederick Barbarossa on the plain of Roncaglia, 1158.

In his *Concordantia canonum discordantium*, usually called *Decretum Gratiani*, Gratian attempted to bring into a harmonious code the statements of councils, popes, and eminent Fathers bearing on all manner of questions concerning the government of the church and its usages. This digest had even greater authority in its department than Peter the Lombard's *Sentences* in the department of systematic theology. In its sections are also contained the fictitious materials of the pseudo-Isidorian decretals, the most notorious portion of which is the donation of Constantine.

As time wore on, the need was felt of supplements to Gratian's work, which were furnished in the Decretals, so-called, collected by order of Gregory IX, 1234,[1] the *Liber Sextus* or Sext, by Boniface VIII, 1298, the *Liber Septimus* or Clementine Constitutions, by Clement V, 1314,[2] and the so-called *Extravagantes*, or fugitive decretals, twenty in number, issued by John XXII and incorporated into the code by John Chappuis in his edition of 1500. Chappuis also added seventy other decretals issued between the pontificates of Boniface VIII and Sixtus IV, 1294–1484. The completed digest, consisting of these parts, was authoritatively issued by Gregory XIII, 1582.[3]

The Glosses and Little Glosses, which Huss frequently quotes—the *Glossa ordinaria*—are comments made upon the original texts by glossators, among whom Cardinal Zabarella,

[1] For Gregory's bull sanctioning the ed. which was made by Raymund of Pennaforte, see Wetzer-Welte, 3 : 1446 1450.

[2] In numbering the supplements of Boniface and Clement the VI and the VII, reference was had to four compilations made during the reign of Innocent III, which constitute the Decretals.

[3] For Gregory's bulls, see Friedberg, 1 : 79 *sqq.*

so prominent in Huss's trial at Constance, d. 1417, occupies a place of distinction.[1]

In this treatise and elsewhere Huss was concerned first of all to base his views upon plain Scripture, and then to find their confirmation in the pages of the canon law. In doing so, he quoted the spurious decretals of pseudo-Isidore, their genuineness in that age being still universally accepted.

It will be seen that, for Huss, the canon law at times was a heavy load to carry. He did the best he could to explain away its language which taught the high-church views which he distinctly repudiated, and to bring its statements into harmony with the teachings of Scripture he adduced. He speaks of the respect due to the body of canon law in a tone which leads us to infer that he accepted it in places with mental reservation.[2] A single case in which he is seen to have absolutely set aside its plain meaning is his exposition of the last clause of the *Unam sanctam* to the effect, that there is no salvation except for those who fully submit to the Roman pontiff, pp. 120, 121. In a fine passage Huss makes the Roman pontiff refer to Christ, the supreme Pontiff and Shepherd, but Boniface had no such idea in mind when he issued his arrogant deliverance.

In regard to Constantine's donation, which established the most pretentious claims made for the papal monarchy and for the sacerdotal office, Huss took the position Dante had taken before him, that Constantine had no right to bestow the privileges he did. For the first time, a generation or two after him, the genuineness of this document was seriously doubted by Laurentius Valla. It was not until 1520 that Valla's destructive criticism was brought to Luther's attention by Ulrich von Hutten.

To have been consistent, Huss would have been obliged

---

[1] See Schulte, 1 : 216, 226–229; 2 : 89, 217 *sqq.*, etc.; and for Zabarella, 2 : 283 *sqq.*

[2] Pp. 94, 211 *sq.*, 215, etc.

to discard Gratian's compilation as Luther did, who, in 1520, threw the ponderous volume into the same flames at Wittenberg which consumed Leo X's bull. And the marvel is that Huss, and Wyclif before him, should have been able to take the advanced views they did with this heavy load of the traditions of men—some good and some utterly anti-Scriptural—weighing them down.

VII. The Translation. This translation has been made from the second edition of Huss's writings, entitled *Historia et Monumenta J. Hus*, published in two volumes at Frankfurt, 1715, with respectively 627 and 542 pages. The edition is a reprint of the earlier edition, Frankfurt, 1558, also in two volumes.[1] The translator has had both editions on his table, using the second on account of the greater clearness of the print. After comparing the two editions almost paragraph by paragraph, he has failed to find a single verbal difference in the text. The only differences are an occasional case of capitalization and punctuation.

With exceptions, Huss's quotations are found to conform exactly to the Vulgate, the text of the canon law and the other texts which he quotes. It was the translator's desire to examine one or more of the original manuscripts of the treatise and through the courtesy of the eminent Huss expert, Dr. Flajshans, of Prague, he received a list of the more important manuscripts.[2] It was found impossible to realize this desire; but from the accuracy with which Huss has transferred quotations to his pages as found in the Frank-

[1] The *de Ecclesia* fills 75 double-columned pages, *Mon.*, 1 : 243–317. To the librarian of Lane Theological Seminary the translator owes his thanks for the use of the original edition as well as other valuable works as he is also indebted to Dr. Henry Preserved Smith for the use of volumes from the library of Union Theological Seminary, of which he is the librarian.

[2] The list of manuscripts, which includes exact descriptions, gives seven in the Royal Library of Vienna, one in the Royal Library of Munich, one in the Cathedral Gymnasium Library of Magdeburg, dated 1414, and four in the university library of Prague. For a list of Huss's works edited by Flajshans, see Schaff, *Life of Huss*, p. 8.

furt text, it is fair to presume that the manuscript would show
no change in any essential matter. It is to be hoped that Dr.
Flajshans will add to his other editions of Huss's writings a
new edition of this, Huss's most important treatise.

Huss's Treatise on the Church is now within the reach
of readers who have known it chiefly by its fame. Its pages
will enable him who reads to feel some of the pious and heroic
spirit of its author, the preacher of Bethlehem chapel, and
at the same time to appreciate more fully what was the
doctrinal and hierarchical system handed down from the
classic period of the Middle Ages to the age of Wyclif and
Huss. According to the letter of this system these two men
were justly pronounced heretics, but not according to the
Scriptures to which they appealed.[1]

To follow Huss's own presentation, the principle upon
which Christ was put to death was stated in the words,
" We have a law and by that law he ought to die." On
the same principle of ecclesiastical usage Huss suffered at
the stake at Constance. When the two principles emphasized in this treatise are given proper recognition—personal
devotion to Christ and a daily life conformed to his teachings and example—the practice of Christian tolerance and all
human tolerance will be advanced. Then will creedal union
and ritualistic prepossessions be softened and the barriers
of denominational self-sufficiency be broken down, barriers
which, at least in part, have been erected on metaphysical
definitions in theological matters or uncertain assumptions
drawn from history concerning the ministry and the sacraments, for which no distinct warrant can be found in the
pages of the New Testament. This treatise will have a
mission to-day, if its pages promote the idea that devotion
to Christ is the condition and the surety of Christian fellowship and co-operation.

[1] This treatise quotes the New Testament at least 347 times and the Old
Testament 72 times. The two books most frequently quoted are the Gospels
of Matthew, 93 times; and John, 67 times.

CONTENTS

CONTENTS

CONTENTS

THE CHURCH

THE CHURCH

CHAPTER I

THE UNITY OF THE CHURCH

As every earthly pilgrim[1] ought faithfully to believe the holy catholic church just as he ought to love Jesus Christ, the Lord, the bridegroom of that church, and also the church herself, his bride; but as he does not love this, his spiritual mother, except he also know her by faith—therefore ought he to learn to know her by faith, and thus to honor her as his chief mother.[2]

Therefore, in order to reach a proper knowledge of her, it is to be noted, (1) That the church signifies the house of God, constituted for the very purpose that in it the people may worship its God, as it is written, I Cor. 11 : 22: "Have ye not houses to eat and to drink in?" Or, to speak with Augustine: "Do you despise the church of God, the house of prayer?" (2) The church signifies the ministers belonging to the house of God. Thus the clerics belonging to one material church call themselves the church. But according to the Greeks, a church—*ecclesia*—is a congregation—*congregatio*—held to-

---

[1] *Viator*, a current word. See Wyclif, *de Eccles.*, 4, 42, 350. Gerson, Du Pin's ed., 2 : 22.

[2] See also chap. II, etc. The designation mother is nowhere given to the church in the N. T. It is derived from the relation the church bears to Christ as his bride. Later on in this chapter Augustine represents her as giving birth to children. So Wyclif, *de Eccles.*, 117: "The church is a virgin since she is the bride of the virgin Jesus Christ, by whom as a mother we are born after a spiritual manner." It followed that Christ was the spiritual father or "father by faith," Wyclif, p. 1, and Grosseteste in this treatise, chap. IV. In his *Com. on the Lombard*, p. 469, Huss speaks of the church as "our most dear mother, the most worthy mother of the predestinate."

gether under one rule, as Aristotle teaches, *Polit.* 2 : 7[1], when
he says: "All have part in the church." In view of this
meaning, therefore, the congregation of all men is called the
church—*ecclesia.* This appears in Matt. 25 : 31–33, which
says: "When the Son of Man shall come in his glory and all
his angels with him, then shall he sit upon the throne of his
glory and before him shall be congregated all nations." What
a great congregation of all men under the rule of Christ the
king that will be! Because, however, the whole of that congregation is not the holy church it is added, "and he will separate them, the one from the other, as a shepherd separates the
sheep from the goats."

From this it is evident that there is one church—*ecclesia*
—of the sheep and another of the goats, one church of the
righteous and another of the reprobate—*præsciti.*[2] Likewise
the church of the righteous is on the one hand catholic, that
is, universal, which is not a part of anything else. Of this I
am now treating. On the other hand, it is particular, a part
with other parts, as the Saviour said, Matt. 18 : 20: "Where
two or three are congregated together in my name, there am
I in the midst of them." From this it follows that two righteous persons congregated together in Christ's name constitute,
with Christ as the head, a particular holy church, and likewise three or four and so on to the whole number of the predestinate without admixture. In this sense the term church
is often used in Scripture, as when the apostle says, I Cor. 1 : 1:
"To the church which is in Corinth, to the sanctified in Jesus

---

[1] Aristotle, the authority of the Schoolmen in philosophy, and called, in the
Middle Ages, The Philosopher. So Huss in this treatise, chap. IV, and often
in his *Com. on the Lombard,* p. 112, etc.

[2] The foreknown, that is, those of whom God knows beforehand that they
are not in a state of permanent grace. Their condition is not the result of an
active decree, though it is a subject of God's previous knowledge. The foreknown are in grace according to present righteousness and desire through merit
at once eternal bliss and at the same time their damnation. This apparent
contradiction Huss explains to lie in this, that they are not willing to use the
means to the attainment of eternal bliss, just as a person may wish a coat and
yet not possess it. *Super IV. Sent.,* 188.

Christ." Likewise Acts 20 : 28: "Take heed to yourselves and to the whole flock in which the Holy Spirit hath made you bishops, to feed the church which he hath purchased with his own blood." And in this sense, all the righteous now living under Christ's rule in the city of Prague, and more particularly the predestinate, are the holy church of Prague, and the same is true of other particular churches of saints of which Ecclesiasticus 24 : 2, speaks: "In the congregations—*ecclesiis*—of the Most High shall she [wisdom] open her mouth," and also 31 : 11: "All the congregation of the saints shall declare his alms." [1]

But the holy catholic—that is, universal—church is the totality of the predestinate—*omnium predestinatorum universitas*—or all the predestinate,[2] present, past, and future. This definition follows St. Augustine on John, *C. Recur.* 32 : 4 [Friedberg, 1 : 1126], who shows how it is that one and the same church of the predestinate, starting at the beginning of the world, runs on to the apostles, and thence to the day of judgment. For Augustine says: "The church which brought forth Abel, Enoch, Noah and Abraham, also brought forth Moses, and at a later time the prophets before the Lord's advent and she, which brought forth these, also brought forth the apostles and our martyrs and all good Christians. For she has brought forth all who have been born and lived at different periods, but they have all been comprised in a company of one people. And the citizens of this city have experienced the toils of this pilgrimage. Some are experiencing them now, and some will be experiencing them, even to the end of the world." How clearly that holy man shows what the

---

[1] See Bissell, *Com. on Apocrypha*, Lange Series, 343, 359. Also *Apocrypha* trsl. out of the Greek and Latin, Cambr., 1895.

[2] Huss takes up the decree of predestination in his *Super IV. Sent.*, 153-188. He makes a slight distinction between elect and predestinate, although he says the Masters use the terms interchangeably. Election may only be for the present life, as in the case of Judas, of whom Christ said: "Did not I elect you twelve, yet one of you is a devil?" John 6 : 70. The predestinate cannot fall, and yet no necessity is placed upon their free will, pp. 165, 168.

holy catholic church is! And, in the same place and in a similar way, he speaks of the church of the wicked. This, he says, "brought forth Cain, Ham, Ishmael, and Esau, and also Dathan and other like persons of that people. And she, which brought forth these, also brought forth Judas, the false apostles, Simon Magus, and other pseudo-Christians, down to these days—all obstinately hardened in fleshly lusts, whether they are mixed together[1] in a union or are clearly distinguished the one from the other." So much, Augustine.

From this statement it appears that the holy universal church is one, the church which is the totality of the predestinate, including all, from the first righteous man to the last one to be saved in the future. And it includes all who are to be saved who make up the number, in respect to the filling up of which number all the saints slain under the altar had the divine assurance that they should wait for a time until the number should be filled up of their fellow servants and brethren, Rev. 6 : 9–11. For the omniscient God, who has given to all things their weight, measure and number, has foredetermined how many shall ultimately be saved. Therefore, the universal church is also Christ's bride about whom the Canticles speak, and about whom Isaiah, 61 : 10, "as a bridegroom decked with a crown, and as a bride adorned with jewels." She is the one dove of which Christ said: "My dove is one, my excellent one," Canticles 6 : 9.[2] She is also the

---

[1] *Permixti*, which the Decretum has instead of *proximi*, Huss's text.

[2] This text *una est columba, una perfecta mea*, was a chief biblical proof used by the Schoolmen for the unity of the church. The Song of Solomon had a great fascination for the Schoolmen—the book upon which, one after another, they exercised their allegorical skill. It was regarded as an inspired anthology of the bodily and spiritual excellences of the Virgin Mary, and the perfections of the church. They found in it a storehouse of devotional meditation, as did Bernard, whose sermons on the Canticles are full of tropical effusions to Christ and to Mary, and the chief source of his mystical theology. Paschasius Radbertus, *de corpore et sanguine*, Migne 120 : 1295, says, "The Canticles treat of the holy church of God, which is called in the Canticles the paradise of delights." Damiani represented God as inflamed with love for Mary, singing

strong woman whose maidens are clothed with double garments, Prov. 21 : 2. She is the queen, of whom the Psalmist says: "The queen stands at thy right hand in vestments of gold" [Psalms 45 : 9]. This is Jerusalem, our mother, the temple of the Lord, the kingdom of heaven and the city of the Great King; and this whole church, as Augustine, *Enchiridion*, 41 [*Nic. Fathers*, 3 : 255, 256], says, "is to be understood not only of that part which sojourns here, praising God from the rising to the setting of the sun, and which, after its old captivity, is singing the new song, but also of that part in heaven which, continuing true to the purpose for which it was constituted, has always been loyal to God, and has never felt misery from any fall. This part among the holy angels remains blessed and, as it behooves it to do, helps the part sojourning upon the earth, because she who is to be one by the companionship of eternity is now also one by the bond of love. And this whole church was constituted to worship God. Therefore, neither the whole nor any part of it wishes to be worshipped as God." So far, Augustine.

This is the holy catholic church which Christians profess immediately after professing their faith in the Holy Spirit.[1] First, because, as Augustine says,[2] she is the highest creature,

the Canticles to her praise. Albertus Magnus, in his elaborate panegyric of Mary, dwells again and again upon its passages, devoting no less than two hundred and forty pages to the words, "a garden shut up is my sister, my bride," Cant. 4 : 12. Alanus ab Insulis speaks of the Canticles as referring to the church, but in the highest spiritual sense to Mary, and another of the saner Schoolmen, Rupert of Deutz, fills his commentary on the Canticles with the most tropical language.

[1] The reference is to the Apostles' Creed, "I believe in the holy catholic church," which is preceded by the confession of God the Father, Son and Holy Ghost. Also the Nicene creed. See Schaff, *Creeds*, 2 : 57 *sq*. With regard to the intercession of the saints in heaven and on earth, the council of Trent, XXV, says: "That the saints who reign together with Christ offer up their own prayers to God for men, and it is good and useful suppliantly to invoke them, and to have recourse to their prayers and help for obtaining benefits from God through his Son, Jesus Christ, our Lord, who is our only Redeemer and Saviour."

[2] In the *Enchiridion*, as quoted above. Augustine makes a similar statement in his sermon to catechumens, *Nic. Fathers*, 3 : 375.

therefore she is placed immediately after the Trinity, which is uncreate, and second, because she is bound to Christ in a never-ending matrimony, and by the love of the Holy Spirit. And third, because, the Trinity being once acknowledged, it is proper that it should have her as a temple in which to dwell.[1] Therefore Augustine, as above [*Enchiridion*, 41] concludes: "That God dwells in his temple—not only the Holy Spirit, but the Father likewise, and also the Son. And of his body —by virtue of which he is made head of the church of God which is among men, in order that in all things he might have the pre-eminence—the Son said: 'Destroy this temple and in three days I will build it up again'" [John 2 : 21]. From these words of Augustine we deduce (1) that the universal church is one, praising God from the beginning of the world to the end; (2) that the holy angels are a part of the holy catholic church; (3) that the part of the church called pilgrim or militant is helped by the church triumphant; (4) that the church triumphant and the church militant are bound together by the bond of love; (5) that the whole church and every part of it are to worship God, and that neither she nor any part of it wishes to be worshipped as God.

From all this the conclusion follows, that the faithful ought not to believe *in* the church, for she is not God, but the

---

[1] The writers of the M. A. also made Mary the dwelling-place of the Trinity, especially the hymn-writers. So the great hymnist, Adam of St. Victor, in the lines

> *Salve mater pietatis*
> *Et totius trinitatis*
> *Nobile triclinium.*

> Hail, mother of piety;
> And of the whole Trinity
> Excellent refectory (monastic hall).

As the church is the bride of Christ, so Mary was also represented as the spouse of the Holy Spirit. Alfonso da Liguori delights so to represent her, as for example, in the prayer: "I thank thee, O eternal Spirit, for the love given to Mary, thy spouse." In his encyclical to the French bishops, Jan. 15, 1907, Pius X spoke "of his full confidence in the Virgin Immaculate, daughter of our Father, mother of the Word and spouse of the Holy Ghost," etc.

house of God, as Augustine in his *Exposition of the Creed* says,[1] but they should believe that the catholic church is the bride of the Lord Jesus Christ—bride, I say, chaste, incorrupt, and never capable of being corrupted. For St. Cyprian, the bishop and glorious martyr, 24 : 1, C. *Loquitur* [Friedberg, 1 : 971, *de Unitate Eccles.*, 5; *Ante-Nic. Fathers*, 5 : 423], says: "The church is one, which is spread abroad far and wide by the increase of her fruitfulness." And he adds: "nevertheless the head is one, the origin is one, and one is the copious mother of fruitfulness. The bride of Christ cannot be defiled. She is incorrupt and chaste. She knows one house and guards with chaste modesty the sanctity of one couch."[2] The holy church is also the husbandman's vineyard, of which Gregory in his Homilies [Migne, 76 : 1154] says: "Our Maker has a vineyard, namely the universal church, which starts from righteous Abel and goes down to the last elect person who shall be born in the end of the world, which bears as many saints as the vineyard sends forth branches." Of the church St. Remigius[3] also says in his Homily Quadragesima on the text: "'The men of Nineveh shall rise up in judgment with this generation and condemn it.' The holy church is made up of two parts, those who have not sinned and those who have ceased to sin." St. Isidore also, in speaking of the church, *de Summo Bono*, 14 [Migne, 83 : 572][4] says: "The holy

---

[1] *Sermo de symbolo*, falsely ascribed to Augustine and given in the Appendix to his Works (Migne, 40 : 1196). Three of Augustine's genuine treatises on the creed are given in translation, *Nic. Fathers*, vol. III, 282 314; 321–333; 369–375.

[2] *Cubilis*. The Decretum has *cubiculi*, bedchamber.

[3] Remigius, d. about 908, a Benedictine monk of Auxerre, who also taught at Paris. He wrote commentaries on the Psalms, Genesis, etc., and 12 Homilies on Matthew, all found in Migne, 131. He supported Paschasius's view of the change of the eucharistic elements.

[4] Usually known as the *de sententiis*, the first Latin compend of theology, and a forerunner of the *Sentences of Peter the Lombard* and the systems of the summists of the Middle Ages. Isidore, archbishop of Seville (d. 636), exercised a large influence over the scholastic studies of the Middle Ages, especially by his encyclopedic works, the *Etymologiæ* and the *de natura rerum*. The former is a general encyclopedia giving curious information derived from

church is called catholic for the reason that it is universally distributed over all the world." Augustine and Ambrose likewise in their canticle, *Praising God*, say: "The holy church throughout all the world doth acknowledge Thee."[1] And Ambrose, 24 : 1 [Friedberg, 1 : 976] speaks thus of her: "What house is more worthy of the entrance of apostolic preaching than is the holy church? Or who else is to be preferred above all others than Christ, who was accustomed to wash the feet of his guests and did not suffer any whom he received into his house to dwell there with soiled steps, that is, works?" And, speaking of this church, Pope Pelagius, 24 : 1, *C. Schisma* [Friedberg 1 : 980,][2] cites Augustine as saying, "There cannot be two churches," and then adds: "Truly, as it has often been said, there can be only one church, the church which is Christ's body, which cannot be divided into two or more bodies." Jerome also says of the church,

---

ancient authors, classic and ecclesiastical, on a large variety of subjects: medicine, law, the Bible, grammar, warfare, etc. See Bréhaut, *An Encyclopedist of the Dark Ages*, New York, 1912. Isidore was one of the very first to write a treatise designed to convince the Jews, *de fide catholica c. Judæos*. The high church fraud, the pseudo-Isidorian Decretals, which appeared about 853, was for centuries ascribed to Isidore. In the chapter quoted by Huss Isidore says, "The holy catholic church tolerates with patience in herself those who live ill, but casts out from herself those who believe ill," and again, "They are heretics who, leaving the church of God, have chosen private societies, that is, they have hewn out broken cisterns for themselves."

[1] The *Te Deum*, or canticle to the Trinity, beginning, "We praise Thee, O God." According to the legend, first noted by Hincmar in the ninth century, Augustine and Ambrose at Augustine's baptism, 387, under supernatural inspiration, improvised the hymn. In the West it became a part of the church service as early as the sixth century, if not earlier. See Julian, *Hymnology*, p. 1119 *sqq.*; Augustine, *Conff.*, 9 : 7, refers to the moving impression made upon him by the "hymns and canticles" sung in the church of Milan. For these reasons, Raphael gave Augustine a place in his painting of St. Cecilia, in Bologna.

[2] Pelagius I, pope, 555–561, witnessed the ravages of the Goth, Totila, in Rome, and helped to repair them during his pontificate. He was Justinian's choice for the papal office. The quotation is from Pelagius's letter to a certain patrician, John, condemning the ordination of Paulinus of Aquileja by the schismatic bishop of Milan as something to be execrated rather than to be regarded as sacred. See Jaffa, *Regesta pontificum*, p. 88. In this letter, Pelagius also quotes for the unity of the church Cant. 6 : 9: "My dove is one."

de Pœn., Dist. 1 : *C. Eccl.* [Friedberg 1 : 1179]: "The church of Christ has no spot or wrinkle or anything of that sort, but he who is a sinner or is soiled with any filth cannot be said to be of Christ's church." This holy universal church is Christ's mystical body, as the apostle says, Eph. 1 : 22: "He gave himself to be the head over all the church, which is his body." Again he said, Col. 1 : 18, "He is the head of the body, which is the church," and again, Col. 1 : 24, "For his body's sake, which is the church," and Eph. 5 : 23, "Christ is the head of the church and himself is the Saviour of his body," and further on: "Christ loved the church and gave himself for it that he might sanctify it, washing it with the washing of water in the word of life that he might present it to himself a glorious church, not having spot or wrinkle or anything of that kind, but that it should be holy and without spot."

Upon this text the holy doctors lean, as when Augustine says, *de doctrina Christi* [3 : 37, *Nic. Fathers*, 2 : 573]: "Christ is the head of the church, which is his body destined in the future to be with him in his kingdom and unending glory." Gregory, *Moralia*, 35 : 9 [Migne, 76 : 762] says: "Because Christ and the church are one, the head and the body are one person." And on Ezekiel, homily 15, he says: "The church is one substance with Christ, its head." And Bernard on the Canticles, homily 12 [Migne, 183 : 831]: "The church is Christ's body, more dear than the body he gave over to death."[1] And Paschasius, *de sacra. corporis Christi* [Migne, 120 : 1284][2] says: "Even as it is found in

---

[1] The passage runs: "The church lives and eats of the living bread which came down from heaven. She is the more precious body of Christ, and lest she should taste of death the other was given over to death."

[2] This treatise of Paschasius, d. 865, usually quoted as *de corpore et sanguine Christi*, is one of the most important treatises bearing on the development of the doctrine of transubstantiation. Without using the word, Paschasius set forth the view that in the Lord's Supper the very body "which was born of the Virgin Mary, suffered on the cross and rose again," is distributed by the priest. He supports this view by the literal interpretation of John 6 : 54:

the Scriptures—the church of Christ, or the bride of God, is truly called Christ's body, truly because the general church of Christ is his body and Christ is called the head and all the elect are called members. From these members the one body of the church is brought unto a perfect man and the measure of the fulness of Christ. But the body of Christ, that is, the bride of God, is called in law the church. This is according to the apostle's words: 'And they twain shall be one flesh.' This, he says, is a great sacrament in Christ and the church.[1] For, if Christ and the church are one flesh, then certainly there is one body, one head, one bridegroom, but different elect persons, members the one of the other." So far, Paschasius.

These quotations from the saints show that the holy catholic church is the number of all the predestinate[2] and Christ's mystical body—Christ being himself the head—and the bride of Christ, whom he of his great love redeemed with his blood that he might at last possess her as glorious, not having wrinkle of mortal sin or spot of venial sin, or anything else defiling her, but that she might be holy and without spot, perpetually embracing Christ, the bridegroom.

"Whoso eateth my flesh and drinketh my blood." Paschasius was a monk and then, 844–851, abbot of the convent of Corbie, nearer Amiens. His tract was written 831 and sent to Charles the Bald 844. His doctrine was opposed by the monk Ratramnus, and others. The next controversy over the Lord's Supper was led by Berengar, d. 1088. Transubstantiation was made a dogma of the church at the fourth Lateran council, 1215. Wyclif denied it, declaring that transubstantiation would involve transaccidentation. Huss was also charged with denying the doctrine, but emphatically repudiated the charge. Ratramnus's work was put on the Index by the council of Trent.

[1] Eph. 5 : 32. The false translation of Jerome, rendering the Greek word mystery by sacrament, a rendering used to justify the inclusion of marriage among the sacraments and repeated in the Rheims version.

[2] Wyclif, *Congregatio omnium predestinatorum, solum numerus predestinatorum, de Eccles.*, 2, 5, etc. In his *Com. on the Lombard*, p. 36, Huss defines the church as "the congregation of all the faithful about to be saved. It is the mystical body of Christ, that is now hidden to us, of which body the damned do not really have part, but they are like dung which in the day of judgment are to be separated from the body of Christ."

CHAPTER II

THE ONE UNIVERSAL CHURCH DIVIDED INTO THREE PARTS

Iт having been said what the holy universal church is—that she is only one just as the number of all the predestinate is one, and also that she is distributed in her members throughout all the word—it must be known that this holy universal church is tripartite, that is, divided into the church triumphant, militant and dormient.

The church militant is the number of the predestinate now on its pilgrimage to the heavenly country, and is called militant because it wages Christ's warfare against the flesh, the world and the devil.

The church dormient is the number of the predestinate suffering in purgatory. It is called dormient because being there she does not enjoy the blessedness which in the present life through God's prevenient and assisting grace she merited that she might get her reward in the heavenly country after the satisfaction made in purgatory.

The church triumphant consists of the blessed at rest in the heavenly country who kept up Christ's warfare against Satan and have finally triumphed. There will, however, be one great church on the day of judgment, made up of all these. And as a symbol of these three parts the doctors say the sacrament of the eucharist is broken into three parts. The first part, the part immersed in the liquid sacrament, they say, signifies the church triumphant which is absorbed and inebriate with the dipping[1] of the divine essence, as says

[1] *Intinctio*, the word used of Judas's dipping the sop, Matt. 26 : 23; John 13 : 26. The custom is for the priest to break the host into two equal parts. He then drops a fragment of one of these parts into the chalice, whose contents

the head of the church, Cant. 5 : 1, making merry with his friends and companions: "Let us be drunken, my beloved," [drink abundantly, Rev. Vers.]. But the two other parts in the hand of the Lord and to be purged through the merit of the church are set forth by those two parts which the priest holds in his hands, the greater, being laid down, signifies the militant church and the lesser, resting upon it, signifies the church waiting in purgatory. For this church in purgatory depends upon the suffrages of the church militant. And for these two parts we pour out our double prayers to the Lamb, who is the head of the church, that he may have mercy upon us. But as for the third part, to whose dwelling-place and rest we look forward, we pray that the same Lamb of the three-fold nature may at last give us peace. For this reason, Christ in his state of humiliation visited three places of the church, (1) the navel of our habitable world, dwelling thirty-three years in Judea and Jerusalem; (2) the limbus, in which the Fathers were purified, by bringing out a fragment of his church in the spirit, and (3) ascending to heaven he led captivity captive, which, after his triumph, he crowned by placing it at God's right hand.[1] This, therefore, is the three-fold division of this one universal or catholic church, although, however, there are particular churches.

he drinks. The priest holds the two larger parts so that the smaller of the two lies upon the other. Thomas Aquinas, *Summa*, 3 : 84 [Migne, 3 : 851], mentions the custom of dropping a fragment into the cup.

[1] Jerusalem was regarded in the Middle Ages as the navel of the earth. The cross, according to Jerome, was erected over Adam's skull, which Shem had carried to Jerusalem after the Flood, and buried on the future Mount Calvary. Noah, according to Jacob of Edessa, had taken Adam's bones with him into the ark. The region *limbus patrum* was, according to the Schoolmen, the future abode, where the patriarchs and faithful Jews were detained until Christ's "descent into Hades." The future world is divided into five abodes, hell, the "place of dolors" (Th. Aquinas), and "the deep prison into whose smoky atmosphere the demons are cast" (Alb. Magnus); purgatory, a sort of reformatory school, where the baptized are purged of sins clinging to them at death; heaven; and the abodes of the fathers and infants, *limbus infantum*. The last is the final dwelling-place of all unbaptized children dying in infancy, where they abide forever without hope of beatitude, without change, and without vision of God or physical light.

But this universal church is a virgin, the bride of Christ
—who is a virgin—from whom as from a true mother we are
spiritually born. A virgin, I say, all beautiful and in whom
there is no spot [Cant. 4 : 7.], "having neither spot nor
wrinkle" [Eph. 5 : 27], holy and immaculate, and so most
chaste even as she is in the heavenly country. Nevertheless
by fornicating with the adulterant devil and with many of
his children she is partially corrupt by wrong-doing. However, she is never received as the bride to be embraced,
beatifically at the right hand and in the bed of the bridegroom, until she has become a pure virgin, altogether without wrinkle. For Christ is the bridegroom of virginity, who,
as he lives forever, can not allow the bride to desert him and
fornicate spiritually. Thus it is said of the multitude of the
heavenly denizens that they are virgins and follow the Lamb
wheresoever he goeth [Rev. 14 : 4]. But in the very first
moment of the world Christ was predestinated to be the bridegroom of the church, and by establishing the angels [in glory]
he gave a dowry to one part of the bride. And so also by establishing righteous Abel and other saints, up to the time of
the incarnation, the church remained continually in her es-
pousals. At the incarnation he made his second marriage by
creating to be a queen a part of the whole church, which by
a certain fitness is called the Christian church. For then
our leader and legislator familiarly addressed his bride, as
the apostle says, Heb. 1. By assuming human nature he put
on our armor and as a giant overcame the enemies of the
church and taught how a part of the church, as a jealous bride,
ought to follow him.

Therefore, the whole of Christian doctrine is involved in
that prayer of the church in which we pray the bridegroom,
by his coming into the flesh, that he may teach us to despise
earthly things and love heavenly things—to despise, that is,
to subordinate, terrestrial things in our affections and to love
Christ the bridegroom above all things.

Hence, it is evident that the universal holy church is Christ's one and only bride, the virgin to be in the end most chaste, whom the Son of God bound to himself in matrimony out of eternal love and by the grace of adoption, and the church we firmly believe, saying with the Creed, "I believe one holy catholic church," and about which the word is added in the second Creed, " and apostolic [church]." It is called apostolic for the reason that the apostles are full participants of this same mother church, which is fully purified in the Spirit, and which they themselves planted with the teaching and blood of Christ; and by whose teaching (*i. e.*, of the apostles) and authority their vicars now rule the young bride, who seeks only the bridegroom of the church. So runs the Decretal 24 [Friedberg, 1 : 968] where pope Leo says: "Peter's authority has its seat wherever its just sentence is carried." For Peter himself dwells in heaven, seeing and looking after what God binds and looses. Hence Boniface VIII, *Extravagante*, says: "We are bound with living faith to believe and hold that the holy catholic and apostolic church is one." [1]

The unity of the catholic church consists in the unity of predestination, inasmuch as her separate members are one by predestination[2] and in the unity of blessedness, and inasmuch as her separate sons are finally united in bliss. For, in the present time, her unity consists in the unity of faith and the Christian virtues and in the unity of love, even as

[1] Boniface's famous bull, *Unam sanctam*, issued 1302 against Philip the Fair of France, which commands subjection to the Roman pontiff as the condition of salvation for every creature. The text goes on, "and we firmly believe it and sincerely confess that outside of it there is no salvation or remission of sins, as the bridegroom announced in the Canticles: 'My bride is one.'" See Schaff, *Ch. Hist.*, V, part 2 : 25 *sqq.* for the original and translation; Friedberg, 2 : 1245; Mirbt, 162. In this treatise Huss quotes this bull a number of times, even to the last chapter.

[2] In his Reply to Palecz, *Mon.*, 1 . 321, Huss says again: "The grace of predestination is the chain by which the body of the church and every member of it are joined to Christ." He also speaks of the unity through love, faith, and hope, *Mon.*, 1 : 326.

Augustine draws forth in expounding John 17 : 21, "that they all may be one," and in his letter to Dardanus,[1] where he expounds the text "it is expedient that one man die for the people" [John 18 : 14]. " Caiaphas," Augustine says: "prophesied that God would gather together in one his children" [John 11 : 52], that is, not in one material locality; " but he has gathered them together into one spirit and one body, whose only head is Christ." To this unity the apostle refers, Eph. 4 : 3: " endeavoring to keep the unity of the Spirit in the bond of peace. There is one body, one Spirit, one Lord, one faith, one baptism, one God and Father of all." Nor is it to be doubted that without this union, as indicated before, is there any salvation.

[1] Dardanus Claudianus Postumus, a Christian prefect of Gaul, the same to whom, probably, Jerome also addressed a letter. For Augustine's letter, Migne, 33 : 832.

CHAPTER III

ALL CHRISTIANS ARE NOT MEMBERS OF THE CHURCH

AGAINST what has already been said the objection is raised (1) that if the treatment is correct then no reprobate would be a part of our holy mother, the universal church. But the consequence is false, for every Christian is a part of that church, as appears from the parable, Matt. 13 : 47: "The kingdom of heaven is like unto a net cast into the sea which gathered in all manner of fish." On this St. Gregory in his Homilies [Migne, 76 : 1116] says: "The holy church is compared to a net cast into the sea because she is committed to fishers and because every one is drawn up through her from the waves of this present world to the eternal kingdom lest they sink in the depths of eternal death." (2) The falsehood of the treatment is confirmed by Matt. 22 : 2: "The kingdom of heaven is likened to a king, who made a marriage feast for his son and sent forth his servants to call them that were bidden to the marriage feast." Going out, they gathered in all whom they found, both good and bad, and the marriage feast was full of guests. Here Gregory says: "By the very quality of the guests it is evident that by this royal marriage the present church is meant, in which the bad meet with the good, a mixed church made up of a diversity of children." [1] (3) It is confirmed by what is said, Matt. 13 : 41, "The Son of man shall send forth his angels and gather together out of his kingdom all things that offend and them that do iniquity"; and (4) by Matt. 5 : 20: "Whoso shall

---

[1] Migne, 76 : 1285. Gregory continues by saying that, though the church brings forth to faith, nevertheless she does not lead all to the liberty of spiritual grace, etc.

break one of the least of these commandments and teach men so, shall be least in the kingdom of heaven." Commenting on both these passages, Gregory, homily 12, says: "The kingdom of heaven is the present church" [Migne, 76 : 1119].

(5) The falsehood appears from Luke 3 : 17: "He shall baptize you with the Holy Spirit and with fire : whose fan is in his hand, and he will cleanse his threshing-floor and gather the wheat into his garner; but the chaff he will burn with fire unquenchable." Here threshing-floor stands for the catholic church as the doctors expound, especially Augustine, who says of faith, *ad Petrum:* "Hold most tenaciously and in no wise doubt that God's threshing-floor is the catholic church and that in it the chaff will remain mixed with the wheat till the end of the world."[1] And this judgment of Augustine is confirmed by Christ's words: "The kingdom of heaven is like unto a man who sows good seed in his field," and Christ afterward says: "Let both grow until the harvest," Matt. 13 : 30.

Now for the right understanding of these things and the things to be said, we must lay down out of the apostle's words that Christ is the head of the universal church, that she is

---

[1] The quotation is taken from the *de fide ad Petrum sive de regula veræ fidei,* wrongly ascribed to Augustine, but printed by Migne, 40 : 753–780, in the Appendix to Augustine's works, and with a Preface stating its genuineness to be a matter of doubt. The work was written by Fulgentius, bishop of Ruspe, in North Africa, not far from Carthage, d. about 533; a vigorous writer against Arianism and semi-Pelagianism. The treatise was addressed to Peter the Deacon, and not to Peter the Apostle, as Huss seems to think. For Peter the Deacon who was sent on a mission to Pope Hormisdas, see Wetzer-Welte, 9 : 1907 *sq.* The treatise is a high church document, and is quoted at least three times in the *Corp. jur. can.,* and under the name of Augustine, viz., *C.* 1 : 1, 55; *C.* 15 : 1, 3; *de consol., D.* 4 : 3, Friedberg, 1 : 379, 746, 1376. The writer follows up the words cited above by saying: "The wicked are mixed with the good in the communion of the sacraments; and in every profession, whether it be the profession of clerics, monastics, or laics, the wicked and the good are mingled. . . . The wicked are to be tolerated for the sake of the good so far as the reason of faith and love demand." Fulgentius declared that "A heretic or a schismatic, though they had been baptized in the name of the Trinity, are outside the catholic church, no matter how much they might give in charity and even though they sweat blood for the name of Christ, yet they could not be saved unless they became incorporated into the catholic church," p. 776.

his body and that every one who is predestinate is one of her members and consequently a part of this church, which is Christ's mystical body, that is, hidden body, ruled by the power and influence of Christ, the Head, and compacted and welded together by the bond of predestination. This underlying proposition follows from that saying of the apostle: "He gave him to be head over all the church which is his body," Eph. 1 : 22. It also follows from the words when, speaking as the representative of the predestinate, he says: "We being many are one body in Christ," Romans 12 : 5. It also follows from Eph. 4 : 11, 15: "He gave some apostles, some prophets, some evangelists, and some pastors and teachers, for the perfecting of the saints for the work of the ministry unto the edifying of the body of Christ." And further on it is said: "Doing the truth in love, let us grow up in all things into him who is the head, even Christ, for whom all the body compacted together by that which every joint supplieth, according to the working in the measure of each several part, maketh increase of the body unto the edifying of itself in love."

Further it is to be noted that Christ is called the head of the church for the reason that he is the most exalted individual of the human family, imparting to all its members motion and feeling. For as in a man the most excellent part is the head, which gives to the body and to its parts motion and feeling, and without which neither the body nor any of its members could live the life of nature, so Christ is the individual, the true God and man, imparting spiritual life and motion to the church and every one of its members and without whose influence it could not live or feel. And as in a man's head are all the senses, so in Christ are hid all the treasures of the wisdom and knowledge of God. Col. 2 : 3. The above judgment is also involved in the apostle's words when he says, Col. 1 : 20: "All things were created by him and in him; and he is before all, and in him do all things consist

and he is the head of the body, the church who is the beginning and the first born from the dead; that in all things he
might have the pre-eminence—*primatum*—for in him it was
pleasing that all fulness should dwell and through him to
reconcile all things to himself."

This unity of the body—that is the church—the apostle
proves by showing, I Cor. 12 : 3, that the diversity of graces,
ministries and operations proceeds from the one spiritual Lord
who works in all. For grace must precede: it is the beginning
of ministration for clerics and of operation for laymen. The
Spirit gives grace, the Lord receives ministration, and God
demands ministration. "To one," the apostle says, "is given
by the Spirit the word of wisdom, to another the word of
knowledge by the same Spirit; to one faith in the same Spirit,
to another the grace of healing, to another the working of miracles, to another prophecy, to another discerning of spirits, to
another divers sorts of tongues, to another the interpretation
of words." These nine the apostle seems to express one after
the other, each in its own logical order in the men who
receive the gifts. God, he says, has placed some in the church,
first apostles, secondarily prophets, thirdly teachers, then
miracles, then gifts of healings, interpretations of words, helps,
governments, divers sorts of tongues, all nine of which seem
to be correlated to the former nine. And in the same passage,
comparing the body of Christ and its members to the body
of the natural man, the apostle says, I Cor. 12 : 12: "As
the body is one and hath many members, but all the members
of the body, though they are many, are one body; so also is
Christ."

There is to be noted a threefold correspondence and a
threefold difference between the members of the mystical
body and the human body. For as the members compose
one body to which the soul is joined, and again as each member
is necessary to every other, the one helping the other in the
performance of its functions, so it is true of the members of

the church by virtue of the power of communion and the bond of love. Again as the members of the body keep themselves in their own function, so do also the members of the church. For, according to Chrysostom, *de opere imperfecto*, a man is as a book in whom the whole Christian religion is written, therefore, just as there is an affinity from the head down to the feet, so reason and feeling are bound together. Also, just as every member, comely or uncomely, serves the spirit without strife, so every member of the church serves Christ, without any strife concerning supremacy and obedience. And, just as the superior members do not boast of their comeliness but perform their functions and follow the soul's rule unto the help of each single member, so ought it to be with members of the church. And just as the eyes and the countenance are in their activities without a covering lest, if veiled, they might defile and prepare for destruction, so Christ and the apostles, out of the fervor of their love and by reason of their exemption from the fervor of lust, were not involved in temporal interests in a secular way; and their vicars, yea, all clerics ought to be like eyes. But the members, less comely, as the secret parts, are more concealed and more tender and multiplex, and so it is with mean[1] persons, by whom the dregs of the church are gotten rid of. But the difference between the members of these bodies is to be stated thus: (1) Since the parts of the church persist by grace, they are not concerned as to their place or corporal location, as are the members of the human body. (2) As the members are mystical, it is not inconsistent but fitting that single members should have functions of different kinds. For a man is, as it were, a totality—*universitas*—so that it is fitting that he should act all at once, so far as he is able. (3) The members of the church should have vital forces flowing into them from Christ, just as the members of the body have vital forces

---

[1] *Contemptibilibus*, a departure from the Vulgate word for " uncomely " used above—*ignobile*.

flowing into them from the soul, from which these forces become part of the very essence of the members; nevertheless, the inflowing comes first, and the operation of the members is voluntary and gracious and meritorious.[1]

Further, it is to be noted that, as there is in the human body an element which is not of the body itself, as spittle, phlegm, ordure,[2] and fluid or urine, and this element is not of the body because it is not a part of the body—and it is another thing to be a part of the human body, as is every one of its members—so also there is something in the mystical body of Christ, which is the church, that is nevertheless not of the church, since it is not a part of it; and in this way every reprobate Christian is of the body just as ordure is of the body and to be finally separated from it. And so it is one thing to be of the church and another thing to be in the church—*aliud esse de ecclesia, aliud esse in ecclesia.* And it is clear that it does not follow of all pilgrims who are in the church, that they are then of the church, but the opposite. For we know that the tares grow together with the wheat, the raven feeds on the same threshing-floor as the dove, and the chaff is gathered into the same garner with the grain. Nevertheless, there is an incommunicable distinction between them, just as has been illustrated by the human body. In this way we ought to think of holy mother church, and to these things I John 2 : 18 has reference where it is said: "Now have there arisen many antichrists. They went out from us, but were not of us; for, if they had been of us, they would have continued with us." For just as superfluity proceeds from food and the solid members and yet is not of them, so the purgaments of the church, namely the reprobate, proceed from her and yet are not of her as parts; for none of her parts can fall away from her finally, because predestinating love, which binds her together, does not fail. This the apostle asserts, I Cor. 13, and this he

[1] The same thoughts are developed in the Reply to Palecz, *Mon.*, 1 : 321.
[2] Jerome's word, *Phil.*, 3 : 8.

proves, Romans 8 : 28 *sqq.*, when he says: "We know that to them that love God all things work together for good, even to them that are called to be righteous according to his purpose," that is, the purpose of predestination. "For whom he foreknew, them he also predestinated to be conformed to the image of his Son, that he might be the first-born among many brethren. And whom he predestinated, them he also called; and whom he called, them he also justified." And he concludes by calling them predestinate after suffering a long trial when he said: "I am persuaded that neither death nor life, nor angels, nor principalities, nor powers, nor things present, nor things to come, nor might,[1] nor depth, nor any creature shall be able to separate us from the love of God which is in Christ Jesus our Lord."

Besides, it is to be noted that, as many say, the relation of pilgrims to holy mother church is fourfold. Some are in the church in name and in fact, as are predestinate Catholics, obedient to Christ; some are neither in fact nor in name, as are the reprobate heathen; some in name only, as are reprobate hypocrites; and some are in the church in fact, although they may seem in name to be outside, as are predestinate Christians whom the satraps of antichrist seem to be damning before the very eyes of the church, for so pontiffs and Pharisees condemned by bitter death our Redeemer as a blasphemer, and consequently as an heretic, "who was predestinated to be the Son of God " (Romans 1 : 4).

Further, it is to be noted that no place, or human election, makes a person a member of the holy universal church, but divine predestination does in the case of every one who persists in following Christ in love. And, according to Augustine —*de predestinatione sanctorum* [*Nic. Fathers*, 5 : 498 *sqq.*]— predestination is the election of the divine will through grace; or, as it is commonly said, predestination is the preparation

---

[1] *Fortitudo* with the Vulgate, but Huss omits the Vulgate's *neque altitudo*— "nor height."

of grace—making ready—in the present time, and of glory in the future. But the position is taken, de Penitentia, Dist. 4 [Friedberg, 1 : 1234], *Hinc propheta*, that predestination is twofold: First, the one predestination by which a person is foreordained here to righteousness and the acceptance of the remission of sins, but not for the obtaining of the life of glory.[1] To this predestination the second definition, as given above, does not apply. The other predestination is that whereby a person is predestinated to obtain eternal life in the future. The first kind of predestination follows this, and not vice versa. For, if any one is predestinated to eternal life, it necessarily follows that he is predestinated unto righteousness, and, if he follows life eternal, he has also followed righteousness. But the converse is not true. For, many are made partakers of present righteousness but, from want of perseverance, are not partakers of life eternal. Hence it is said, *de Penitentia*, 4, *Hoc ergo*: "Many seem to be predestinate by the merit of present righteousness and not by the predestination of eternal glory." And Gratian grounds this position in the words of the apostle, Eph. 1 : 3–7: "Blessed be the God and Father of our Lord Jesus Christ who has blessed us with every spiritual blessing in the heavenly places in Christ: even as He chose us in Him before the foundation of the world, that we should be holy and without blemish before Him in love: who predestinated us unto the adoption of sons through Jesus Christ, according to the good pleasure of His will to the praise of the glory of His grace, which is freely bestowed on us in His beloved Son, in whom we have our redemption through His blood unto[2] the remission of sins."

Further, it is evident that men may be of holy mother church in two ways—either by predestination to life eternal, the way all who are finally holy are of holy mother church,

---

[1] Augustine is quoted at length in the *de Penitentia*, 4 : 7–12 [Friedberg, 1 : 1229 *sqq.*]; Huss does not quote Augustine, but Gratian's comment.

[2] *In* is lacking in the Vulgate, which, following the Greek, puts "remission" into apposition with "redemption."

or by predestination to present righteousness only, as are all such who at one time or another accept the grace of the remission of sins but do not persevere unto the end.

And, further, it is evident that grace is twofold—namely, the grace of predestination unto eternal life, from which a person foreordained cannot finally fall away. The other is the grace related to present righteousness, which now is present and now is absent, now comes and now goes. The first kind of grace makes sons for the holy universal church and makes a man infinitely more perfect than the second kind, because it bestows an infinite good to be enjoyed forever. But not so the second kind of grace. Again, the first makes sons of an eternal heritage, while the second makes officials acceptable to God only for time. Hence it seems probable that just as Paul was at the same time a blasphemer according to present unrighteousness and yet of holy mother church, and, consequently, one of the faithful and in grace in virtue of predestination unto eternal life—so Iscariot was at one and the same time in grace according to present righteousness and yet never of holy mother church by predestination unto life eternal, for that predestination was wanting in his case. And so Iscariot, howbeit he was an apostle and bishop elected by Christ—"bishop" being the name of an office—was nevertheless never a part of holy mother church. Even so Paul was never a member of the devil, howbeit he committed some acts which were like the acts of the church of the wicked. Similar was the case of Peter, who, by the Lord's permission, fell into grave perjury, but in order that he might rise the stronger; for, as Augustine says: It is expedient that the predestinate fall into sins of that sort.

From what has been said, it is evident that there is a twofold separation from holy church. The first is permanent [cannot be lost—*indeperdibilis*], and here belong the reprobate who are separated from the church. The second may be lost—*deperdibilis*—and here belong heretics, who are separated by ruinous sin from holy church itself, but, nevertheless, are able by God's grace to come to the sheepfold of the Lord Jesus Christ. Of the latter Christ says: "Other sheep I have which are not of this fold, and them I must bring," John 10 : 16. Other sheep he had by virtue of predestination, which are not of this fold and of his church according to present righteousness, which sheep of his grace he brought to life.

This distinction between predestination and present grace deserves to be strongly emphasized, for some are sheep by predestination and ravening wolves according to present righteousness, as Augustine deduces in his Commentary on John [*Nic. Fathers*, 7 : 253 *sq.*]: "In like manner some are sons by predestination and not yet by present grace." And this same distinction in both its parts Augustine touches upon in his Exposition of John 11 : 52 [*Nic. Fathers*, 7 : 278], where it is said: "That they might gather together into one the children of God who are scattered abroad." "Caiaphas," Augustine says, "was prophesying of the Jewish people only, to whom the sheep belonged whom the Lord had in mind when he said: 'I am not sent but unto the lost sheep of the house of Israel,' but the Evangelist knew that there were other sheep who were not of this fold which he had to bring. Therefore, he added: 'And not for that nation only, but that he might gather together into one the sons of God who are scattered abroad.' These things, moreover, were said according to the law of predestination. For, up to that time, they were neither his sheep nor the sons of God." So much Augustine. And in reference to these things it is said, *de Penitentia, Dist.* 4, *Hoc ergo* [Friedberg, 1 : 1235]: "In this way they are not children except as they are partakers of eternal blessedness." And it is added: "They are called children in three ways: either by predestination alone, as those of whom John spoke that 'he might gather into one the children of God who are scattered abroad'; or by predestination and the hope of

eternal blessedness, as were those to whom the Lord said:
'Little children, yet a little while I am with you'; or, thirdly,
by the merit of faith and present righteousness, but not by
predestination to eternal glory, as was the case with those of
whom the Lord said: 'If his sons forsook my law and walked
not in my statutes' [Psalm 89 : 31]."

CHAPTER IV

CHRIST THE ONLY HEAD OF THE CHURCH

In view of what has been said, the conclusion is (1) that
Christ alone is the head of the universal church, which church
is not a part of anything else. This is clear because, if any one
is the head of the universal church, then is he made better
than the angels and than any blessed created spirit, Heb.
1 : 4; but this befits Christ alone, for it behooved him to be
the first-born among many brethren, Romans, 8 : 29, and
consequently it behooves him to be the chief by the right of
the law of primogeniture, Col. 1 : 15. This conclusion also
follows from the apostle's words, Eph. 1 : 20: "Which God
wrought in Christ when he raised him from the dead and
made him to sit at his right hand in the heavenly places, far
above all rule and authority, power and dominion, and every
name which is named not only in this world but also in the
world which is to come, and has put all things under his feet
and gave him to be head over all things to the church, which
is his body." From this it is clear that, if any Christian were
to be the head of the universal church with Christ (for the
church cannot be a monster having two heads, as is set forth
in Boniface VIII's bull, beginning *Unam sanctam;* therefore,
the bull says, "the church is one body and has one head,
not two heads, like a monster "), it would be necessary to
concede that the Christian who was the head of that church
was Christ himself, or otherwise it would be necessary to
concede that Christ is inferior to that Christian and a lowly
member of him. The conclusion shows that the thing is impossible. Hence, the holy apostles agreed in confessing that

they were servants of that one Head and humble ministers of the church, his bride. No one of the apostles ever presumed to claim that he was the head or the bridegroom of the church, for this would have meant to adulterate with the queen of heaven and to arrogate the name of dignity and office—the dignity by which, according to the eternal predestination, and the office through which, by eternal appointment, God ordained that Christ should be supreme ruler of his bride. This also appears from St. Augustine's letter to Dardanus [Migne's ed., 33 : 832 *sqq.*], where he says: "She only has one head, namely him who rules over her, excelling all and typifying in one union the spiritual and secular rule."

Therefore, it is possible to understand the " Head of the Church" in a twofold sense: inward and outward. In the inward sense, as the chief person of his church, and he is this in two ways: either by superintendence over the material goods of his church or by ruling over its spiritual things. As outward head he is a person that superintends persons inferior to his nature, but he is called the head to those outside of this number whom he rules by his influence in virtue of his nature. And so Christ is the outward head of every particular church and of the universal church by virtue of his divinity, and he is the inward head of the universal church by virtue of his humanity and these two natures, divinity and humanity, are one Christ, who is the only head of his bride, the universal church, and this is the totality of the predestinate. For this divinity is the man who descended from heaven and who ascended again into heaven, as is said in John 3 : 13, not the whole of the divinity considered as divinity, but according to the headship whose descent was not a local movement but an incarnation or self-emptying. And the ascent was a local movement by which he took with himself the other parts of the body.

Hence, it is plain that there is nothing inconsistent in a

particular church having several heads. For it may have three heads, namely the divinity of Christ, his humanity, and the chief appointed by God to rule over it. But there are degrees of subordination in these heads, because the divinity is supreme, Christ's humanity is intermediate, and the chief is the lowest. But the universal church, as has been said, has two heads, the outward head which is the divinity and the inward which is the humanity.

Further, from these things it is seen that Christ from the very beginning of the world down to his incarnation was, in virtue of his divinity, the outward head of the church, but from the incarnation on he is the inward head of the church, by virtue of his humanity. And so the whole holy catholic church always has had and now has Christ as its head, from whom it cannot fall away, for she is the bride knit to him, her head, by a love that never ends, for the bridegroom says to the church herself, Jer. 31 : 3: "I have loved thee with an everlasting love, therefore with loving kindness have I drawn thee." Therefore, always, from the very beginning, the bridegroom has been present with the whole church by virtue of his divinity, who later was with the holy fathers by virtue of his humanity. Hence Augustine says, commenting on Psalm 37 : 25, "I have been young [*junior*, younger] and now I am old": "The Lord himself in his heart, that is, his church, was younger than the first men. And, behold, now that he is old, ye know and do not know, and ye understand because ye are fixed in this, and so ye have believed, because Christ is our head, we are the body of the head. Are we alone the body and not those also who were before us? All who were righteous from the beginning of the world have Christ for their head. For they believed that he was for to come whom we now believe to have come, and in the faith in him they were healed, in which faith we also are healed; that he verily might be the head of the whole city of Jerusalem, all the faithful being included from

the beginning even unto the end, and all the legions and
armies of the angels being also added—that so there might
be one city under one king, and one province under one
emperor, happy, lauding God in its never-ending peace and
salvation, and blessed without end. Christ's body, which is
the church, is, as it were, like a young man. And now in the
end of the world the church is of plump old age, because, with
reference to this, it was said of her: 'They shall be multiplied
in her plump old age.' She has been multiplied among all
nations." So much Augustine, in whose words it appears how
Christ is the head of the holy church, in whom the fathers
believed as the one who was for to come in virtue of
his humanity that he might be their head in his humanity
as he had always been present with them in his divinity.
And in this head all the elect are united, together with the
holy angels.

(2) The second point concerns the objection that no reprobate is a member of our holy mother, the Catholic church.
For, not only is our holy mother, the Catholic church, one
from the beginning of the world, which without mixture has
been embraced with never-ending love by the right hand of
the bridegroom, as is plain from what has been said above
and on Augustine's authority: Inasmuch as the church, after
the day of judgment, will have no other members than she has
and will have before the day of judgment, but all who are
to be saved after that day of judgment are predestinate,
therefore none of them, before that day of judgment are reprobate. And consequently no reprobates have ever been
members of the church, the bride of Christ. By the same kind
of reasoning this will always be true, that no reprobate whatsoever is a member of our holy mother, the Catholic church.

Likewise, it is not possible that at any time Christ does
not love his bride or any part of her, for he necessarily loves
her as he loves himself. But it is not possible that he should
love any reprobate in this way; therefore it is not possible

that any reprobate should be a member of the church. The antecedent is clear from that notable principle, "that God is not able to know or love anything *de novo*," as Augustine says, *de Trinitate*, 6 [*Nic. Fathers*, 3 : 103]. For God is not able to begin to know anything or to give up knowing anything or to call forth an act of his will, for he is unchangeable and also because the divine knowledge or volition is not conditioned by anything from without.

From this it is evident that Christ loves the whole church as he loves himself, because he loves her now, just as he will love her after the day of judgment, when she will reign with him as is plain from the Canticles. For, otherwise, there would not be a true marriage out of the never-ending love of Christ, a party to the divine nuptials, if the bridegroom who is one person with the bride did not love her even as he loves himself. To this the apostle was speaking when he said: "Christ loved the church and gave himself for it that he might purify it, washing it in the laver of water, the word of life, that he might present it unto himself a glorious church, not having spot or wrinkle or any such thing, but that it should be holy and without blemish," Eph. 5 : 26, 27. For this reason Bernard, in his 12th homily on the Canticles [Migne, 183 : 831] says: "The church is Christ's body, dearer to him than the body he gave to the grave." It is plain, therefore, that it is befitting that Christ always love his bride, the holy church, just as he will love her after the day of judgment; and in the same way he hates every reprobate, just as he will hate him after the day of judgment. For, inasmuch as God knows fully what the end of every reprobate will be, and what penance every predestinate person who falls will, with God's unending grace, do—it is evident that God loves a predestinate person who sins more than he loves any reprobate person, no matter what measure of grace the latter may enjoy in time, because God wills that the predestinate have perpetual blessedness and the repro-

bate eternal fire. Thus, the Psalmist [5 : 6] says: "Thou
hatest all who work iniquity." Hence, because the pride
of the reprobate, in proportion as they hate God, always
ascends after final impenitence, they are not of Christ's
body. For St. Augustine says: Sermon on the Lord's Words,
53 [Migne's ed., 354, vol. 39 : 1568]: "A lowly head and a
proud member! Nay. He who loves pride does not wish to
be of the body of Christ the head." And again, Sermon 50
[Migne's ed., 138, vol. 38 : 765], he says: "Christ spoke truly
in regard to certain shepherds, for he holds all good shepherds
in himself, when he said: 'I am the chief Shepherd and all ye
are one in me.' [1] But the reprobate, who is a member of the
devil, is not duly joined together in the same structure with his
head." Augustine also, de doct. Christi, 3 : 32 [Nic. Fathers,
2 : 569], after he shows that Christ and his body, which is the
church, are one person, censures Tychonius,[2] who in his second
rule calls the whole human family the twofold—bipartitum—
body of the Lord. This, he says, "was no proper name to apply
to the body of Christ. That in truth is not the Lord's body
that will not be with him through eternity. Tychonius ought

[1] Huss's text differs from Augustine's, which runs: ego sum pastor bonus, etc.—
"I am the good Shepherd. I am, I am one. All are one with me in unity.
He who feeds apart from me, feeds against me. He who gathers not with me,
scattereth abroad. Hear how greatly this unity is commended! 'I have other
sheep which are not of this fold.'" Augustine then goes on to say that "among
the nations there were predestinate persons, who were not of the people of
Israel according to the flesh. These will not be outside of that fold—ovile—
for he must bring them also that there may be one flock—grex—and one shepherd." Here Augustine departs from the text of the Vulgate, which has unum
ovile—fold—in both places, and conforms to the Greek original, which has two
different words.

[2] Tychonius, a scholarly North African belonging to the Donatist party,
flourished about 400 and was an extensive author. Bede quotes him as essentially orthodox except on the question of the Donatist schism. He departed
from the Donatist teachings, however, in denying the visible millennial reign
of one thousand years and in accepting non-Donatist baptism. Both he and
Augustine were involved in the confusion of identifying the true church with
a visible communion, although both made the church a mixed body. Tychonius set forth seven rules of exegesis. Huss's quotation is drawn from Augustine's treatment of the second rule. Tychonius's Book of Rules has been published by Burkitt in Texts and Studies, 4 : 1, 1894.

to have spoken about the real body and the mixed body of Christ, or about the real body and the simulated body, for, not only through eternity but now, hypocrites cannot be said to be with him." How plainly does that holy man show that the reprobate are not truly of Christ's church! To refer to Augustine again, *de Pen.*, 4 [Friedberg, 1 : 1230], he draws the conclusion that no one belongs to Christ's kingdom, which is the church, except the son whom the Father gave to him, about whom it is said, John 3 : 16: "That he should not perish but have everlasting life." Therefore, he says: "Let it not move us that God does not give to some sons that gift of perseverance, for surely this could not be the case if these were of the predestinate and of those who are the called according to his purpose, who are truly the sons of promise. But, because these live piously, they are called sons of God; but those who shall continue to live wickedly and shall die in their wickedness, these he does not call sons."

And again Augustine, treating the words of I John 2 : 18 [Friedberg, 1 : 1231], "They went out from us but were not of us," says: "They were not of the number of sons, and when did they have the faith of sons? Because those who are true sons are foreknown and predestinate to be conformed to the image of God's Son and according to His purpose are called to be holy even as they are elect. For not does the son of the promise perish, but the son of perdition. These, therefore, were of the multitude who were called and not of the few who were chosen." A little further on he remarks: "For he knew from the beginning who would believe on him and who would betray him, and he said: 'Therefore, have I spoken to you, because no one can come to me, except it be given him of my Father.' After that, many of his disciples went back and no longer walked with him. They were for a time called disciples in the Gospel, nevertheless they were not true disciples, for they did not abide in his words as he said: 'If ye shall abide in my words, then are ye my disciples.' Therefore, as they did not have perseverance, they were not Christ's true disciples, and so they were not true children of God, although for a time they seemed to be so and were called so. Therefore, we call those the elect, disciples of Christ and God's children, and they are to be called children whom we see living regenerate and pious lives. And then they truly are what they are called when they abide in that on account of which they were so called [which is the ground of their receiving these names]. But if they have not the gift of perseverance, that is, do not abide in that on account of which they started out to be, then they are not truly called on account of that which they are called [for that which gives them their name], and such they are not [that is, they are not what their names indicate]; for those things do not exist with Him to whom is known what they will be in the future, that is, evil persons who have proceeded from being good" [that is, from being by name and in appearance good they will at last appear to be what they really are, namely, evil]. Thus much St. Augustine. How clearly does not he show that many are in the church who are nominally called "sons" by men, who nevertheless are not of the church, for they are not truly sons of God predestinated unto the life of glory!

This also is made plain by St. Chrysostom in his *de opere imperfecto*, Hom. 9, who says: "Those who are of God cannot perish, because no one can pluck them out of God's hand." This appears also from John 10 : 28: "My sheep hear my voice and I know them and they follow me, and I give unto them eternal life and no one shall pluck them out of my hand." And later Christ, the best of teachers, proves by the greatness of God's gift, which is the Holy Spirit, that no one is able to do this, because his Father is almighty, and from his hand no one is able to pluck anything. But, because Christ and his Father are one with the Holy Spirit—who is Christ's gift, by whom the church is knit together with him—therefore, no one is able to pluck his sheep out of his hand. For he himself from eternity has chosen every member of his church into the bridal relation. Therefore he will desert no such member; because, if this were not so, he would choose without foresight and proper provision to glory. And to this the conclusion of the great philosopher applies when he says of the reprobate who abode for a time in grace: "If they had been of us, they would have continued with us," I John 2 : 19. For this conditional clause cannot be impossible or heretical, for it is formulated by the Holy Spirit. To this text may be added Matt. 10 : 20, "It is not ye who speak, but the Spirit of your Father which speaketh in you"; and also Romans 8 : 35, where the apostle, as I have quoted above, speaking of himself and of the predestinate who are members of the church, proves that no creature shall be able to separate them from the love which is in Christ Jesus. And he gathers his members together gently, for the love of predestination does not fail, I Cor. 13. Hence the apostle says: "Ye are not in the flesh but in the Spirit, if so be that the Spirit of God dwelleth in you. But if any one hath not the Spirit of Christ, he is none of his," Roman 8 : 9. And he understands that such an one is not a part of his body.

And if, after all, it be objected that the reprobate living in this present time in love has this bond [of perfectness] and consequently is united with Christ, and the predestinate living in sin lacks this bond and consequently is not united with Christ, it is evident that, as in the human body there is fluid moisture and a radical moisture, so in Christ's mystical body there is, so it must be granted, a grace according to present righteousness and also a perfecting grace. As ulcers develop and display themselves through the moist fluid and are not continuous on account of a difference of nature [from the body itself], so for the present it is with the members of the devil who are known according to present righteousness. But the predestinate, although they may be for a time deprived of fluent grace, nevertheless have radical and abiding grace, from which they cannot fall away, and so the predestinate, being now righteous and having twofold grace, are bound by a twofold bond.

But here the objection is made that, in view of the things said above, we ought to grant that at one and the same time the same person may be righteous and unrighteous, one of the faithful and an unbeliever, a true Christian and a heretic, in abounding grace and without grace[1] (not to use other such contradictory expressions), it follows that there is a manifest contradiction. In this objection it is said that it should be granted that the same person is at one and the same time both righteous and unrighteous; but it is inconsistent with the truth, that the same person is at one and the same time both righteous and unrighteous in respect to the same thing. Even as contraries cannot at one and the same time inhere in the same person in respect to the same thing, so the names given above are, on account of their ambiguity, not contrary one to the other, for, according to the Philosopher[2] only one thing can be opposed to one thing, and so the same man is righteous by virtue of predestinating grace and unrighteous by virtue of destructive vice, as was Peter in his denial of Christ and Paul in his persecution of him. For they were at that time not fallen away from the love of predestination. Consequently they were, in view of this love, in grace and therefore righteous; and because they were at that time in sin they were deprived of fluent temporal grace and therefore were unrighteous. And if the inference be drawn: therefore they were at that time not righteous and consequently were not righteous at all, the inference is drawn by denying the first consequence. For a consequence which is drawn by proceeding from a denial to a negation does not hold except with modification as follows in this proposition, namely:

[1] Here, as a little further down, Huss uses the Greek *acharis*.

[2] Aristotle, whom the Schoolmen regarded as the forerunner of Christian truth in method and knowledge of natural things—*precursor Christi in naturalibus*.

Peter and Paul were unrighteous; therefore, according to present grace, they were not righteous. This conclusion is true. As it was properly conceded that they were righteous according to the grace of predestination and were not righteous according to present grace, so, in a similar way, Paul was one of the faithful in view of predestination and one of the unfaithful by reason of his persecution, an Israelite by predestination and a blasphemer by the law of present unrighteousness, was in the love of predestination and yet was without grace, that is, without the love of present righteousness.

Paul's own words, drawn from Hosea, confirm this: "I will call that my people which was not my people, and her my beloved that was not my beloved; and her to have acquired mercy which did not acquire mercy, and in the place where it was said unto them, Ye are not my people, there shall they be called the sons of the living God," Romans 9 : 25, 27. Hence it is evident that this Scripture and other Scripture like it are not understood except by those who know that there is not a contradiction, unless opposites are predicated of the same person according to the same thing and for the same instant of time. Those who know how to carry on such discussion acknowledge that Christ was both dead and alive during the three days; yea, as Ambrose says: "He was dead and was not dead, for he lived in the spirit and was dead in the flesh; died as a man and did not die as God." So the apostle says, I Tim. 5 : 6, that "a widow living in pleasure is dead while she liveth," because she lives in the flesh but does not live in the spirit. It is clear that neither what is contrary nor self-contradictory follows.

Finally, to sum up what has been said, it is evident that no reprobate is truly a part of holy mother church. For, if St. Thomas[1] or any one else should be found to call a reprobate who is in grace a member of the church, then he is speaking ambiguously with Augustine and sacred Scripture, giving

[1] Thomas Aquinas, the angelic doctor, d. 1274.

heed to the popular mode of speech and the popular notion
of the militant church. Hence it was stated above that St.
Augustine said [*Dist.* 4 : 8, *de Pen.;* Friedberg, 1 : 1232]:
"If they have not perseverance, that is, if they do not abide
in that for which they started out to be, then they are not
truly called what they are called, and they are not what they
are callèd. For these things do not exist for Him who knows
what they will be in the future, that is, evil persons who have
proceeded from being good"—*ex bonis mali.* This saying of
Augustine should stand against all objections wherein ambiguity is to be noted.

CHAPTER V

GOOD AND BAD IN THE CHURCH

IN answer to the proofs cited in Chapter III, urging the contrary to what is here laid down, this is to be said: To understand them we must be on our guard to note that men are said to be in holy church in different senses. For some are said to be in it by virtue of an unformed faith[1] only, as are reprobate Christians involved in sins, to whom the Lord said: "Why call ye me Lord, Lord, and do not the things which I bid you?" Luke 6 : 46. And of them he also said, "Many will say unto me in that day, Lord, Lord, did we not prophesy by thy name, and by thy name cast out demons, and by thy name do many mighty works? and then will I profess unto them, I never knew you," namely, as persons to be saved, Matt. 7 : 22. Hence Psalm 6 : 9 says: "Depart from me all ye workers of iniquity."

Some are in the church only according to present faith

---

[1] *Fides informis*, as opposed to *fides formata*, that is, faith working by love, or, as we might say, intellectual belief and living faith. The distinction of *formata* and *informis* was first made by Peter the Lombard. In his *Com. on Peter the Lombard*, Huss treats the subject at length, pp. 452–455, defining the different sorts of faith. He says, to believe God, *credere Deo*, is to believe that the things He says are true. Such faith the wicked have. To believe God, *credere Deum*, is to believe that He is God. To believe in God, *credere in Deum*, is by believing to love Him. The faith which the demons and bad men have is a quality of the intellect, but it is unformed, *informis*, faith because it is unaccompanied by love, and this unformed faith is an acquired habit and not a habit infused from above. This *fides informis* precedes hope and love, but the *fides formata* is contemporary with hope and love. Peter the Lombard, 4 : 23, quotes Ambrose as saying: "Love is the mother of all virtues, which forms all within us—*informat*—and without which there is no virtue." Luther denounces this distinction as a pestilential ecclesiastical invention. Denifle, in his *Life of Luther*, 1 : 637 *sqq.*, makes the astounding assertion that the faith which Luther required was simply an intellectual assent—faith without love and the works of love.

and grace, as the reprobate righteous, who are not in the church by virtue of predestination to life eternal. Others are in the church by virtue of predestination only, as are unbaptized children of Christian parents and pagans, or Jews destined to be Christians in the future. Others are in the church by virtue of an unformed faith and predestination, as are predestinate Christians who are now in sins, but will return to grace. Others are in the church by virtue of predestination and present grace, as are all predestinate Christians who imitate Christ in their lives, who, however, may in this life fall away from fluent [operating] grace. Still others are in the church now triumphant, confirmed in grace. But all are divided into the reprobate and the predestinate, the former being ultimately the members of the devil and the others members of the mystical body which is the holy church, the bride of our Lord Jesus Christ.

Therefore, in the first proof taken from the net, the predestinate are represented by the good fish, and the reprobate by the bad fish which they cast out. On this Gregory [Migne, 76 : 1116] has this to say: "Holy church is compared to a net cast into the sea, for she also is committed to fishermen. This is the first resemblance, and by her every one is drawn from the waves of this present age into the eternal kingdom, namely by call, lest he be drowned in the depths of eternal death. This is the second resemblance. She gathers together fish of every kind, because she calls to the forgiveness of sins the wise and the foolish, the free and the bond, the poor and the rich, the strong and the weak. This is the third resemblance."

Therefore, let the false writer be on his guard against inferring that, because holy church gathers together by her call men of every kind, therefore all men are called to faith which is in Christ and are members of holy church, Christ's bride. Hence St. Gregory conclusively shows who are the elect and who are the reprobate, when he says that "at the end

of the world the good fish will be gathered into vessels, but
the bad cast out, because every elect person is received into
everlasting habitations, and the reprobate, having lost the
light of the eternal realm, are cast into outer darkness.   For
now the net of faith holds the good—that is, the elect—and
the evil—that is, the reprobate—mingled together, like the
fishes.   This is the fourth resemblance.   And the net which
she drew, namely, by the call of faith, represents the shore of
holy church."   And St. Gregory adds: "And the fish of the
sea which were caught cannot be numbered.   But we who are
bad when we are caught are thoroughly changed in the element of goodness."   In this he finds a sign that the wicked
who are predestinate are permanently and thoroughly changed
into what is good.   Therefore, the voice of St. Gregory is the
voice of the predestinate who, being smitten with badness, are
through baptism and penance called back by holy church to
goodness.

From these things is evident the exposition of the second
proof from the parable of the marriage supper, in which are
gathered by faith the good and the bad, who are mingled in
holy church.   But the bad are not true sons, just as those are
not true friends, because they lack the marriage garment,
which is predestinating love.   Hence the king of the wedding
will say to them, as he said to the one: "Friend, why did'st
thou come in hither not having a wedding-garment?"   At
this point Gregory says: "It is very remarkable, my dear
friends, that he at one and the same time calls this one friend
and condemns him, as if he might more aptly say: 'Friend and
no-friend—friend by faith and no-friend by works.'"   Thus
much Gregory [Migne, 76 : 1289].

The exposition of the third proof is clear because they
gather up from the kingdom of holy church all that offend,
that is, those who commit iniquity, namely, the sin of final impenitence [the parable of the tares, Matt. 13 : 41].   Here the
reprobate are referred to.

As to the fourth proof, which runs, "Whosoever therefore shall do one of these least commandments"—to this St. Augustine aptly replies, Com. on John 21 : 11 [*Nic. Fathers*, 7 : 443], where Simon Peter is said to draw "the net to land full of great fishes, a hundred and fifty and three." St. Augustine says: "'Whosoever will break one of these least commandments and shall teach men so, shall be called least in the kingdom of heaven; but whoso shall do and teach them shall be called great in the kingdom of heaven.' The latter, therefore, would belong to the number of the great fishes. But the former, that is, 'the least,' who in act breaks what he teaches in word, may be in such a church, which contains those who are represented by that first catch of fishes, which had both bad and good, because this catch is also called the kingdom of heaven—for he said, 'The kingdom of heaven is like unto a net cast into the sea, which gathers in all kinds of fish,' a parable by which he wishes both the good and the bad to be understood. And of these he says that they are to be separated on the shore, namely, at the end of the world. Then, in order to show that these 'least' are the reprobate, who teach good things with their lips and break them by their bad living, and will not be as the 'least' in the future in the life eternal, yea will not be there at all, for he had said, 'He shall be called least in the kingdom of heaven,'—Christ went on to say: 'For I say unto you, except your righteousness shall exceed the righteousness of the scribes and Pharisees, ye shall not enter into the kingdom of heaven.' Certainly, these are the scribes and Pharisees who sit in Moses' seat and of whom Christ said: 'Whatsoever things they say, these do ye, but whatsoever things they do, these do not ye, for they say and do not,' Matt. 23 : 2. They teach in words what they break in their lives. Therefore the conclusion is that he who is 'least in the kingdom of heaven,' the church now being made up of such as it is, will not enter into the kingdom of heaven, the church being then what it is to be; because, in teaching the things which he is in the habit of breaking, he will not belong to the company of those who practise what they teach. Therefore, will this one not be of the number of the great fishes, for he who both practises and teaches, he shall be called great in the kingdom of heaven. And because he was great here, therefore he will be in the place where that least person is not. Yea, and so very great will they be there [that is, in heaven] that the one who there is the least is greater than he than whom here no one is greater. Nevertheless those who are great here, that is, those who are in the kingdom of heaven, where the net gathers together the good and the bad, and do the good things they teach—these shall be the greater in that eternal kingdom of heaven, even those who belong at God's right hand and to the resurrection of life, and those are they whom the fish represent." Thus far Augustine.

Augustine's words have the same meaning as the words of Gregory, namely, that the church gathers together the elect and the reprobate in the faith; and, secondly, that those who teach in the church and fill its seats of dignity and break God's commandments are reprobate. For he says: "Finally, in order to show that those least are the reprobate, who teach good things with their lips and break them with bad living, they will not only not be as the least in the eternal life in the future, but will not be there at all." In the third place, he teaches that faithful Christians, doing God's commands, indeed are great in God's holy church, and that prelates who occupy commanding offices and break the commandments are the least; and, if they are reprobate, then they will not be in the kingdom of God. Therefore, let the disciples of antichrist blush who live contrary to Christ and yet say they are the greatest in God's holy church and are most proud, and who, flourishing in public places by the covetousness and haughtiness of this world, are called the heads and the body of holy church, but who, according to the Gospel of Christ, deserve to be called the least. The fourth teaching is that the hun-

dred and fifty and three great fishes, caught on the right side
of the boat, stand for the predestinate, amongst whom, other
things being equal, are the greater ones who teach and do
God's commandments.

As for the fifth proof from the Gospel: "He shall baptize
you in the Holy Spirit, etc.," it is conceded that holy church
is the Lord's threshing-floor in which are now mingled together
in virtue of faith the good and the bad, predestinate and
reprobate; the predestinate as the wheat, and the reprobate
as the chaff. The first shall be gathered into the heavenly
garner, the rest burnt with fire unquenchable, as say the
Gospel and Augustine's exposition. And as the chaff always
remains chaff, so a reprobate always remains reprobate, even
though for a time he may be in grace according to present
righteousness. Nevertheless, he is never a part of holy church.
And just as the wheat always remains wheat, so the predestinate always remains predestinate and a member of the church,
howbeit for a time he may fall away from accidental grace,
but never from the grace of predestination. On this subject
Augustine, 32 : 4, *C. Recurrat* [Friedberg, 1 : 1127], thus
expresses himself: "Therefore, whether they seem to be turned
over within or are evidently outside, what is flesh is flesh;[1]
or whether they continue in their sterility on the threshing-
floor or are carried away on occasion of temptation as by a
wind without, what is chaff is chaff; and he will always be
separated from the unity of the church, which is without spot
and wrinkle, who continues in carnal obduracy and is mingled
with the company of the saints. Nevertheless, of no one
should we despair, neither of him who appears to be of this
kind and is within, nor of him who is outside and is more
manifestly whirled about."[2] Thus much Augustine.

[1] I have corrected Huss's text from the text of the *Corp. jur. can.* For example, Huss has *qui carior est, carior est* for *quod caro est caro est*, and *veritate*
for *unitate*. The first part of the passage, "to turn within," has some reference
to the time before birth, in the womb. Augustine has been speaking of Re-
becca and the births of Jacob and Esau, and also of Sarah and Hagar.

[2] Huss text has *manifestus* and above *veritate* for *unitate*—unity of the church.

Hence, John the Baptist aptly says that "he will purge,"
that is, on the day of judgment, "his threshing-floor," that is,
holy church, and "gather the wheat into the garner," namely,
the predestinate into the heavenly country; but "the chaff,"
namely, the reprobate, "he will burn with fire unquenchable." And Augustine, commenting in his Letter to Peter on
Faith [Migne, 40 : 777], as already quoted, says: "Hold fast
most tenaciously and never doubt that God's threshing-floor
is the catholic church, and that unto the end of the world will
be found in it chaff mixed with wheat. Here also the wicked
and the good are mingled in the communion of the sacraments;
and in every calling, whether of clerics or laymen, there are
both good and bad." And further on he says: "But in the
end of the world the good are to be separated with the body
from the bad, when Christ shall come with his fan in his hand
and shall purge his threshing-floor and gather the wheat into
the garner and burn the chaff with fire unquenchable, yea,
when by righteous judgment he shall separate the righteous
from the unrighteous, the good from the wicked, the strait
from the crooked. The good he will place at his right hand,
and the wicked at his left. And from his mouth will go forth
a sentence, unending and immutable, of righteous and eternal
judgment, and all the wicked will go into eternal burning, but
the righteous into life eternal. The wicked will always be
burning with the devil, the righteous be reigning without
end [with Christ]."[1] Thus far Augustine. From the exposition of the saints it is clear how in Christ's parables the
reprobate are symbolized by the bad fishes, by the bad guests
at the wedding, by the man not clad in a wedding-garment
at the feast, by the chaff, by the tares, by the bad seed, by the
evil tree, by the foolish virgins, and by the goats. On the
other hand, in an opposite way, the predestinate are symbolized by the good fishes, the good guests, the man clad in a

---

[1] "With Christ," a part of the original, is omitted by Huss. The quotation
is not from Augustine, but from Fulgentius's Letter to Peter the Deacon. See
note, chap. III.

wedding-garment, by the wheat, the good seed, the good tree, the wise virgins, and the sheep.

Reflecting upon these things, the faithful should be on his guard against this conclusion: the reprobate are in God's holy church, therefore they are a part of it. For it has already been said that it is one thing to be in the church and another to be of the church or to be a part or member of the church. For as it does not follow, because the chaff and the tares are among the wheat or mixed up with the wheat, therefore the chaff is the wheat, so the conclusion does not follow in the above proposition. Similarly as it does not follow that, because ordure or a sore is in the body of a man, therefore it is a part of his body, so it does not follow that because a reprobate is in Christ's mystical body of the church, therefore he is a part of it. Again, the following conclusion is not valid, namely: he is in grace according to righteousness, therefore he is a member or a part of the holy catholic church. But this is right reasoning, namely: a man is in the grace of predestination, therefore he is a part or member of holy church. And again this reasoning is not valid: Peter is in sin, therefore he is not a part or member of the holy church. But it is good reasoning to say that at that time he was not in the church according to the grace of present righteousness. Arguing of this kind will be understood by reflecting what it is to be in the church and what it is to be a member or part of the church; and that it is predestination which makes one a member of the holy catholic church, which predestination is the preparation of grace in the present time and of glory in the future. No place of dignity, no human election, and no other outward sign makes one a member of the church. For the devil Iscariot, who did not refuse Christ's election and the temporal charisms given unto him by virtue of his apostolate and episcopate—even though the people believed that he was one of Christ's true disciples—was not a true disciple of Christ, but a wolf clad in sheep's clothing, as Augustine says; and consequently he was not predestinate and so not a part of the church, the bride of Christ.

From this it is clear that it would be a great presumption for any one without revelation and godly fear to assert of himself that he is a member of that holy church.. For no one except the predestinate, in his time without spot or wrinkle, is a member of that church. No one, however, without godly fear or revelation may assert of himself that he is predestinate, and holy without spot or wrinkle. Hence the conclusion is properly drawn. Wherefore it is exceedingly wonderful with what effrontery they who are given up to the world, live completely a worldly and vicious life, removed from companionship with Christ, and even more barren in the fulfilment of Christ's counsels and precepts—that they assert without godly fear that they are heads or the body or the chief members of the church, which is Christ's bride. Do we ever think that these are without spot of mortal sin or wrinkle of venial sin? By forsaking Christ's counsels, by neglect of their sacred office, and by their works they teach that we should rather feel the opposite, for the bridegroom of the church says, "By their fruits ye shall know them," Matt. 7 : 20, and "believe the works," John 10 : 38, and "do not after their works, for they say and do not," Matt. 23 : 2.

But against these things the objection is raised, first, on the ground that every cleric, being stamped with the clerical character or the outward sign by a prelate in the judgment of the church, is a part of holy mother church, and alone the body of such clerics is by antonomasia[1] called the church, which (body) we ought especially to honor, because otherwise it would follow that Christians would not recognize their mother. Yea, and, thus not being recognized, they would not

---

[1] A rhetorical term for the substitution of a title for a general term, as "his honor" for "judge." Wyclif also uses it, *de Eccles.*, 1 : 400. In the first case he says: "Christ's bride is antonomatically our mother."

pay to it the material gifts due, such as oblations and tithes, and in consequence inordinate confusion would follow in the church militant.

Here, by way of denying the antecedent statement, it is said: An instance is furnished in the case of Judas, chosen for the service of the episcopate by Christ, who could not err. For that reprobate never was Christ's true disciple, as Augustine shows, but a wolf clad in sheep's clothing, and he was always chaff and a grain of weed or tares. Similarly, the second part of the antecedent is denied. For the church is by antonomasia called the bride of Christ, which is the totality of the predestinate, as has already been said. For, if that totality is in the highest sense the bride of Christ, then the church herself is holy, for she is the one dove and the queen standing at the King's right hand, to whom the young virgins are led. Wherefore, as in the days when Christ walked on the earth and companied with the clergy, the high priests, priests and Pharisees—the different grades of the priesthood— observing the traditions of their own making, and asserting that they had God for their Father and that they were of Abraham's seed, and at no time served any man and enjoying a reputation among the people, did not do all these things, so that the clergy might by antonomasia and truly be called the holy church, inasmuch as Christ himself said of them, Matt. 15 : 14, that the disciples should allow them to take offense, because "they were blind leaders of the blind," so also it is certain that a particular multitude of the clergy is not the holy church simply because it chooses to affirm itself to be the holy church. Such conclusions, it is plain, do not follow. In the first, the inference was drawn [that the clergy is the church] because otherwise it would follow that Christians would not be able to recognize their mother. For we must know our mother by faith, just as we know the church triumphant, Christ and also his mother by faith, and likewise Christ's apostles and all the blessed angels and the multitude of saints. But we know imperfectly and indistinctly enough those who are now pilgrims and those who are sleeping. But when that which is perfect is come that which is in part shall vanish away, because in heaven we shall distinguish our mother clearly and also her individual members. And let not the faithful [Christian] complain but rejoice in the truth that holy mother church is to so great a degree unknown to him here on the way, because over him stands the merit of Christian faith. For, according to the apostle, Heb. 11 : 1, "Faith is the substance of things hoped for, the assurance of things which do not appear," that is, which do not appear palpably to our senses here on the pilgrim way. And the ground of predestination or of charity, which never faileth and which is the nuptial garment, distinguishing a member of the church from a member of the devil, we do not here-by our senses discern. For, according to Augustine, "an act of faith is believing what thou dost not see." And the very opposite of the second conclusion is clear. For we pay what is due to holy church when we, who have Christ as our supreme pontiff, provide with temporal gifts for their material support Christ's ministers, whom by an indistinct faith we respect as ministers and fathers for their works' sake, and whom we by uncertain knowledge regard as members of Christ.

And, if it be objected that a layman is expected and bound to believe of his prelates that they are the heads of the church and parts of the church either by virtue of predestination or present righteousness, it is to be said in reply that a layman is not expected to believe anything of his superior except what is true. It is clear that no one is held to believe anything which he is not moved by God to believe. But God does not move a man to believe what is false. Howbeit good may come by a false faith under certain circumstances, and howbeit God moves to the essence of an act, nevertheless, God does not so move a man that the man is deceived. Therefore, if a layman believes about his prelate that he is a holy member of the church while in fact he is not, his faith or his believing will be false. Therefore, a pastor is expected, by giving instruction in works that are more virtuous, to influence those under him to believe that he is such. Hence, if an inferior does not discern the works of his superior to be virtuous, he is not bound to believe that he is a member of the church by the law of present righteousness, or to believe with godly fear and conditionally that he is such genuinely, *simpliciter*, namely by virtue of predestination. And, if he certainly knows his sin, then he ought to conclude from his works that at that time he is not righteous but an enemy of Jesus Christ. . And so it is clear that the third conclusion is false. For there is no confusion in the church militant, by reason of the fact that without revelation we do not know certainly who are members of Christ's mystical body on earth.

Up to this point the objection is: Seeing that grace makes sons of the church, just so sin makes members of the devil and also unbelievers, it is clear that a man may become a member of the church after being an unbeliever, just as from being a member of the church one may become a member of the devil. For who doubts that Iscariot, when he was a true apostle, was not also a member of the church?[1] Even so Paul, when he was a blasphemer, was separate from holy mother church. What is here said is said because the church is conceived of in a true sense or in a nominal sense— in the true sense she is, as has been said, identical with the predestinate; in the nominal sense the church is called the

---

[1] Huss is constantly using Judas as an example of how a prescitus, a reprobate, may be a pope or a bishop, having present righteousness, it may be, but not among the elect. Judas was legitimately elected, as Christ says, John 6 : 70, and yet he had a devil. So a pope may well be elected according to the ritual, and yet be of the lost, Replies to Palecz and Stanislaus, *Mon.*, 322, 323, 339, 340, etc. In his *Com. on Peter the Lombard*, Huss says, p. 188: "In truth, Judas Iscarioth wanted to be a bishop, and it pleased God to choose him to the episcopate. But what good did he get thereby? Certainly he lost his episcopate because he committed simony; and he gave himself up body and soul to damnation because he would not conform his will to the will of God."

assembly of the reprobate. It is by a sheer error that men living on the earth speak in this way of the true holy mother church, and so many according to common fame are called heads or members of the church, although according to God's foreknowledge they are members of the devil, who for a time believe and afterwards fall away or are now and always were unbelievers, and of this sort, as already said above and to follow Augustine, were those disciples of Christ who went back and no longer walked with him. Similarly, it was with Iscariot who was falsely reputed to be a disciple of Christ, about whom Augustine, in his Commentary on John [*Nic. Fathers*, 7 : 253], speaks when he shows how the sheep heard Christ's voice. "But what," he says, "are we to think? Those who heard—were they the sheep? Did not Judas hear and he was a wolf? He followed but was clothed in sheep's clothing and plotted against the Shepherd." In this way, therefore, many are reputed according to present righteousness to be of the church, but they are not really so by virtue of predestination unto glory. And who these are Augustine teaches in his Commentary on John, when he says: "The Lord knows who are his. He knows who will hold out till the conferring of the crown, who will hold out unto the flames. He knows in his threshing-floor the wheat, he knows the chaff, he knows the good seed, he knows the tares. But to the rest it is unknown who are doves and who are ravens."

CHAPTER VI

CHRIST THE HEAD OF THE ELECT

TREATMENT having been made of the holy catholic church, which is Christ's mystical body and of which Christ is the head, a statement must also be made of the church of the wicked—*malignantium*—which is the body of the devil, he being its head.[1] For St. Gregory says, *Moralia*, 4 : 9 [Migne, 75 : 647]: "As our Redeemer is one person with the assembly of the good (for He is the head of the body and we the body of that head), so is the old enemy one person with all the company of the reprobate, for he as their head presides over them unto iniquity. Hence it is evident that all the reprobate constitute one body. For Christ said to the Jews, the high priests and Pharisees, who were called the chiefs—*capitales*—of the church: 'Ye are of your father, the devil, and the lusts of your father ye will do,'" John 8 : 44. This shows that there must be one generation—brood—which was bad in the case of the common people, worse in the case of secular rulers, but worst of all in the case of the prelates, just as the generation of the righteous has three opposite classes, corresponding grade for grade to these three classes. If, therefore, the generation of the perverse is one, it is fitting that there should be one evil man [being] with parts, who are the members of the devil. And as there cannot be a head or a member except as these are related to the entire body, it is plain that there is one body of the devil.

---

[1] In his *Super IV. Sent.*, 36, 733, Huss also calls the kingdom of Satan *ecclesia malignancium*, or *civitas diaboli*. "This is the congregation of all the damned, as the holy church is the congregation of all the faithful—those who are to be saved. In the present time this church of the wicked is dispensing its evil odor and infection and the virus of false doctrine."

When, however, the body of Christ is called the mystical body on account of the mystery of the heavenly marriage between Christ and the church, the body of the devil is not likewise mystical but dark, because to be joined with the devil as one of his members does not express itself directly in mystery but in the scourge. Thus the body of the devil has something natural about it, because, as Augustine says, *de natura Boni*, all evil must root itself in the good, so all evil in morals is founded in what is good by nature. And besides having that which is natural, the body of the devil has the essence of vice, just as the mystical body of Christ has the essence of virtue. Hence St. Augustine denies, *de doct. Christi*, III [*Nic. Fathers*, 2 : 569], that the body and members of Christ are one in the same sense as the members of the devil are one.

Now, if it be asked what is the form in which the members of the devil are united in that body, the answer is that there is an outer form and an inner deformity. The outer form is God's eternal foreknowledge which knows and ordains all the foreknown members of that diabolical body to be bound to perpetual punishment. But the inner deformity is the final disobedience or pride, which the saints call the guilt of final impenitence or the sin against the Holy Spirit. And so the same sin both continues on and disjoins. For it holds on in the members of the devil, binding them together in their wickedness for Tartarus and separating them from the companionship of the blessed, just as heat, first dissolving a mixture, gathers together the homogeneous parts, making each element of the dissolved mixture to seek its own place. But it separates the heterogeneous constituents, when it dissolves what seems on the surface to be harmonious by resolving the parts of the mixture, each into its original, separate element. For in the day of judgment, by the contrary principles, the coldness of the devil's body and the heat of the love of Christ's body, the bipartite body must be dissolved according to the law of the final form, when the light parts will hasten upward with their head, who is a consuming fire, to their appropriate mansions among the saints, but the parts terrestrial, weighted, as of lead, will go down to hell, even as John said, 21 : 13: "In a moment they went down into hell" [sheol].

But the objection is drawn from St. Thomas [*Summa*, III, q. 8 : 3–7, Migne], 3 : 100 *sqq.*, when he says: "Christ is the head of all men, both the faithful who are united unto himself in deed through grace, and also the unbelieving who are his members only potentially"—*in potentia*. And later on, he makes a division according to the predestinate and reprobate who, passing away from this world, cease wholly to be members of Christ. This he thus explains: As for this statement of St. Thomas, it seems to me he speaks ambiguously, saying truly that in virtue of his deity, Christ is the outward head of the whole human race which, taken as an aggregate, may be termed one natural body on which Christ confers benefits as he does on the whole world. In virtue of his humanity a secondary perfection was won by the merit of Christ's passion for the whole world, and so in virtue of his humanity he does good to the whole human race—when he punishes all the damned, whether they are damned (1) because of unbelief, like those who did not believe in the Lord Jesus Christ, or (2) because of despair which they ought to have put aside, aspiring to heavenly things, or (3) because of a rash and foolish judgment, which they ought to have put aside, and finally accepted the Lord Jesus Christ in love.

Thus it appears how Christ is head of all men and how he is also head of the predestinate; and how it is not contradictory to speak of the body of the devil (which is the synagogue of Satan) and at the same time to speak of the church of Christ on the ground of creation, beneficence, and preservation, but not on the ground of a union based on love, on which ground it is called Christ's church which he loved, that he might present it as his bride without spot and to be cherished forever. But what the church of Christ or the synagogue of Satan are or will be—whether in the case of men or—more numerously—in the case of the angels—we shall fully know after Christ the Lord has pronounced the final judgment. For he himself says: "Enter ye in at the strait gate, for wide is the gate and broad is the way which leadeth unto perdition and many there are who go in thereat, for strait is the gate and narrow is the way which leadeth unto life and few there are who find it." Matt. 7 : 13. On this passage Chrysostom says, Homil. 18 [*Nic. Fathers* 10 : 163]: "The way of Christ is said to be strait and narrow, because Christ received to himself only those who divested themselves of all sins, laid down all the care of this world and were made refined and spiritual—*subtiles et spirituales.*"

Almighty Lord, who art the way, the truth, and the life, Thou knowest how few in this present time walk in Thee, how few imitate Thee as their head, in humility, poverty, chastity, diligence, and patience. Open is the way of Satan; many walk therein. Help Thy weak flock, that it may not forsake Thee, but follow Thee unto the end in the narrow way.

CHAPTER VII

THE ROMAN PONTIFF AND THE CARDINALS NOT THE UNIVERSAL CHURCH

IT has been said that Christ is the sole Head of the holy universal church and all the predestinate, past and future, are his mystical body and every one of them members of that body. It remains now briefly to examine whether the Roman church is that holy universal church, the bride of Christ. This seems to be the case because the holy catholic apostolic church is one, and this is none other than the Roman church. What seemed a matter of question is therefore true. The first part of the statement appears from Pope Boniface's bull: "By the urgency of faith we are compelled to believe and hold that the holy catholic apostolic church is one."[1] Likewise, the second statement appears from the same decretal, which says: "Of the one and only church there is one body, one head, and not two heads like a monster, namely, Christ and Christ's vicar, Peter, and Peter's successors, even as, when the Lord said to Peter himself, 'Feed my sheep,' he spoke in a general sense, not of individuals, of these or those sheep. It is plain that he regarded all the sheep as committed to him. Therefore, if the Greeks and others say that they were not committed to Peter and his successors, they thereby confess that it is not necessary to be of Christ's sheep; for did not the Lord say, in John: 'They shall become one fold and one shepherd'?" Is it not evident, therefore, that the holy Roman church is that holy universal church, because

---

[1] The first clause of Boniface's bull, *Unam sanctam*, Friedberg, 2 : 1245; Schaff, *Ch. Hist.*, V, part 2, p. 25.

all are Christ's sheep, and the one fold is of one shepherd? This is the meaning of the aforesaid decretal of Boniface, which closes with these words: "Further we declare, say and determine that to be subject to the Roman pontiff is for every human being altogether necessary for salvation"—*subesse Romano pontifici omni humanæ creaturæ . . . omnino esse de necessitate salutis.* If, therefore, every man is of necessity subjected by this declaration to the Roman pontiff, the aforesaid proposition will follow as true, and, on the other hand, the proposition that the Roman church is the church, whose head is the pope and whose body the cardinals, and these together constitute that church. But that church is not the holy catholic and apostolic church. Therefore, what seemed a matter of doubt is false. The first proposition is made out by the statements of certain doctors—among the statements being that the pope is the head of the Roman church and the body is the college of cardinals. The second is manifest from the fact that the pope with the cardinals is not the totality of all the elect.

For the understanding of this subject the notable passage of the Gospel must be meditated upon, namely, Matt. 16 : 16–19: "And Simon Peter answered and said, Thou art the Christ, the Son of the living God. And Jesus answered and said, Blessed art thou, Simon Bar-Jonah: for flesh and blood hath not revealed it unto thee, but my Father which is in heaven. And I also say unto thee, that thou art Peter, and upon this rock I will build my church; and the gates of hell shall not prevail against it. I will give unto thee the keys of the kingdom of heaven: and whatsoever thou shalt bind on earth shall be bound in heaven: and whatsoever thou shalt loose on earth shall be loosed in heaven." In this passage are designated Christ's church, its faith, the foundation, and the authority. In these words Christ's church is designated, "I will build my church"; in these Peter's faith, "Thou art the Christ, the Son of the living God"; in these the foundation, "on this rock I will build"; and in these the authority, "I will give unto thee the keys of the kingdom of heaven." These four are to be touched upon briefly, namely, the church, faith, the foundation, the church's power.

As for the first point, in view of the things set forth above the proposition is to be laid down that, if we put aside the church, nominally so called and as she is generally esteemed to be, then the church is said to be threefold. In one sense it is the congregation or company of the faithful in respect to what is for a time or in respect to present righteousness alone, and in this sense the reprobate are of the church for the time in which they are in grace. But this church is not Christ's mystical body nor the holy catholic church nor any part of it. In the second sense the church is taken to be the admixture of the predestinate and the reprobate while they are in grace in respect to present righteousness. And this church is in part but not in whole identical with God's holy church. And this church is called mixed in character—grain and chaff, wheat and tares—the kingdom of heaven like unto a net cast into the sea and gathering fish of every kind and the kingdom of heaven like unto ten virgins, of whom five were foolish and five wise, as was said above. This church, Tychonius falsely called the bipartite body of the Lord, as appears in *de doct. Christi*, 3 : 32 [*Nic. Fathers*, 2 : 569]. For the reprobate are not the body of the Lord or any part of it.

In the third sense the church is taken for the company of the predestinate, whether they are in grace in respect to present righteousness or not. In this sense the church is an article of faith, about which the apostle was speaking when he said, Eph. 5 : 26: "Christ loved the church and gave himself for it, cleansing it by the washing of water in the word of life, that he might present it to himself a glorious church not having spot or wrinkle or any such thing, but that it might be holy and without spot."

This church the Saviour calls his church in the Gospel

quoted, when he said: "On this rock I will build my church."
And that he means this church is plain from the words which
follow: "And the gates of hell shall not prevail against it."
For seeing that Christ is the rock of that church and also the
foundation on whom she is builded in respect to predestination, she cannot finally be overthrown by the gates of hell,
that is, by the power and the assaults of tyrants who persecute her or the assaults of wicked spirits.   For mightier is
Christ the king of heaven, the bridegroom of the church,
than the prince of this world.   Therefore, in order to show his
power and foreknowledge and the predestination wherewith
he builds, protects, foreknows, and predestinates his church,
and to give persevering hope to his church, he added: "And
the gates of hell shall not prevail against it."   Here Lyra
says: "From this it appears that the church is not composed
of men by virtue of any power of ecclesiastical and secular
dignity, because there are many princes and high priests and
others of lower degree who have been found apostates from
the faith."   This comment has its proof, in part, in the case of
Judas Iscariot, both apostle and bishop, who was present when
Christ said: "On this rock I will build my church and the
gates of hell shall not prevail against it."   But he himself
was not built upon the rock in respect of predestination and
therefore the gates of hell prevailed against him.

From the aforesaid words of Christ it is evident that the
church is taken to mean all, in a special sense, who after his
resurrection were to be built upon him and in him by faith
and perfecting grace.   For Christ commended Peter, who
bore [represented] the person of the universal church and
confessed his faith in the words: "Thou art the Christ, the
Son of the living God."   And Christ said to him, "Blessed art
thou, Simon Bar-Jonah."   This commendation befits Peter
and the whole church, which from the beginning was blessed
in the way, by confessing humbly, obediently, heartily, and
constantly that Christ is the Son of the living God.   This

faith in regard to that most hidden article, the flesh—that is, the wisdom of the world—does not reveal; nor does blood reveal it, that is, pure philosophical science—but alone God, the Father. And because the confession was so clear and positive, the Rock—*Petra*—said to Peter—the rock: "And I say unto thee that thou art Peter," that is, the confessor of the true Rock—*Petra*—who is Christ, and "on this Rock," which thou hast confessed—that is, upon me—"I will build" by strong faith and perfecting grace "my church"—that is, the company of the predestinate who, the probation being over, are appointed to glory. Wherefore, "the gates of hell shall not prevail against it." Up to this point it has been deduced from the Saviour's words that there is (1) one church—namely, from the very word "church"; (2) that it is Christ's church—from the word "my"; (3) that it is holy—from the words, "the gates of hell shall not prevail against it." The conclusion, therefore, is that there is one holy church of Christ, which in Greek is *katholike* and in Latin *universalis*. She is also called apostolic, *apostolike*, because she was established by the words and deeds of the apostles and founded upon the Rock, Christ, as Jerome says in the Prologue to his *Commentary on the Apocalypse*.[1]

Hence I lay it down that it is to be called the holy Roman church, for the *Decretum, Dist.* 21 [Friedberg, 1 : 70], says that "although there is only one bridal couch[2] of the universal catholic church of Christ[3] throughout the world, never-

---

[1] Jerome referred the rock now to Christ, *Com. on Amos*, 6 : 12, now to Peter, now to Peter and his confession. The notable passages in which he makes Peter the rock are his letter to Marcella, and especially his letter to Damasus, bishop of Rome, *Nic. Fathers*, 6 : 18, 55. In commenting on Matt. 16 : 16, Jerome combined the interpretations Christ and Peter. He can, therefore, be cited for both interpretations.

[2] The word transl. couch—*thalamus*—is used in the Vulgate, Deut. 33 : 12: "He will abide the whole day on his couch," where the proper transl. of the Hebrew is: "He covereth him all the day long." Gilbert of Hoiland, Sermon on the Cant., Migne 184 : 64, says: "There is a couch on the breast of Jesus, yea and also a treasure," *in pectore Jesu thalamus*, etc.

[3] I have substituted for Huss's text, *Christus*, the text of the *Decretum, Christi*.

theless the holy Roman catholic and apostolic church is by
the decisions of no synods[1] set above the other churches."
This it proves by the passage already cited, Matt. 16—
namely: "Thou art Peter and upon this rock I will build
my church." And a little later it calls this church "the
Roman church, the primal seat of the apostle, which has
neither spot nor wrinkle." This church, however, cannot
be understood to mean the pope with his cardinals and his
household, for they alike come and go. Therefore, the Gloss
on this text has this to say: "The argument is, that wherever
the good are, there is the Roman church." And so the *Decretum*, 24 : 1 [Friedberg 1 : 970]: *a recta* is to be understood.
Where the canon on the Roman church speaks in this way:
"This is the holy and apostolic mother church of all the
churches of Christ, which [2] by God's omnipotent grace is
proved never to have erred from the path of apostolic tradition, nor has ever been corrupted by or succumbed to
heretical novelties." This, it must here be noted, cannot
be understood of any pope or the members of his household,
on which point the Gloss also says: "I ask, therefore, of which
church do you understand that it cannot err?" But it is
certain that the pope can err. See *Decretum, Anastasius*, 19,
and *Si papa*, 40 [Friedberg, 1 : 64, 146]. Therefore, neither
the pope himself nor his family is that church of which it is
here said, she cannot err. Hence the Gloss says: "The
company of the faithful itself is called this church." So also
is to be understood St. Jerome's statement, *Dist.* 25: 1, *Hæc
est fides* [Friedberg 1 : 970]: "The Roman church is holy,
which always has remained thoroughly unspotted, will in the
future by the Lord's providence and the blessed Apostle
Peter's care remain without any dent from heretics and abide

---

[1] Instead of "no synods" Huss's text has "many—*multis*—synods." The
text of the *Decretum* is *nullis*. This was the famous decree of Gelasius, pope
about 495 or 496, and I have substituted the right reading above; for the mistake of the editor makes Huss prove the very opposite of what he was intending.
[2] Huss here has *qui*, the *Decretum quæ*.

unmoved and unmovable for all time." Here no pope with his college of cardinals can be understood. For often these are as soiled with wicked, deceitful depravity and sin, as at the time of pope Joanna, the Englishwoman, who was called Agnes. How, therefore, did that Roman church—that Agnes, pope Joanna with college—remain always unspotted, seeing she bore? And the same is true of other popes who were heretics and deposed on account of their manifold enormities.

Since, therefore, according to the Decretals, the Roman church has the primacy and the dignity, so far as God is concerned, over all other churches, it is evident that she is the whole militant church, which God loves more than any of its parts. And so it is evidently of faith that not that college [of the cardinals] but the whole mother dispersed among all peoples and tongues is that holy Roman church of which the laws [the canon law] accord in speaking with the holy doctors. Hence, in order to impress upon us this judgment by St. Augustine and St. Ambrose, the hymn is ordained for the church, "The holy church throughout the world doth acknowledge thee." And in the canon of the mass, first and chiefly, we offer prayer for the holy catholic church, that God would condescend to give her peace, to keep her, and to grant her unity in all the world. Hence prayer is undoubtedly offered for the principal—*principalissima*—militant church, which, I lay down, is the Roman church. And truly among its parts, when we compare in the matter of greatness, the pope and his college are in dignity its chief part, so long as they follow Christ closely and, putting away the pomp and ambition of the primacy, serve their mother diligently and humbly. For in doing the opposite they are turned into the desolation of abomination —into a college at direct variance with the humble college of the apostles and our Lord Jesus Christ.

But it is to be noted that the Roman church was properly called a company of Christ's faithful, living under the obedience of the Roman bishop, just as the Antiochian church was called the company of Christ's faithful, under the bishop of Antioch. The same also was true of the faithful in Alexandria and Constantinople. And in this way Peter, Christ's apostle and Roman bishop, speaks of the church when, addressing the faithful in Christ in Pontus, Galatia, Cappadocia, Asia, and Bithynia, he says: "The church which is gathered together[1] in Babylon saluteth you," I Peter 5 : 13. Is not the church here taken to mean the faithful of Christ who were at Rome with St. Peter? After the same manner also, the apostle designated particular churches when he wrote from Corinth to the Romans, "all the churches of Christ salute you," and a little further on: "I, Tertius, salute you, who wrote the epistle in the Lord. Gaius my host and the whole church saluteth you." Romans 16 : 16, 23. Here the whole church is taken for all Christ's faithful, who with Paul were waging warfare in Corinth. Likewise we have the words: "To the church of God which is in Corinth, sanctified in Christ Jesus," I Cor. 1 : 2, and "Paul and Sylvanus and Timotheus to the church of the Thessalonians," I Thess. 1 : 2. We have the same often in other places, so that those are properly called particular churches which separately are parts of the universal church, which is the church of Jesus Christ.

But the Christian church had its beginning in Judea and was first called the church of Jerusalem, as it is said: "In that day there arose a great persecution in the church which was in Jerusalem, and they were all scattered throughout the regions of Judea and Samaria, except the apostles," Acts 8 : 1. The second church was the Antiochian, in which Peter, the apostle, resided, and there, for the first time, the name Christian was employed. Hence, the faithful were first called disciples and brethren, and later Christians, for we read: "The apostles and brethren which were in Judea,"

---

[1] *Collecta.* The Vulgate has *coelecta* with the Greek.

and at the close of the chapter it is stated how Barnabas led
Paul to Antioch and they were together for a whole year in
the church and taught great multitudes, so that "the disciples
were called Christians first in Antioch," Acts 11 : 1, 26.

In the second sense, the Roman church is taken to mean
any pope together with any cardinals, wherever they may
happen to reside, whether their lives are good or evil. And
in the third sense, it is taken for the pope. These two last
senses are wrested by scholars. For there is no good reason
for calling the Roman church our mother either (1) on account of its pride or (2) on account of the emperor's clement
goodness in endowing the church or on account of the pope's
haughtiness and self-assertion because of imperial rule drawn
from the pope's primacy or dominion, (3) or, again, is this
a good reason that men should believe that it is incumbent
upon every Christian to have recourse to the pope and that
it is of necessity for salvation to recognize him as the head
and as the most holy father, but for other reasons than this.
For since the term Roman church was established aside from
any foundation in sacred Scripture, it is enough to give a
probable reason. For the holy church of Christ flourished
first in Jerusalem during the days of the apostles, who companied with Christ, and afterwards in Antioch at the time of
Peter's incumbence as bishop—*cathedrationis*—and afterwards
in Rome at the time of the preaching and martyrdom of
Peter and Paul. And so is to be understood the Saviour's
saying, Matt. 12 : 28, "Finally is the kingdom of God come
unto you," and also Luke 17 : 21, 37, "The kingdom of God
is within you . . . for where the body is, thither will the eagles
also be gathered together." For, although the Christian
church began in Judea and Christ suffered martyrdom in
Jerusalem, nevertheless with reason Christ's church is called
the Roman church in view of a certain pre-eminence and for
three causes: (1) Christ knew that the peoples under the
Roman empire would be brought in in the place of the unbe-

lieving Jews, as the apostle says, Romans 11 : 2, 12. (2) A larger multitude of martyrs triumphed there than in any other city, for so, where a man is born from the womb and triumphs gloriously, from that place he takes his name. Inasmuch, therefore, as holy church, so far as many of its parts go, was born in Rome, having been gathered out of the womb of the synagogue, and there triumphed, growing among the nations, so it was thought proper that she should take her name from the metropolitan city which is Rome. Hence *Dist.* 22 [Friedberg, 1 : 74] runs: "She is called most holy, because Peter and Paul on the same day and at one and the same time consecrated the whole Roman church and exalted her above all other cities in the whole world by their presence and by their glorious triumph." (3) Not the locality or the antiquity, but the formulated faith establishes the church of Christ, for, both as regards personalities and time, Christ's church had existed before in its earlier seats. And in this sense it is said: "The Lord did not choose people on account of the place, but the place on account of the people," II Macc. 5 : 19. For this cause, I believe it is permitted to name Christ's church from any locality which the righteous faithful inhabit, just as Christ was called the Nazarene on account of his conception which occurred in Nazareth, and as he may be called a Bethlehemite from the place of his nativity, and a Capernaumite from Capernaum where he worked miracles, and a Jerusalemite from his most glorious passion in Jerusalem.

In view of these things it is plain what ought to be said with regard to the doubtful statement made at the beginning of this chapter. For it should be granted that the Roman church is the holy mother, the catholic church, the bride of Christ. To the argument in favor of the opposite, by which it is argued that the Roman church is the church of which the pope is the head and the cardinals the body—this is said by way of concession and by defining the church in the second way, that is, as the pope—whoever he may be—in conjunction with the cardinals—whoever they may be and wheresoever they may live. But it is denied that this church is the holy, catholic and apostolic church. And so both parts of the argument are granted, but the conclusion is denied. But if this be said, namely, "I lay down that the pope is holy together with all the twelve cardinals living with him," this being laid down and admitted as highly possible, it follows that the pope himself in conjunction with the cardinals is the holy, catholic and apostolic church. This conclusion is denied, but it follows well that a holy pope in conjunction with holy cardinals are a holy church which is a part of the holy, catholic and apostolic church. Therefore Christ's faithful must hold firmly as a matter of faith to the first conclusion and not to the second; for the first is confirmed by Christ's words: "The gates of hell shall not prevail against it." But the second is a matter of doubt to me and to every other pilgrim, unless a divine revelation makes it plain. Hence neither is the pope the head nor are the cardinals the whole body of the holy, universal, catholic church. For Christ alone is the head of that church, and his predestinate are the body and each one is a member, because his bride is one person with Jesus Christ.[1]

[1] It was a popular definition which regarded the pope in conjunction with the body of the cardinals as the church. So Wyclif, "the public—*communitas* —holds the church to be the pope and the cardinals, which it is necessary for all to believe." *De Eccles.*, p. 92, and often. In his Replies to Palecz and Stanislaus, Huss represents these two magisters as defining the church in the same way, the "pope is the head and the cardinals the body of the church." *Mon.*, 1 : pp. 333, 335.

CHAPTER VIII

THE FAITH WHICH IS THE FOUNDATION OF THE CHURCH

So far as the second thing is concerned [involved in Matt. 16 : 16–18], that is, faith, which is touched upon in the words, "Thou art Christ, the Son of the living God"—it is to be noted that faith is now taken for the act of believing by which we believe, now for the inward state or disposition—*habitus*[1]—of believing through which we believe, and now for the truth which we believe, as Augustine lays down, *de Trinitate*, 13 [*Nic. Fathers*, 3 : 166 *sqq.*].

In the second place, it is to be noted that there is one faith which is the explicit belief of a faithful man and that there is another faith which is implicit faith as the catholic, who has the disposition—*habitus*—of faith infused or explicitly acquired, believes in the catholic church in common with others and by reason of that common faith believes implicitly whatever single thing is included under holy mother church.[2] Likewise in believing whatsoever Christ wished to be believed

---

[1] In his *Super IV. Sent.*, 452, Huss defines the meaning of the word when he says "*fides est habitus vel virtus*—provided faith is formed in love."

[2] The distinction between implicit and explicit faith, which starts with Augustine, is the distinction between acceptance of doctrines on the ground of obedience to the church and a real assent to them as doctrines. So Thomas Aquinas, who says, in essence, that implicit faith is acceptance of things to be believed as things contained in the Scriptures, and explicit faith is their acceptance with the understanding and heart. *Summa*, 2 : 2, *q.* 2, 5. Innocent IV, in his *Com. on the Decretals*, said that it is enough for laymen to believe in God as the God of justice and in all other matters, dogmas, and morals—*implicite*—that is, to think and say, I believe what the church believes. Innocent went on to say that clerics were under obligation to follow the commands of a pope that were unrighteous. Döllinger, *Akad. Vort.*, 2 : 49.

about himself and refusing to believe what he did not wish to be believed about himself, he believes every article, affirmative or negative, which is to be believed about Christ. This faith Peter had implicitly when he expressly confessed Christ to be true God and true man, saying: "Thou art Christ, the Son of the living God." And yet the same Peter explicitly set himself against Christ and his Gospel when, after Christ had said, "All ye shall be offended in me this night" [Matt. 26 : 31], he denied and said: "Though all be offended in thee, yet will I never be offended." Thus also many of the faithful in common [that is, as a body] believe implicitly all the truth of Scripture, and when a truth unknown to them is proposed, they search to see if it is laid down in holy Scripture, and if this is shown to be the case they at once acknowledge the sense which the Holy Spirit insists on. Therefore, whoever has in common with others faith formed in love, this suffices for salvation when accompanied with the grace of perseverance. For God, who gave the first faith, will give to his soldier clearer faith, unless he puts some hindrance in the way. For God does not demand of all his children that they should continuously during their sojourn here be in the particular act of thought about any particular point of faith, but it is enough that, putting aside inertia and callousness, they have faith formed as a habit.

Faith, therefore, we must understand, is twofold: the one unformed, which is exercised by the demons who believe and tremble; the other faith formed in love. The latter, accompanied with perseverance, saves, but not the former. Hence with reference to the faith formed in love the words were spoken: "Whosoever believeth in the Son of God, hath eternal life," John 3 : 15. And the Saviour said to Peter, who had that faith and professed it: "Blessed art thou, Simon Bar-Jonah." This faith is the foundation[1] of the other virtues

---

[1] It would seem that Huss gets his expression *fundamentum*, foundation, from the word *substantia*, used in the Vulgate, Heb. 11 : 1 (hupostasis), *sub-*

which the church of Christ practises. Likewise it is to be noted that, inasmuch as faith is not of things which appear to the senses but of hidden things and inasmuch as it is difficult to believe hidden things, therefore two elements are necessary to faith in order that we may believe anything truly: (1) the truth which illumines the mind, (2) the authority [evidence] which confirms the mind. Here belongs one property of faith, that it is concerned alone with the truth—all falsehood being excluded—the truth which the faithful ought to defend even unto death. The second property of faith is, that without proof and special knowledge it is obscure to the faithful, for what we see with the eye we cannot be said to believe. And the saints in heaven who see the articles clearly, which we know obscurely, are not said to believe them but to see. In the place of faith they have clear vision and in the place of hope unending fruition. The third property of faith is, that it is the foundation [assurance] of the things which are to be believed for the pilgrim who is to come to the peaceful dwelling. Therefore, the apostle says that faith is "the substance," that is, the foundation, "of things hoped for": "the evidence of things which do not appear," that is, to the senses, Heb. 11 : 1. For now we hope for our blessedness and believe, but do not see with the eyes of the flesh. And, because it is not possible without faith to please God, therefore every one who is to be saved ought first of all to be faithful—*fidelis*—[have faith]. A faithful person, however, is he who has faith infused by God and has no fear of ill to himself mixed with his faith. But all open offenders according to the law of present unrighteousness are unfaithful—*infideles*—[without faith], for it is impossible for any one to sin mortal sin except

stantia rerum, that which underlies, and trsl. "assurance" in the Rev. Vers. The same word *substantia* is used in the Vulgate, II Cor. 9 : 4, 11 : 17; Heb. 3 : 14. Huss may also have been influenced by the Vulgate *fundamentum*, Heb. 6 : 1, "not laying the foundation of repentance and good works and of faith toward God." Huss quotes Heb. 11 : 1 in his *Com. on Peter the Lombard*, p. 453.

in so far as he lacks faith. For, if he were mindful of the penalty to be inflicted on those sinning in that way and fully believed it and had the faith which comes from divine knowledge—wherewith God knows all things clearly and is present with such sinners—then, without doubt, he would not sin mortal sin.

A person may lack faith in three ways: (1) By weakness, and in this way he is lacking who vacillates in believing and does not persist unto death in the defense of faith. (2) He is lacking in faith who firmly believes the many things which are to be believed and yet is lacking in many things to be believed, which unbelieved things are as holes, and thus he has a shield of faith which is full of holes. (3) He is lacking in faith who lacks in the use of this shield; and this happens in this way: that, though he has the firm habit of things to be believed, he nevertheless lacks in acts of meritorious living because of an undisciplined life. These things are referred to in Titus 1 : 16: "They confess that they know God, but in deeds deny him." Every one, therefore, who is lacking in faith in any of these three ways is wanting in the abiding strength of faith.

And we must remember that faith differs from hope: (1) In this, that hope has reference to the future prize to be obtained, but faith concerns the past, namely such things as that God created the world, that Christ was incarnate, etc. And it concerns also the present, as that God is, that the saints are in heaven, and that Christ sits at the right hand of the Father. Faith also concerns the future, as that Christ will come again in judgment; that all who have not arisen at that time will arise in the day of judgment; and that God will finally reward in bliss all the saints who finish this present life in grace. (2) Hope does not reach the knowledge of faith in that which it hopes for, but it rests in a certain middle act between doubt and belief, so that there are many things which are to be set before the faithful to accept which, when the distinction is removed, they should neither doubt, nor grant, nor deny but only hope for. For example, if it were proposed to me, "Thou shalt be saved," I ought not to grant it, for I do not know whether it is true, nor should I deny it, for I do not know whether it is false, nor should I doubt it—but I should hope for it. (3) Faith also differs from hope in this, that hope is only of good which is possible to him who hopeth, but faith is about the evil as well as about the good, for we believe the forgiveness of sin, which is most certainly a good thing for all who are to be saved; and we believe also that the sin of blasphemy will not be forgiven either in this world or in that which is to come.

And for the reason that believing is an act of faith, that is, to put trust in—*fidere*—therefore know that to believe that which is necessary for a man to secure blessedness is to adhere firmly and without wavering to the truth spoken as by God. For this truth, because of its certitude, a man ought to expose his life to the danger of death. And, in this way, every Christian is expected to believe explicitly and implicitly all the truth which the Holy Spirit has put in Scripture, and in this way a man is not bound to believe the sayings of the saints which are apart from Scripture, nor should he believe papal bulls, except in so far as they speak out of Scripture, or in so far as what they say is founded in Scripture simply. But a man may believe bulls as probable, for both the pope and his curia make mistakes from ignorance of the truth. And, with reference to this ignorance, it can be substantiated that the pope makes mistakes and may be deceived. Lucre deceives the pope, and he is deceived through ignorance. How far, however, faith ought to be placed in the letters of princes, the instruments of notaries, and the descriptions of men, experience, which is the teacher of things, teaches. For she teaches that these three often make mistakes. Of one kind is the faith which is placed in God. He cannot deceive or be deceived; of another is the faith placed in the pope, who may deceive and be deceived. Of one kind is the faith placed in holy Scripture; and another, faith in a bull thought out in a human way. For to holy Scripture exception may not be taken, nor may it be gainsaid; but it is proper at times to take exception to bulls and gainsay them when they either commend the unworthy or put them in authority, or savor of avarice, or honor the unrighteous or oppress the innocent, or implicitly contradict the commands or counsels of God.

It is, therefore, plain which faith is the foundation of the church—the faith with which the church is built upon the Rock, Christ Jesus, for it is that by which the church confesses that "Jesus Christ is the Son of the living God." For Peter spoke for all the faithful, when he said: "Thou art the Christ, the Son of the living God." "This is the victory," says John, "which overcometh the world—even our faith. Who is he that overcometh the world but he that believeth that Jesus is the Son of God?" I John 5 : 4.

CHAPTER IX

THE CHURCH FOUNDED ON CHRIST, THE ROCK

THE third foundation, included in the proposition (Matt. 16 : 18) is touched upon in the words: "On this rock I will build my church." And in view of the fact that in their utterances the popes most of all use this saying of Christ, wishing to draw from it that they themselves are the rock or the foundation upon which the church stands, namely upon Peter, to whom it was said, "Thou art Peter,"—in view of this fact, in order to understand the Lord's word it must be noted that the foundation of the church by whom it is founded is touched upon in the words: "I will build," and the foundation in which it is laid is referred to in the words, "on this Rock," and the foundation wherewith the church is founded is referred to in the words, "Thou art the Christ, the Son of the living God." Christ is therefore the foundation by whom primarily and in whom primarily the holy catholic church is founded, and faith is the foundation with which it is founded—that faith which works through love, which Peter set forth when he said: "Thou art the Christ, the Son of the living God." The foundation, therefore, of the church is Christ, and he said: "Apart from me ye can do nothing," John 15 : 5; that is, apart from me as the prime and principal foundation. But Christ grounds and builds his church on himself, the Rock, when he so influences her that she hears and does his words, for then the gates of hell do not prevail against her. Hence Christ says: "Every one that cometh unto me and heareth my words and doeth them, I will show you to whom he is like: he is like a man building a house, who built a house deep and laid the foundation on a rock: and when the flood arose, the stream brake against that house, and could not shake it: for it was founded on the rock," Luke 6 : 47. And what this foundation is, the apostle Paul shows in I Cor. 3 : 11: "Other foundation can no man lay than that which is laid, which is Christ Jesus"; and I Cor. 10 : 4: "But the rock was Christ." Therefore, it is in this foundation and on this rock and from this rock up that the holy church is built, for he says: "Upon this Rock I will build my church."

And on this foundation the apostles built the church of Christ. For not to themselves did they call the people, but to Christ, who is the first, the essential and most effectual foundation. For this reason the apostle said: "Other foundation can no man lay." Therefore this apostle, seeing how the Corinthians might err concerning the foundation, condemned them, saying: "Each one of you saith I am indeed of Paul, and I of Apollos, and I of Cephas, and I of Christ. Is therefore Christ divided, or was Paul crucified for you, or were ye baptized in the name of Paul?" I Cor. 1 : 12, 13. It is as if he said, No! Therefore, neither Peter nor Paul nor any other besides Christ is the chief foundation or head of the church, so that later the holy apostle said: "What then is Apollos and what is Paul? His ministers whom ye believed and each one as the Lord gave to him" to minister to the church, I Cor. 3 : 5. He said: "I planted," that is by preaching; "Apollos watered," that is by baptizing; "but God gave the increase," that is through the founding by faith, hope, and love. Therefore, "neither he that planteth," as Paul, "is anything, nor he that watereth," like Apollos, "is anything," that is anything upon which the church may be founded, but only God who giveth the increase; He is the church's foundation. And the words follow: "Let every one take heed how he buildeth thereon, for other foundation can no man lay than that is laid, which is Christ Jesus."

Now, this foundation is the rock of righteousness of which

Christ spoke in the Gospel to St. Peter: "Thou art Peter, and upon this Rock I will build my church." On these words St. Augustine says, in his *Sermons on the Words of the Lord*, 13 [*Nic. Fathers*, 6 : 340]: "Our Lord Jesus Christ thus spake to Peter, Thou art Peter and upon this rock I will build my church—on this Rock, which thou hast confessed, on this Rock which thou hast recognized, when thou saidst, 'Thou art Christ, the Son of the living God'—'I will build my church': I will build thee upon myself, not myself upon thee. For wishing that men should be built upon men, they were saying, 'I am of Paul, I of Apollos, and I of Cephas,' that is, Peter. And others who did not wish to be built upon Peter—*Petrum*— but upon the Rock—*Petram*—said, 'I am of Christ.'" Again, in his last Homily on John [*Nic. Fathers*, 7 : 450], Augustine says: "Peter the apostle, because of the primacy of his apostleship, had a symbolic and representative personality, for what belonged to him as an individual was that by nature he was one man, by grace one Christian, and by a more abundant grace he was one and the same chief apostle. But when it was said to him: 'I will give unto thee the keys of the kingdom of heaven, and whatsoever thou shalt bind on earth shall be bound in heaven, and whatsoever thou shalt loose on earth shall be loosed in heaven,' he represented the universal church which in this world is shaken by divers temptations, even as by torrents of rain, by rivers, and tempests, and yet doth not fall, because it is founded upon the Rock, the word from which Peter got his name. For Rock —*Petra*—does not come from Peter—*Petrus*—but Peter from Rock, just as the word Christ is not derived from Christian, but Christian from Christ.

"Hence the Lord said: 'On this Rock I will build my church,' because Peter had said before, 'Thou art the Christ, the Son of the living God.' Upon this Rock which thou hast confessed, he said, 'I will build my church.' For Christ was the Rock. Therefore, the church, which is founded on Christ, received from him the keys of the kingdom of heaven in the person of Peter, that is, the power of binding and loosing sins. For what the church is essentially in Christ, that Peter is symbolically in the Rock—*Petra*—by which symbolism Christ is understood to be the Rock and Peter the church. Therefore, this church which Peter represented, so long as she prospers among evil men, is by loving and by following Christ freed from evil, but much more does she follow in the case of those who fight for the truth even unto death."

These things Augustine teaches throughout, in agreement with the apostle, that Christ alone is the foundation and Rock upon which the church is built. To this the apostle Peter speaks, when he says: "Unto whom coming, a living stone, rejected indeed of men, but of God elect and precious, ye also, as living stones, are built upon into spiritual houses[1] to be a holy priesthood to offer up spiritual sacrifices unto God through Jesus Christ," I Peter 2 : 4 *sq.* For this reason the Scripture continues: "Behold I lay in Zion a chief cornerstone, elect, precious, and he that believeth on Him shall not be put to shame. For you, therefore, that believe is the honor, but for such as disbelieve, the stone which the builders rejected, the same was made the head of the corner and a stone of stumbling and a Rock of offense. For they stumble at the word and do not believe that whereunto they were appointed." Paul also said: "Israel following[2] after a law of righteousness did not arrive at the law of righteousness. Wherefore? Because they sought it not by faith but[3] by works. They stumbled at the stone of stumbling, as is written, Behold I lay in Zion a stone of stumbling and a rock of offense, and he that believeth on him shall not be put to shame," Romans 9 : 31 *sqq.* Behold how these two Roman apostles and bishops, Peter and Paul, prove from Scripture that the Lord Jesus Christ is

---

[1] In *domos spirituales*. The Vulgate: *domus spiritualis*, etc.
[2] The text here has *non*, not, which must be a mistake for the Vulgate's *vero*.
[3] Vulgate adds *quasi*.

himself the stone and the Rock of foundation, for the Lord says: "Behold I will lay for a foundation in Zion a corner-stone tried and precious, a stone of sure foundation," Isaiah 28 : 16. And also in the Psalms 118 : 22. "The stone which the builders rejected has been made the head of the corner."[1] Therefore, Christ himself is the foundation of the apostles and the whole church, and in him it is fitly framed together.

For this reason the apostle says: "So then ye are no more strangers and sojourners, but ye are fellow citizens with the saints and of the household of God, being built upon the foundation of the apostles and prophets, Jesus Christ himself being the chief corner-stone, in whom each several building fitly framed together groweth into a holy temple unto the Lord," Eph. 2 : 19–21. Here St. Remigius says [Migne's ed., 117 : 711]: "The foundation of the apostles and prophets and of all the faithful is Christ because they are established and grounded in faith in him, just as he himself said, 'On this Rock' that is, 'on myself, I will build my church,' which consists of angels and righteous men. For every one that hath faith in Christ is founded upon him, Christ Jesus himself being the chief corner-stone. How, then, is Christ the foundation and the chief stone? For this reason, that faith begins with him and is perfected and completed in him and by him so that all the elect are grounded in him." Thus Remigius Haymo.[2]

From these things it is plain that Christ alone is the chief foundation of the church, and in this sense the apostle thought of that foundation, because he did not dare to speak of anything except what was built upon that foundation. Hence he says: "I will not dare to speak of any thing save those which Christ wrought through me by the obedience

---

[1] I Cor. 10 : 4, the Rock that followed them was Christ, is the only passage of the sort Huss applies to Christ in the *Super IV. Sent.*, p. 559.

[2] Remigius, bishop of Auxerre, d. about 910, wrote in part under the pseudonym of Haymo of Halberstadt.

of God[1] in word, and in deeds, and in the power of signs and wonders, in the power of the Holy Spirit. And so I have preached this Gospel not where Christ was already known, that I might not build upon another man's foundation," Romans 15: 18–20. Was not this that apostle, a vessel of election, who said he did not dare to preach anything save those things which Christ spoke through him; for otherwise he would not be building on Christ, the most effectual foundation, if perchance he should say and teach or do anything which did not have its foundation in Jesus Christ. And from this it is plain, that not Peter but the Rock, Christ, was intended in Christ's Gospel, when Christ said: "On this Rock I will build my church."

But the objection is drawn from Ambrose, *Dist.* 50 [Friedberg, 1 : 198], where he says: "Peter became more faithful after he had wept over having relinquished his faith and so he found greater grace than he lost. For as a good shepherd he received the flock to care for it so that, as he had been weak to himself, he might become a buttress—*firmamentum*—to all, and he who faltered,[2] under the temptation of a question, might establish others by the steadfastness of his faith. Finally, in order to strengthen the devotion of the churches, he was called rock, as the Lord said: 'thou art Peter and upon this rock I will build my church.' For he is called *petra*—rock—because he was to be the first to lay the foundations of the faith among the nations,[3] and, as an immovable bowlder—*saxum*—he held up the structure and weighty edifice of the whole of Christ's work." So much Ambrose, showing that Peter is called the rock. The exposition of Augustine, the foremost of Scripture expositors, seems to me here to be more efficacious and is more efficacious because it

---

[1] The Vulgate: *in obedientiam gentium.*

[2] *Nutaverat.* Huss here has *mutaverat se.* The *se* is retained in Friedberg's ed. of the *Corp. jur. can.*, although, as there indicated, many MSS. and editors omit it.

[3] *In nationibus ;* Huss's text has wrongly *imitationis.*

is founded in the very words of Scripture which says that Christ is the Rock and the corner-stone and the effectual foundation. But nowhere in Scripture do we expressly read that Peter is a rock. Nor did Christ, who was able to say it easily—*leviter*—say: "Thou art the Rock, and on thee, the Rock, I will build my church." What he said was: "Thou art Peter," that is the confessor of the true Rock, "and upon this Rock," which thou hast confessed, "I will build my church." But Christ builds the church upon himself, by faith, hope, and love. Hence we believe and hope in Christ and not in Peter, and we are bound to have more love and affection for Christ than for Peter. For the fathers of the Old Testament did not believe or hope in Peter, who was to come, but in the Rock. Nor did the saints of the New Testament believe and hope in Peter but in Christ, who is objectively [the object of] our faith and hope.

It must be granted that the apostles are foundations of the church but not in the same way as Christ is the foundation. For Christ is the foundation of foundations, as he also is the holiest of the holy. This is expressed by St. Augustine on Psalm 86 [*Nic. Fathers*, 8 : 420]: "His foundations are in the mountains," etc. Here he shows that the chief foundation of the New Jerusalem, the city of Zion, and also its corner-stone is Christ; and the mountains are the prophets and apostles in whom are the foundations of the church. And Augustine says: "That ye may come to know that Christ is the first and the great foundation, the apostle says, 'other foundation can no man lay than that which is laid, which is Christ Jesus.'" How, then, can the prophets and the apostles be foundations and at the same time Christ be the foundation beyond whom there is nothing? How do we think but figuratively of the foundation of foundations, except as he is expressly called the holiest of the holy? If, therefore, thou thinkest of the sacraments, Christ is the holiest of the holy; if thou thinkest of an obedient flock, Christ is the shepherd of shepherds; if thou thinkest of the edifice, Christ is the foundation of foundations.

And later he [Augustine] gives the reason for the prophets and apostles being called the foundations of the structure of the city of Jerusalem, and asks: "Why are they the foundations? Because their authority bears up—*portat*—our infirmity. How are they gates—*portæ?* Because by them we go into the kingdom of God, for they preach to us. And as we go in by them, so we go in by Christ, for he is the door. And there are said to be twelve gates of Jerusalem, and Christ is the one gate and Christ is the twelve gates, because Christ is in the twelve gates." Thus much Augustine. And on that text of Rev. 21 : 14, "The wall of the city having twelve foundations," the Gloss says: "that is the prophets in whose faith the apostles were grounded, for from them faith passed on by succession to the apostles, whose preaching had the same belief as had the prophets who also said the same thing. Or let us accept the apostles as the foundations in whom the whole fortification of the church is grounded. Again, in this passage it is said: "All the foundations of the wall of the city are adorned with a precious stone, and the first foundation was jasper." The Gloss says: "The foundations, that is, the prophets and apostles, are adorned in themselves with graces of every kind."

Behold how Christ is the foundation of the church and the apostles are the foundations! Christ is by a figure of speech—*antonomastice*—the foundation because the edifice of the church begins from him and is finished in him and through him. But the prophets and apostles are the foundations because their authority bears up our weakness. And this was the sense intended by Ambrose when he said: "That Peter was called the rock because he was the first to lay in the nations[1] the foundations of the faith; and, like an immovable rock," that is, by the steadfastness with which he endured to the

---

[1] Huss's text has *imitatoribus* instead of *in nationibus*.

end, "he held together the structure and weighty edifice of
the whole of Christ's work." For truly the foundation with
which the church is grounded in Christ is the faith which
Peter confessed, when he said: "Thou art the Christ, the
Son of the living God." And of this foundation Paul said,
I Cor. 3 : 10: "According to the grace which is given unto
me, as a wise master builder, I laid the foundation," that
is to say, by teaching the faith of Christ. And he adds:
"And another buildeth thereon," that is, he does good works
on the basis of faith. "But let each man take heed how he
buildeth thereon," that is, his spiritual life in Christ. For
Paul adds: "Other foundation can no man lay than that is
laid, which is Christ. And if any man build upon this foundation gold"—that is, the doctrine of deity and heavenly
things—"silver"—that is, the doctrine of the humanity of
Christ and created things—"precious stones"—graces which
adorn the soul and its faculties—he without doubt is built
upon Christ. So the apostles built when they taught with
clearness and fervor the doctrine of the deity and humanity
and the Christian graces and, when they lived in the flesh,
planted with their blood the church of Christ. But which
of them built upon Christ and planted the church on Christ
more industriously, this we shall no doubt know when we
reach the heavenly country, the Lord himself being our
leader.

It is conceded, however, that Peter had his humility, poverty, steadfastness of faith, and, consequently, his blessedness from the Rock of the church, which is Christ. But that
by the words "On this Rock I will build my church" Christ
should have intended to build the whole militant church upon
the person of Peter, the faith of the Gospel, as expounded
by Augustine, and reason declare untrue. For on the Rock,
which is Christ, from whom Peter received his strength,
Christ was to build his church, since Christ is the head and
the foundation of the whole church, and not Peter. On the

other hand, St. Dionysius,[1] *de divinis nominibus*, 3, calls St.
Peter the peak, that is, the capital or captain. And in his
book which he wrote on the death of the apostles Peter and
Paul, he thus addresses Titus: "As Peter and Paul were
being led to the place of martyrdom and were about to be
separated, one from the other, Paul addressed to Peter these
words: 'Peace be to thee, O foundation of the churches and
shepherd of Christ's sheep and lambs!'" In the same way
Augustine, in his *Questions on the Old and New Law*, says
that "Peter was the first among the apostles." So likewise
Pope Marcellus, 24 : 1, *Rogamus* [Friedberg, 1 : 970],[2] says:
"We beseech you, brethren, that ye teach no otherwise than
as ye have received from St. Peter and the other apostles,
for he is the head of the whole church, to whom the Lord
said: 'Thou art Peter and upon this rock I will build my
church.'" Likewise Pope Anacletus, *Dist.* 21,[3] *in novo* [Fried-
berg, 1 : 69]: "In the New Testament after Christ's death,
the priestly order began with •Peter, because to him as the
first was given the pontificate in Christ's church even as the
Lord said to him: 'Thou art Peter and upon this rock I will
build my church.' He, therefore, was the first to receive
from the Lord the power of binding and loosing and he was
the first to lead the people to the faith by the power of his
preaching. And truly the other apostles received with him
in virtue of equal fellowship honor and power." Likewise,
it is commonly said that Peter was the head of the church
because he was called Cephas, which by interpretation is head.

---

[1] Dionysius the Areopagite, once identified with St. Denis and regarded
as first bishop of Athens, wrote probably about 500, as he is first quoted 533,
and shows the influence of Alexandrian neo-Platonism. He was much quoted
in the Middle Ages and has a strong mystical vein. His *Eccles. Hierarchy* and
his *Heavenly Hierarchy* were issued by John Colet and reissued by Lupton with
trsl., London, 1869.

[2] Marcellus, pope, 308–309. The quotation is from Pseudo-Isidore.

[3] Anacletus, 79?–91?, placed by the Catholics in the list of popes second
after Peter. Linus, Anacletus, Clement were probably contemporary presbyters in Rome, as Lipsius says. This quotation is from Pseudo-Isidore. Thirty
quotations are ascribed to Anacletus in the *Corp. jur. can.*

By what was said above in Chapters II, III, IV, namely, that the holy universal church is one and consists of all the predestinate that are to be saved and that Christ alone is the head of the church, just as he alone is the most exalted person in the church, imparting to it and to its members motion and understanding unto the life of grace, so it is evident that Peter never was and is not now the head of the holy catholic church.   And the dictum of St. Dionysius is true, that Peter was the captain among the apostles and was the foundation of churches, as is said in the next chapter of the apostles.   And the dictum of Augustine is also true, that by a certain prerogative Peter was the first among the apostles.   And the dictum of Marcellus is also true, that Peter was the head of the whole church which he ruled by his teaching and example.   But he was not a person higher in dignity than Christ's mother; nor was he equal to Christ or made the governor of the angels who, at that time, were the church triumphant.

Therefore, it is not a matter of much doubt to the simple Christian—faithful—that Peter did not dare to claim to be the head of the holy catholic church, for the reason that he did not rule over the whole church and did not excel above the whole church in dignity, nor was he the bridegroom of the catholic church.   John the Baptist, than whom, according to the testimony of the truth in Matt. 11 : 11, "There hath not risen a greater among those born of women," did not dare to call himself the bridegroom, but in humility confessed himself the bridegroom's friend.   And when his disciples in their zeal for him said, "Rabbi, he that was with thee beyond Jordan to whom thou hast borne witness, behold the same baptizeth and all men come to him," John answered them and said: "A man can receive nothing except it have been given from heaven. Ye yourselves bear me witness I have said I am not the Christ, but that I am sent before him.   He that hath the bride is the bridegroom: but it is sufficient for me that I am the bridegroom's friend that standeth and heareth with joy[1] the bridegroom's voice," John 3 : 27-29. And the bridegroom said: "Ye `are my friends if ye do whatsoever I command you," John 15 : 14. Thus it is evident that it would be the highest arrogance and folly for any man, Christ excepted, to call himself the head and the bridegroom of the holy catholic church.

But the reason for Christ's appointing Peter after himself as captain and shepherd was the pre-eminence of virtues fitting him to rule the church. For otherwise the Wisdom[2] of the Father would have unwisely appointed him the bishop of his church. And as all moral virtues are bound together in a class—in genere—it is evident that Peter had a certain pre-eminence in the entire class of virtues. But there were three virtues in which Peter excelled, namely, faith, humility, and love. Faith, which properly is the foundation of the church, excelled in Peter because of what the best of Masters ordained, Matt. 16 : 16, in answer to that question which he asked about himself: "Whom do men say that I the Son of man am?" To this Peter replied for all, saying: "Thou art the Son of the living God." Here he confessed Christ's humanity by which he meant that Christ was the Messiah promised to the fathers. The second part confesses Christ as the natural Son of the living God, and so Peter confessed Christ to be very God and very man. And among all the articles of faith, this one appertains most to the edification of the church, for, according to St. John, the Son of God overcometh the world: "Who is he that overcometh the world but he that believeth that Jesus is the Son of God?" I John 5 : 5. For, when this foundation is laid, the belief follows that all things which Christ did or taught are to be accepted without any detraction by the whole church.

---

[1] *Audiens cum gaudio.* The Vulgate: *audiat eum, gaudio gaudet propter vocem.*
[2] Referring to Prov. 8, Wisdom being interpreted to mean the second person of the Trinity by the old commentators.

And so Peter heard from the Lord's lips the words: "Blessed art thou, Simon Bar-Jonah, for flesh and blood hath not revealed this unto thee, but my Father which is in heaven." And because of this faith Peter received the burden of the church's prefecture. And the Rock said: "I say that thou art Peter and upon this Rock I will build my church." Hence, on account of these things Peter's vicars and those appointed to rule in the church are bound to preach the church's faith. Therefore, the Saviour said: "I have prayed for thee, that thy faith fail not; and do thou, when once thou hast turned again, establish thy brethren," Luke 22 : 32. Therefore, praying for faith, "he was heard for his godly fear," Heb. 5 : 7.

In the second place the Lord joined with him the primacy of office. After my death, he said: "I will give to thee the keys of the kingdom of heaven," that is, the keys of the church, which I will strengthen and defend against the church of the wicked by giving to thee the power of binding and loosing that thou mayest, not without avail, hold the keys of the church which I have given thee for thy meritorious confession of my humanity and deity, of which, taught by the Father, after a heavenly manner, thou didst say: "Thou art the Christ, the Son of the living God." Therefore, because of his confession, so confident and profound, he was called Cephas, which is by interpretation Peter, John 1 : 42. For this reason Jerome, expert in languages, says: "that Cephas means Peter, or firmness, and that it is a Syriac not a Hebrew word." This affords the solution of the last objection; for Cephas does not mean head, according to the Gospel and Jerome, but Peter.

Peter's second virtue was humility. Inasmuch as Peter heard from his Master the words, "Learn of me, for I am meek and lowly of heart," Matt. 11 : 29 and, "whosoever will be great among you, let him be your minister; and whosoever will be first among you, let him be your servant," Matt.

23 : 11; Mark 10 : 43—how should he not be of an humble spirit, above others, in regard to the prerogative which he had from the Lord Jesus Christ? Hence it is said with probability that Peter asked questions and answered questions with humility just as he bore himself, above others, in humility to perform his ministry in the church. For, sent by the apostles to Samaria, he went humbly with John, Acts 8 : 14. And so, called to Joppa, he went humbly, and there for many days he tarried with Simon the tanner. Called by Cornelius from Joppa, he proceeded humbly to Cæsarea, Acts 10 : 18. And also at the council of the apostles and the church [at Jerusalem, 51 A. D.], after he had finished his speech, when James stated the case and said: "Hearken unto me; Simon hath declared," etc. And then James adds a statement: "Wherefore my judgment is that we trouble not them that from among the Gentiles turn unto God," Acts 15 : 19. It is also narrated how Peter went everywhere throughout all parts, preaching humbly the Word of God, Acts 9 : 32. Being sharply rebuked by Paul, he bore it humbly, Gal. 2 : 11. And all these things he did, not for worldly honor and advantage but in an humble and obedient spirit and to support the honor of the law of Christ. Therefore, in these things we read the full greatness of Peter the apostle which is to be measured by the humility of his service, as appears from the definition of the Master: "Whoso humbleth himself shall be exalted," Matt. 23 : 12.

As for the third virtue, love, it is plain that Peter had this in certain respects above the others, as appears from the fervor of his acts which fittingly proceed from greater love. This is confirmed by the fact that otherwise he would have been ungrateful, if he had not loved his Master, in a way corresponding to Him who had loved him in so peculiar a way, and wiped him clean from his great blasphemy and graciously placed him over his sheep. Again it is confirmed by this, that otherwise there would have been no fitness in the

Master asking him, "Simon, son of John, lovest thou me more than these?" and then immediately committing to him his sheep to feed, John 21 : 15. But here it should be noted that the reasons for loving Christ are manifold. Some love Christ more than others on the ground of his divinity, as is believed to have been the case with John the Evangelist; others because of his humanity, as is believed to have been the case with Philip; and others love Christ because of his body which is the church, and so men love him for many other reasons, for which, in the case of a certain saint, they quote Ecclesiasticus 42: "No one has been found like unto him in keeping the law of the Most High." Peter's pre-eminence is manifest from his faith, humility, love, yea, and also from his poverty and endurance. For he said to the man asking an alms: "Silver and gold have I none, but such as I have give I thee," Acts 3 : 6. And, because he heard from the Master the words, "In your patience possess ye your souls," Luke 21 : 19, it seems probable that, after his denial of the Master, Peter stood for that very reason more ready to endure martyrdom and especially for the reason that, recognizing his weakness, he had fresh in his mind the memory of his own frailty in denying his Master. And for this reason he stooped in humility to others and was more ready to suffer imprisonments, even unto death, for the Lord whom he denied. Nor is it to be doubted that he bore with an humble mind Herod's prison in Jerusalem, the prison of Theophilus in Antioch, and Nero's prison at Rome.

If he, who is called to be Peter's vicar, follows in the paths of the virtues just spoken of, we believe that he is his true vicar and the chief pontiff of the church over which he rules. But, if he walks in the opposite paths, then he is the legate of antichrist at variance with Peter and Jesus Christ. Therefore, St. Bernard, *de consideratione*, IV,[1] writes

---

[1] The most famous book ever written on the papal office, prepared at the request of Eugenius III, by St. Bernard of Clairvaux, d. 1153. It was much

as follows: "Among these things thou walkest in the van a shepherd overornamented with gold even in the midst of an environment so varied. Why do they seize the sheep? If I may dare, I will say that these are the pasture grounds of demons rather than of sheep. Not in this way[1] did Peter act, or Paul frisk about." And he adds: "Either deny to the people that thou art shepherd or show thyself such. Thou wilt not deny it lest he whose place thou holdest deny thee to be the heir. He is Peter who is not known to go about in processions, ornamented with gems or silks, not clad in gold or carried by a white horse, or compassed about with soldiers, and surrounded by bustling servants. Without such things, Peter believed he was able to fulfil sufficiently the salutary commandment: 'If thou lovest me, feed my sheep.' In things like these thou hast followed not Peter, but Constantine." Thus far Bernard.

That holy man knew that Pope Eugenius ought to be a vicar in poverty and humility, not in pride but in feeding the sheep, following Peter. For that man is a true vicar of him whose place he fills and from whom he has lawfully received the procuratorial power. But no one can truly and acceptably to Christ rule in Christ's stead or the stead of Peter without following him in his life—*moribus*[2]—since there is no other fitting way of following him except he receive subject to this condition from God procuratorial power. Thus

quoted by Huss, also in other writings, and by the title *ad Eugenium*. Although Eugenius was his spiritual son, Bernard addressed him as "most holy father." He recalls the pope from the love of pomp and wealth to spiritual humility and the proper business of the pope who, although pastor of pastors, is greatest when he is servant of all. He is in the line of the primacy of Abel, Abraham, Moses, Aaron, and Peter. Both Ultramontanes and Gallicans claim the treatise for their position. Bp. Reinkens's trsl., Münster, 1870, pp. 170, the Old Catholic divine, represented the second view. Besides the ed. of Migne, Schneider's ed., Berlin, 1850. The passage quoted is Schneider, pp. 75 *sq.* Reinkens, pp. 114, 116. See Schaff, *Ch. Hist.*, V, pt. 1 : 776 *sq.*

[1] *Non sic.* Bernard has *scilicet*, the words being spoken in irony. Below Huss has *neges* instead of *neget*, deny.

[2] Literally, morals denoting the disposition or principles as well as the outward act.

there is required for such an office as that of vicar conformity of life and authority from the person instituting it, and to this one [such a vicar] the Saviour at the Last Supper committed the institution of the venerable sacrament. And constituting his disciples his vicars that they might so do in remembrance of him, he said: "I have given you an example that ye also should do as I have done to you," John 13 : 15. He also said: "Whosoever shall do and teach them he shall be called great in the kingdom of heaven," Matt. 5 : 19.

On this point St. Jerome *ad Heliodorum*, also *Decretum*, *Dist.* 40 [Friedberg, 1 : 145], says: "It is not easy to fill the place of Peter and Paul in occupying the chair—*cathedra*—of those who reign with Christ, because it was said, 'they are not the children of saints who hold the places of saints, but they who do their good works.'" St. Gregory [Friedberg, 1 : 146] says the same: "Neither places nor orders make us near to our Creator, but our good works bind us together or our evil works separate us." Likewise Chrysostom, *Dist.* 40 : 12 [Friedberg, 1 : 147], says: "Many priests there are, and few; many in name, and few in works. See, therefore, how ye sit in the official chair, for the chair does not make the priest, but the priest makes the chair: the place does not sanctify the man, but the man the place. Not every priest is holy; but every holy person is a priest. He who sits well in the official chair gives[1] honor to the chair; he who sits there ill does injury to it. Therefore a bad priest gets criminality from his priesthood not dignity."

Likewise, we have this from the *Acts of Boniface-Martyr* [Friedberg, 1 : 146]: "If a pope neglect his own and his brother's salvation and be reproved as useless, remiss in his acts, and above all keeping silent about the good[2] because

---

[1] *Facit.* In the *Decretum, accipit,* "has received the honor of the chair."
[2] *De bono*, omitted by Huss.

he serves himself rather than the sheep,[1] none the less he leads an innumerable company of people in flocks with himself to be beaten together with himself, as the property of hell, with many stripes throughout eternity." Nor is it necessary to refer to many saints, for the Chief Pontiff, the holiest of the holy said: "All that came before me are thieves and robbers," John 10 : 8. Again he said to his disciples: "Ye are the salt of the earth; but if the salt hath lost its savor, wherewith shall it be salted . . . it is neither useful for the land nor for the dunghill, but it is cast out," Matt. 5 : 13; Luke 14 : 34.

Wishing to impose this judgment upon the minds of men, that most good Saviour and best of masters immediately added: "Who hath ears to hear let him hear." Therefore, let every priest see to it, if he has entered well, that he live pure of offense, with the sincere purpose of honoring God and profiting the church, and in case he demean himself well, that he lay little store by mundane honors and the world's lucre. For, otherwise, he is a lying antichrist, and the higher his office the greater antichrist he is. Let the humble pilgrim look at Christ who said: "I am the way, the truth, and the life," John 14 : 6. Behold he who wants to go, hath the way, for Christ is the way, and whither he wants to go, for Christ is the truth, and where he wants to abide, for Christ is the life.

[1] The *Decretum* has *omnibus* instead of *ovibus*.

CHAPTER X

THE POWER OF BINDING AND LOOSING

Now as to the power—authority—of Christ, given by himself to his vicars, which is touched upon in the words, "I will give unto thee the keys of the kingdom of heaven," that is, the power to bind and to loose sins,—Augustine says, Com. on John 21: "The effects of this power are shown, when Christ adds, 'And whatsoever thou shalt bind on earth, shall be bound in heaven, and whatsoever thou shalt loose on earth shall be loosed in heaven.' This power is a spiritual power. Therefore, it is to be noted, that spiritual power is a power of the spirit, determining its acts of itself so that a rational creature, so far as gracious gifts go, may be guided and have his own distinctive place both as determined from the standpoint of the subject and the object." Every man, however, is a spirit, since he has two natures; as the Saviour in speaking to his disciples said: "Ye know not what spirit ye are of" [Luke 9 : 55], and "every spirit that confesseth not Jesus is not of God," I John 4 : 3. Here the spirit is subtle and heretical, denying Jesus to be very God and very man. And it is evident that whether power in respect to God and power in respect to rational creatures are analogous or the analogy is to be restricted to the powers of men and the powers of angels, it is true that all spiritual power is a power of the spirit. And, although a man does not give grace, he nevertheless administers the sacraments, so that the inferior is guided as to gifts of grace.

But although bodily power may be the result of gifts of grace, nevertheless it is immediate, so that the creature of

God is ruled according to the law of natural things or of fortune. So every man is seen to have a double power; for every man ought to have the power over the movements of his members, and therefore has the power of walking in grace, so also the spiritual power has manifold subdivisions, for there is one power of orders and another common to all. The power of orders is called the spiritual power. This is that which the clergy has to administer the sacraments of the church that the clergy may profit itself and the laity, and such power is the power of consecrating the mass, absolving and performing the other sacramental acts—*sacramentalia*. For the power of consecrating the mass exists of itself and immediately, that the priest may consecrate just as dispositions of moral virtue are ordained because of acts better than the dispositions. And as the priest, in order that he may consecrate worthily, is guided as to the gifts of grace, the above description holds.

But the spiritual power, which is common, is the power which every priest[1] has in doing spiritual works whether in his own person or among others, and about these the verse reminds us:

Doce, consule, castiga, solare, remitte, fer, ora.

Teach, counsel, punish, console, remit, bear, pray.[2]

For as many as received Christ by faith to these hath he given the power to become the sons of God, so that they may guide themselves and their brethren in the way of their Father Christ, and by rebuking in love as Christ said: "If thy brother sin against thee, go show him his fault between thee and him alone," Matt. 18 : 15.

---

[1] Plebanus, the term common in the M. A. for the parish priest.

[2] The seven spiritual gifts of mercy, namely, teach the ignorant, direct the doubting, reprove the erring, console the sorrowing, forgive those indebted to thee, bear the infirmities of others, pray for all—in opposition to the seven bodily works of mercy: *Visito, poto, cibo, redimo, tego, colligo, condo*, namely, I visit the sick, give drink to the thirsty, feed the hungry, release the imprisoned, clothe the naked, care for the stranger, bury the dead. See Huss, *Super IV. Sent.*, p. 596.

Secular power is twofold, civil and common.   Civil power, which is authoritative, belongs only to the civil lord.   But civil power, which is vicarious, belongs to officials or servants. But secular power, which is common to all, is the power by which a man is able to rule himself and his own according to the gifts of nature and of fortune.   And thus, just as a man cannot be a whole man without body and soul, nor is the adopted child of God complete without the gifts of nature and of grace, so the pilgrim cannot get along as a pilgrim unless he has both secular and spiritual power which are common to all, although this is bound in the case of infants and the dead.   But spiritual power is everywhere the more perfect and the sacerdotal power exceeds the power of kings in dignity as appears from Heb. 7 : 7: "Greater is he that blesses and less is he who is blest."

Hence the spiritual power, which is sacerdotal, excels the royal in age, dignity, and usefulness.   In age it excels, because the priesthood was instituted by God's command, as appears from Ex. 28.   Later at God's command the kingly power was instituted by the priesthood, as appears from Deut. 17 and I Sam. 12.   In dignity it excels, as already said, because the priest as the greater blesses, consecrates and anoints the king.   And the usefulness is evidently greater for the reason that the spiritual power is in and of itself sufficient for the ruling of the people, as appears from the history of Israel, which down to the time of Saul was salubriously administered independent of the kingly authority. Therefore, the spiritual power, inasmuch as it concerns the best things—things having their sufficiency in themselves— excels the earthly power, since the latter is of no avail independent of the spiritual power which is the chief regulative force.   On the other hand, the spiritual power may act by itself without the aid of the earthly power.   And, for this reason, the priests who abuse this power, which is so exalted, by pride or other open sin, fall all the lower with the devil into hell, and this is in accord with the rule of St. Gregory and other saints: "The higher the position the deeper the fall."

And it is to be noted, that power now means absolutely the ability to regulate and rule and now collectively such ability through authoritative notification and announcement. And when these senses are equally known, it is evident, there is nothing contradictory in the principles that there is no power but of God and yet to give power from God, that is, make an authoritative announcement before the church that a created being has from God power of this sort. Indeed such a bestowal, so far as part of it is concerned, is given by man but not unless God primarily authorizes it. And from this we may further understand that power is not relaxed or stiffened, increased or diminished, so far as its essence goes, but only in respect to the exercise of the act which proceeds from the power itself. And this exercise ought only to be used when a reasonable ground exists for it from the side of God. This meaning is set forth in *Decretum* 24 : 1, *Miramur* [Friedberg, 1 : 981], which says: "The official power is one thing, the exercise of it another. And official power is for the most part held in restraint in the case of monks and of others, such as those under suspension, who are inhibited from ministering, though the power itself is not taken away from them."[1] In like manner it is conceded that the natural power, which is free will, may now be relaxed by grace and now tightened [*i. e.*, increased and lessened]. And in this way the seeming discordances of the doctors which arise by ambiguity of language are solved, some of whom, as Anselm, say, "that free will cannot be lost or increased or diminished," while others,

---

[1] In regard to the bishop, Thomas Aquinas made the distinction between the power—potestas—of doing episcopal acts and jurisdiction. Even a bishop who becomes schismatic or heretic retains the former, but loses the latter. *Summa Supplem.*, 39 : 2 [Migne, 4 : 1065]. The problem of the validity of acts done by priests who have become schismatic or heretic was so difficult that Peter the Lombard and Gratian thought it well-nigh if not altogether insoluble.

like Augustine, *Enchiridion* [*Nic. Fathers*, 3 : 247], say, that free will may be lost through sin and increased through grace. On this account there is in the church great strife about the power of bestowment, withdrawal or restriction. Nevertheless, it is known that when God and reason make it necessary for the profit of the church that a thing should be done by man, then and not otherwise does God give or withdraw or restrict power of this sort.

Hence, when Christ said to Peter: "I will give thee the keys of the kingdom of heaven," that is the power of binding and loosing sins, he said in the person of Peter to the whole church militant, that not does any person whatever of the church without distinction hold those keys, but that the whole church, as made up of its individual parts, as far as they are suitable for this, holds the keys. These keys, however, are not material things, but they are spiritual power and acquaintance with evangelical knowledge, and it was on account of this power and knowledge, as we believe, that Christ used the plural "keys." For this reason the Master of Sentences, 12 : 18, *cap.* 2 [Migne's ed., p. 375], says: "He speaks in the plural ' keys,' for one is not sufficient. These keys are the wisdom of discernment and the power of judging, whereby the ecclesiastical judge is bound to receive the worthy and exclude the unworthy from the kingdom." And it is to be noted, that to the Trinity alone does it belong to have the chief power of this kind. And the humanity of Christ alone has chief subordinate power from within himself, for Christ is at the same time God and man. Nevertheless, prelates of the church have committed unto them instrumental or ministerial power, which is a judicial power, consisting chiefly of two things, namely, the power of knowing how to discriminate, and the power of judging judicially. The former of these is called in the court of penance the key of the conscience, reasonably disposing the mind to the exercise of the second function, that is, the judicial; for no one legally has the power of pronouncing a definite sentence unless he has the prior power of discerning in a case in which he is called upon to discriminate and pronounce sentence.

The first key, therefore, is neither an act nor a state of knowledge, but the power of antecedent discernment. Consequently, all the power of the sacerdotal order, namely, of being the instrument in opening to man the gate, which is Christ, or of shutting to an inferior the said kingdom, is the key of the church given to Peter and to others, as appears from the Saviour's words: "Verily I say unto you whatsoever ye bind on earth, shall be bound in heaven, and whatsoever ye shall loose on earth shall be loosed in heaven," Matt. 18 : 18. He also said: "Receive ye the Holy Spirit. Whosesoever sins ye forgive they are forgiven unto them; and whosesoever sins ye retain they are retained," John 20 : 22. To Peter and the church in him were the words spoken: "Whatsoever thou shalt loose on earth," etc., Matt. 16 : 19.

These words, because of a defect in their understanding, frighten many Christians so that they are filled with servile fear, while others are deceived by them and presume because of the fulness of power [they are supposed to convey]. Therefore, the following things are to be laid down: (1) That the Saviour's dictum about the virtue of the words is necessary, because it is not possible for a priest to loose or bind anything, unless such loosing and binding take place in heaven, not only in the heavenly realm which also comprises the sublunary world and all things which are therein, but also take place with the divine approval and the approval of angelic beings which are heavenly. Hence, it is to be noted, that guilt inheres in the soul of him who sins mortally and grace is corrupted or ceases to be, for which reason he who sins mortally is under the debt of eternal damnation, provided he does not do penance, and, if he persists in this guilt, he is separated from the companionship of pilgrims in grace. But in penance there is a remedy, by which guilt is deleted, grace conferred, the chain of damnation broken, and man reunited with the church. This penance is performed by contrition, confession and satisfaction.[1] Contrition, which is sorrow or full pain for sin committed, must include displeasure with the sin already committed, and the sin which may be committed and, in the case—*articulo*—of necessity, such contrition is enough for salvation. Hence the Saviour, knowing that the mind of the adulteress was full of sorrow, added the words: "Go and sin no more," John 8 : 11. For this reason St. Augustine, St. Ambrose and St. Gregory agree in saying that to be penitent is to lament evils done and not to wish to do evils that are to be lamented.

Secondly, it is to be noted that, for the justification of the wicked man there is needed infinite power by which God cleanses from spot and stain and grants grace. Again, God's mercy is needed whereby he relaxes the offense done his Majesty, and the eternal punishment for the debt which would follow if he did not do penance. Therefore, the church often prays, "Almighty and most merciful God," urging the infinite power and mercy of God. But that infinite power is required for the justification of a wicked man is evident because, as Augustine says, "it is easier to create a world than to justify the wicked; the first demands infinite power and consequently also the second [act], and this is the reason why, in the justification of the wicked, the active bestowal

---

[1] Penance is treated by Thomas Aquinas as a restoration to health. This sacrament is the second plank thrown out for the sinner, as baptism is the first. After the close of the twelfth century the four elements were considered necessary parts of penance: contrition, confession to the priest, satisfaction, and absolution. Peter the Lombard still taught that confession to God was sufficient for forgiveness. Alexander of Hales, d. 1245, made confession to the priest essential, and he was followed by Thomas Aquinas. Absolution, which from 1200 on has been regarded in the Catholic church as a judicial act, was treated by Peter the Lombard as a declarative act, and the petitionary form was still common in his day. Schwane, *Dogmengesch. d. m. Z.*, p. 670, pronounces it the most important part of the sacrament of penance. In his *Com. on the Lombard*, p. 598 sqq., Huss takes a moderate view, and on the basis of the cases of the penitent thief and publican, leans toward the opinion that contrition of heart and confession to God are sufficient.

of the Holy Spirit is required, which cannot be secured except from God," as Augustine proves in many places, as I have shown in my *Tract on Indulgences*. And the Master of Sentences, 1 : 14 [Migne's ed., p. 49], concludes from these words of Augustine and says, "Therefore no men, however holy, can give the Holy Spirit," and the same reasoning applies to the active remission of sins.[1]

Hence in a unique sense the Baptist said of Christ: "Behold the Lamb of God that taketh away the sins of the world," John 1 : 29. On these words Augustine says, Hom. on John, 4 [*Nic. Fathers*, 7 : 28]: "Let no one presume and say of himself that he takes away the sins of the world. Now, observe the proud against whom John lifted his finger were not yet heretics and yet they were already shown to be such against whom he cried from the river." Wherefore the Jews often ascribed blasphemy to Christ because, esteeming him, though falsely, to be a mere man, they said he was not able of himself to forgive sins, because sin is not forgiven by a mere word except only as the offense against God is relaxed. But who forgives an injury except the person against whom it is done or against whose subject it is done? For God, in giving power of this kind, first forgives the injury against Himself before His vicar can forgive. Hence on this point Ambrose says: "He alone forgives sins who alone died for us. The Word of God forgives sins. The priest is the judge. The priest performs his function and does not exercise the

---

[1] The *Treatises on Papal Indulgences*, *Mon.*, 1 : 215–237, was called forth by John XXIII's two bulls, calling for a crusade against Ladislaus, king of Naples, 1412, and promising liberal indulgence for participation in the campaign. The bulls created a great sensation in Prague, where the billets of pardon were openly sold at three different places. Huss attacked the whole system of wars against fellow Christians started at the pope's instance, and entered into the question of papal and priestly absolution. He declared that if the pope had the right to give indulgences, he was a criminal if he did not empty purgatory. He took up the same position as here that the priest cannot absolve whom God has not before absolved, and that the priest's power is essentially the same as the priest's power under the O. T. in pronouncing a leper clean. See Huss, *Super IV. Sent.*, 606 *sqq.*, and Introd. to this volume.

way[1] of any power," *de Penitentia*, 1 [Friedberg, 1 : 1170].
To the same purport speaks Jerome, whom the Master of
Sentences quotes (see above), and Gregory, 1 : 1, *Paulus*.
The same holds good for the retention and binding of sins.
Hence the Master of Sentences, 4 : 18, 4 [Migne, p. 376], ad-
ducing these authorities and reasons, concludes, that "God
alone washes a man within clean from the stain of sin and
from the debt of eternal punishment," and he closes thus:
"By these and many other testimonies it is taught that God
alone and of Himself forgives sins; and just as He forgives
some so He retains the sins of others."

But some one will say, if God alone can forgive and retain sins, why did He say to the apostles and their vicars:
"Whatsoever ye shall loose," etc., . . . and "whosesoever sins
ye retain," etc.?   What, therefore, is it for a priest to loose or
bind sins, to remit or retain?   To the first the Master of
Sentences (see above) gives answer and says: "Priests also
bind when they impose the satisfaction of penance upon
those who confess.   They loose when in view of the satisfaction they forgive anything or admit those purged by it
to participation in the sacraments."   To the second Richard
answers well in his *Power of Loosing and Binding* [Migne,
196 : 1164 *sq.*], when he says:[2] "What is it to remit sins
except to relax the sentence of punishment which is due for
sins, and by relaxing to absolve?   And what is it to retain sins
but not to absolve those not truly penitent?   For many of
those who confess seek absolution who nevertheless do not

---

[1] *Viam.* The *Decretum* has *jura*, rights.

[2] Richard of St. Victor, d. 1173, was born in Scotland, and was the pupil of
Hugo of St. Victor.   Both were mystics, but their mysticism differed from that
of St. Bernard by being developed into a scientific system and brought within
the limits of careful definition.   In addition to the book above quoted, Richard
wrote commentaries on the Canticles, the Apocalypse, etc., *Emmanuel*, a treatise
directed to the Jews, *Preparation of the Mind for Contemplation*, etc.   While
he was prior of St. Victor, Alexander III and Thomas à Becket visited the
convent.   It was located within the present bounds of Paris, and its buildings
were destroyed during the French Revolution.

want to wholly abandon their sins. Many promise caution for the future but do not want to make satisfaction. All of this sort, in so far as they do not truly repent, beyond doubt ought not to be forgiven. For truly to repent is to be sorry for past wrong-doing, to confess with a strong purpose, to make satisfaction, and to take heed to oneself with all caution. Those who do penance in this way, they ought to be forgiven; and to be remitted in any other way without absolution, this is to retain sins. Now, from the things already said we may clearly understand that, in the forgiveness of sins, the Lord does by and of Himself what is done through his minister, that is, he does not by Himself and through the office of ministers, but He fully of Himself looses the bond of obduracy; and He looses by Himself and His minister the debt of eternal damnation; truly He looses by his ministers the debt of future purgation. The power of the first kind of forgiveness He reserves for Himself alone. The second kind of forgiveness He imparts by Himself and His minister. But the third kind, the Lord is accustomed to impart not as much by Himself as by his minister. Properly, indeed, is it said that the Lord absolves..the truly penitent from the bond of damnation. None the less it is true that the priest does this and the Lord, [1] the Lord in view of the conversion of the heart, and the. priest in view of the confession of the mouth. For the confession of the heart alone suffices in the case of the truly penitent unto salvation. And the case—*articulus*—of necessity excludes both the confession of the mouth and absolution by the priest." Thus much Richard.

From these things the conclusion is drawn that God predestinates from eternity, and He executes in time the absolution of a person who is to be saved and the remission of his sin, before such a person is absolved on earth by the min-

---

[1] The expression, "and the Lord" is not in Richard's text. Otherwise Huss's quotation is exact.

49607

ister of the church. Again the minister of the church, the
vicar of Christ, is not able to absolve or to bind, to forgive sins or to retain them, unless God has done this previously. This appears from John 15 : 5: "Apart from me
ye can do nothing." That vessel of election knew this, and
so he said: "Not that we are sufficient of ourselves to account anything as from ourselves, but our sufficiency is from
God," II Cor. 3 : 5. Therefore, if we are not sufficient to
think except as God imparts the thought, how are we sufficient to bind and loose except God have previously loosed
and bound? And this the philosophers recognize when they
say that a second cause can effect nothing without the
coagency of a first cause.

Further, it is clear that no man may be loosed from sin
or receive the remission of sins, unless God have loosed him or
given him remission. Hence the Baptist says: "A man can
receive nothing except it first be given him from heaven," John
3 : 27. Hence as an earthly lord first forgives in spirit the sin
committed against himself, before this is announced by himself or by another, so it is necessary for God to do. Therefore,
the presbyters are wildly beside themselves who think and say
that they may of their own initiative loose and bind, without
the absolution or binding of Jesus Christ preceding their act.
For loosing and binding are in the first instance the simple
[absolute] act of God. Therefore, the Gospel says, "Whatsoever is bound on earth shall be bound in heaven," but it does
not say that it is bound in heaven at a later time and not
previously.

Hence, the ignorant think that the priest binds and looses
in time first and after him God. It is folly to have this
opinion. But the logicians know well that priority is twofold: the one, priority of origin, taken from the material cause,
and the other the priority of dignity, taken from the final
cause. And these two priorities meet at one and the same
time, and in this way the binding and loosing of the church

militant is in a sense prior to the binding and loosing of the church triumphant and vice versa.

But God's act of binding or loosing is absolutely first. And it is evident, it would be blasphemy to assert that a man may remit an offense done to so great a Lord, with the Lord himself approving the remission. For by the universal law and practice followed by the Lord, He himself must loose or bind first, if any vicar looses or binds. And for us no article of the faith ought to be more certain than the impossibility of any one of the church militant to absolve or bind except in so far as he is conformed to the head of the church, our Lord Jesus Christ.

Hence, the faithful should be on his guard against this form of statement: "If the pope or any other pretends that he binds or looses by a particular sign, then by that very fact the offender is loosed or bound." For by conceding this, they have to concede that the pope is impeccable as is God, for otherwise he is able to err and to misuse the key of Christ. And it is certain that as impossible as it is for the figure of a material key to open anything when the substance is wanting, so impossible is it for Christ's vicar to open or shut except as he conforms himself to the key of Christ which first opens and shuts. For just as Christ the first-born of many brethren and the first-fruits of them that sleep was the first ·to enter the kingdom, so he alone and above all could have had committed to him the spiritual kingdom[1] which was altogether closed from the time our first parents lied until he himself came. And the same is to be said in regard to any opening or closing whatever which pertains to the heavenly country. And it is plain that every vicar of Christ, so long as he continues to walk in this world, may err, even in those things which concern the faith and the

---

[1] The kingdom of bliss to which the worthies of the Old Testament dispensation were not admitted till they were released from the limbus patrum during the three days after Christ's crucifixion.

keys of the church as those knew who wrote the *Chronicles ;* [1]
for Peter himself, Christ's first vicar, sinned in these regards.

Likewise, God is the only being who cannot be ignorant
as to whose sins may be remitted, and He the only being who
cannot be moved by a wrong motive and judge unjust judgment.   But any vicar may be ignorant as to whose sins ought
to be remitted, and he may be moved by a wrong motive in
binding or loosing.   Therefore, if he refuse to impart absolution to one truly penitent and confessing, moved by anger or
greed, he cannot by his act bind such a person in guilt.   Similar would be the case with one who came with a lying confession, as happens very often, and the priest, not knowing
his hypocrisy, should impart to him the words of absolution.
Undoubtedly he does not thereby absolve, for the Scriptures
say, Wisdom [of Solomon] 1 : 4: "The Holy Spirit evades
a feigned act of worship."   In the first case, just noted, the
vicar alleges that he bound or forgave sins and did not; and
in the second case he alleges that he loosed or remitted sins and
did not.   And it is evident how great the illusion may be of
those who administer the keys and of those who do not truly
repent.   For it is necessary that a person, wishing to be absolved, be first so disposed in his will that he is sorry for his
guilt, and then have the purpose to sin no more.   Hence,
all priests combined—who are at the same time vicars—are
not able to absolve from sins him who wishes to go on sinning and who does not wish to lament his sins.

So all together are not able to bind a righteous man or
retain his sins when he humbles himself with his whole heart
and has a contrite heart, a thing which God does not despise.
Wherefore St. Jerome, commenting on Matt. 16 : 19 [Migne's
ed., 26 : 118], "I will give unto thee the keys of the kingdom of heaven, and whatsoever thou shalt loose on earth
shall be loosed in heaven," etc., says: "Some not under-

---

[1] The histories of the church of Ranulph Higden, Martinus Polonus, etc.,
mentioned by name in a subsequent chapter.

standing this passage appropriate something of the arrogance
of the Pharisees so as to think that they can damn the guilt-
less and loose offenders, for with God not the judgment of
priests is sought but the life of the guilty."[1]   To these words
the Master of Sentences, 4 : 18, *cap.* 6, adds [Migne's ed.,
p. 375]: "Here it is plainly shown, that God does not follow
the sentence of the church which judges in ignorance and
deceitfully."   He also adds, *cap.* 8: "Sometimes he who is
sent outdoors, that is, outside of holy church, by the priest,
is, nevertheless, inside.   And he who, by virtue of the truth,
is outside, seems to be kept inside by the priest's false sentence."   And again he says, 4 : 19, *cap.* 4 [Migne, p. 382]:
That the priest who binds and looses others ought himself
to be prudent and just, for otherwise he will put to death
souls who do not die and revive souls which do not live, and
in this way he turns his power of pronouncing judgment into
an instrument of cursing—so that it is said in Mal. 2 : 2:
"I will bless your cursings and curse your blessings."   Therefore the vicars of Christ ought to take heed that they do
not lightly presume to bind or loose whenever it pleases
them.

   But the objection is offered concerning higher rank and
obedience from the Canon *Solitæ* [Friedberg, 2 : 196–199],
where Pope Innocent [III] says: "The Lord said to Peter,
and in Peter to his successors, 'Whatsoever thou shalt bind
on earth shall be bound in heaven,' making no exception
when he said, 'Whatsoever,' etc."   Here it is to be noted
that in virtue of the words, "Whatsoever thou shalt loose,"
Peter could not loosen the Scriptures, for Christ our Saviour
said: "The Scripture cannot be broken," John 10 : 35.

   [1] Jerome adds that, according to Lev. 14, the lepers were commanded to
show themselves to the priest and, if they had leprosy, they became unclean
by the priest—*a sacerdote immundi fiant*—"not that the priests made them
leprous and unclean, but that the leprous and those who were not might have
the knowledge of their condition."   For Huss's treatment of the power of the
keys as set forth in his *Com. on Peter the Lombard*, see Introduction to this
volume.

Nor, secondly, could he loose one who would not repent, and so he said to Simon Magus: "Repent, therefore, of this thy wickedness and pray the Lord if perhaps it may be forgiven you," Acts 8 : 22. Thirdly, Peter had no power to loose the marriage bond, for the Saviour said: "What God hath joined together, let not man put asunder," Matt. 19 : 6. And fourthly, he was not able to absolve Judas from sin, because the Saviour said: "Not one of them perished but the son of perdition, that the Scripture might be fulfilled," John 17 : 12.

Therefore, if Peter in virtue of that saying of Christ, "Whatsoever thou shalt loose on earth shall be loosed in heaven," had presumed to have power to loose in any of the four cases just adduced, would they have been loosed in heaven? Certainly not! For the will of God would have opposed it in the case of the Scriptures, marriage, Judas, and in the case of the one refusing in his pertinacity to repent. Therefore, it does not follow that the vicar, who thinks that he is able to loose or to bind whomsoever he chooses, really does it. On this point, St. Augustine, *de vera et falsa Penitentia*,[1] speaks, when he says: "God, who had already raised up Lazarus from the grave, offered Lazarus to the disciples that they might loose him,[2] thereby showing the power of loosing imparted to priests: and God said, 'Whatsoever ye shall loose on earth shall be loosed in heaven,' that is, I, God, and all the ranks of the heavenly army and all the saints who give praise in that heavenly glory join with you in confirming those whom ye bind and loose. He did not say, 'whom ye think ye bind and loose, but those towards whom ye exercise works of righteousness or mercy. But your other works done towards sinners I do not recog-

---

[1] Migne, 40 : 1122. The work is printed in the Appendix of Augustine's Works. It is quoted by Gratian and Peter the Lombard as Augustine's. That the work was not from Augustine's hand, Erasmus showed.

[2] "Jesus said unto them, loose him and let him go," John 11 : 44. Richard of St. Victor also uses Lazarus, Migne, 196 : 1166.

nize.'" Thus much Augustine, who limits the clergy's power to loose or bind as it stands in their own estimation.

To the same purport are the words of Richard, *de potest. ligandi et solvendi* [Migne, 196 : 1167]. He says: "So far thou goest and sayest: if I am not able to bind or absolve anything or to retain and remit the sins of all persons whatsoever, what does that mean, which was said in a general way unto Peter: 'Whatsoever thou shalt bind, whatsoever thou shalt loose'? Just as it was also laid down as a general rule spoken to the apostles in common: 'Whosesoever sins ye remit, they are remitted unto them; and whosesoever sins ye retain, they are retained.' Properly should this question move you had the Lord said to Peter, 'Whatsoever thou shalt wish to bind shall be bound, and whatsoever thou shalt wish to loose shall be loosed,' but he did not say this nor did he wish to be understood in this way—namely, if any one shall wish to bind what he is not able to bind, shall that sin, therefore, be bound? Who said this? Therefore, he did not say, whatsoever thou shalt wish to bind, but whatsoever thou shalt bind, shall be bound in heaven. He verily is bound who is bound by the just debt of satisfaction in accordance with the nature of his confession. That person is really absolved by the sacerdotal office whose sin is justly remitted in view of a deserved satisfaction. God, therefore, binds and absolves those who by a priest's sentence justly deserve absolution,[1] but, beyond any doubt, the sins of those are retained to whom the absolution of sins has been justly denied and not those to whom it has been unjustly denied.

"What the Lord, therefore, said to Peter means the same as if he had said in other words: 'What has been bound or loosed by thee, shall be bound or loosed with me. He who is held with thee by the command of a required satisfaction is held with me as a debtor owing the same satisfaction. And because[2] he deserved from thee the just absolution for

---

[1] An important clause is here omitted from Richard's treatise.
[2] *Quia.* Richard has *qui.*

his sins he shall not at my bar be held bound any further.'
After this manner we should also understand that which
Christ said to all his apostles: 'Whosesoever sins ye remit,
they shall be remitted unto them, and whosesoever sins ye retain, they are retained.' Assuredly the sins of offenders will
be remitted or retained with the Lord which have been properly remitted or retained by his ministers, the priests—both of
which are truly and really done by them when done in accord
with the canonical rite; nevertheless, neither of these things
can priests do at their personal pleasure, but only for desert
—merito—and according to the rite as instituted." Thus
much Richard.

From Augustine and from this declaration by Richard,
it is plain that it does not follow: Christ said to Peter or
to any vicar of his: "Whatsoever thou shalt loose on earth,"
that is, in the church militant, "shall be loosed also in heaven,"
that is, in the church triumphant—therefore, whatsoever thou
shalt wish to loose on earth shall be loosed also in heaven.
And it is evident that by this clause the bestowment falls on
every person that is truly penitent. And also, in view of the
words, "Whatsoever thou shalt bind," the bestowment falls
upon the impenitent, for the loosing applies to every truly
penitent person, the binding to the impenitent. The same is
true of retaining and remitting.

Therefore, Christ's disciple ought to be on his guard
against the fallacy of antichrist, when the following course
of argument is pursued: Whatsoever Christ's vicar shall bind
upon earth shall be bound also in heaven, but this faithful
layman who does not wish to give money for his absolution,
him he binds on earth. Therefore, this layman is bound in
heaven. Likewise, whatsoever Christ's vicar shall loose on
earth shall be loosed also in heaven, but him who is not
contrite and yet is willing to give money, him he looses on
earth. Therefore, is he loosed also in heaven. The case is
similar if it be argued: Whatsoever Christ's vicar looses on

earth shall be loosed also in heaven, but him, who is evidently a reprobate, he looses on earth in the agony of death, therefore he is loosed also in heaven. In these arguments the minor premise is wanting in strength; for unless the said man, in the case of the minor premise, binds himself by a bad will or looses himself by true contrition, the minor premise is false. And, according to Richard, the argument is to be rectified in this way: "Whatsoever Christ's vicar shall properly bind on earth shall be bound also in heaven. But this faithful layman who does not wish to give money, him he binds properly on earth." Thus the falsehood of the minor premise is made to appear. In a similar way the other arguments are to be corrected. And, if the objection be raised that a Christian ought to be in doubt as to when a priest binds and looses according to the rite and when not, the reply is to be made that the opposite follows [we should not be in doubt], since we ought to believe that the priest binds and absolves only in cases when he ministers according to the rules of Christ's law. And when he exceeds that law, then he alleges that he is binding and loosing, but does not bind and loose.

Then as to Innocent's words: "The Lord made no exception when he said to Peter: 'Whatsoever,' etc." If Innocent understands a bestowment in any case whatsoever, when Peter or his vicar might allege they were binding, then Innocent's meaning would be false. For then, through a subordinate assumption, an improper conclusion would follow, the argument running thus: whatsoever Peter or his vicar shall bind on earth, shall be bound in heaven. But this holy man he alleges he is binding on earth: therefore he is bound in heaven. The conclusion is false and impossible. The minor proposition is true or may be true. Therefore the application of Innocent's major proposition would be false. But, if Innocent means with Richard, Augustine, and Gregory that the bestowment is for that for which binding and loosing are intended then it is true that when the Lord said, "whatsoever," he made no exception. For it means this: Whatsoever that is of true penitence thou shalt loose on earth shall be loosed in heaven. Likewise, whatsoever that is of impenitence thou shalt bind on earth shall be bound also in heaven. And with this the Little Glosses[1] of the Decretists agree, which say that, when the key does not make a mistake, and consequently when a righteous thing is done on earth, it shall be confirmed in heaven.

For every man who, being penitent, is according to the rite loosed on earth by Christ's vicar on the earth, he also is loosed in heaven—just as he who has believed and is baptized shall be saved, and he who has believed in love shall be saved finally. For "believe" here is to be accepted as in John 3 : 36, "He that believeth on the Son hath eternal life," and if it shall be argued that whosoever believeth on the Son hath eternal life: every Christian believes on the Son of God, therefore every Christian hath eternal life—or, again, if it be argued that whosoever believeth on the Son of God hath eternal life but that reprobate, who is in grace, believes on the Son of God, therefore that reprobate has eternal life—in these cases the conclusion is false. And both these conclusions are invalid, because "to believe" is one thing in the major premise and another thing in the minor. Hence, in order to correct the statement the argument must run in this way: Whosoever believes with love in the Son of God and perseveres. In this case the consequence is good [he shall be finally saved]. But the minor statement the objector should prove [namely, that every Christian believes with love of God]. Similar is the case with the second conclusion and its minor premise: namely, "that reprobate who is in grace believes with love in the Son of God and perseveres." This reasoning is false.

From the things already said, it is clear what the power

[1] See Introduction.

of the keys is and what is catholic belief on the subject,
namely, that every priest of Christ ordained according to
the rite has the sufficient power to confer the sacraments ap-
pertaining to him and consequently to absolve a person truly
contrite from sin, howbeit power of this kind, so far as the
exercise of it goes, is for good reasons bound in the case of
many persons, as appears near the beginning of this chapter.
But how this power belonged to the apostles equally is stated
in the *Decretum, Dist.* 21, *in novo* [Friedberg, 1 : 69], where
it is said:[1] "The other apostles with him, that is, Peter, by
reason of equal fellowship received honor and power. . . .
When these died, the bishops arose in their place." And
here the Gloss, *Argumentum,* says that the bishops are all
equal in apostolic power, so far as the order and ground of
consecration go. St. Cyprian, 24 : 1, *cap. Loquitur* [Fried-
berg, 1 : 971], says: "He gave to all the apostles after his
resurrection equal power."

Hence it would be foolish to believe that the apostles received from Christ no spiritual gifts except what were derived by them immediately and purely—*simpliciter*—from
Peter, for Christ said to all: "Whatsoever ye shall loose on
earth," Matt. 18 : 18; also, "Receive ye the Holy Spirit:
whosesoever sins ye remit they are remitted unto them," John
20 : 23; and again, "This do ye in remembrance of me,"
Luke 22 : 19; and still again, "All power is given unto me
in heaven and on earth. Go ye therefore and teach all
nations, baptizing them in the name of the Father, and the
Son, and the Holy Spirit, teaching them to observe all things
whatsoever I have commanded[2] you; and lo, I am with you
all the days, even unto the consummation of the ages,"
Matt. 28 : 19, 20.

[1] A letter of Pope Anacletus to the bishops of Italy asserting the gift of the
primacy to the Roman church.

[2] *Præcepi.* Vulgate: *Mandavi.*

CHAPTER XI

THE ABUSE OF SCRIPTURE IN THE INTEREST OF CLERICAL POWER

BECAUSE many priests abandon the imitation of Christ, the high priest, and boast of the power committed to the church, without doing works that correspond, therefore up to this time we have been speaking of the power of this kind. For they extract out of Matt. 18 : 16, "Whatsoever thou shalt bind on earth shall be bound in heaven," that whatsoever they do, every man ought altogether to approve. And from the words of Matt. 23 : 2, "The scribes and Pharisees sit on Moses' seat, therefore all things whatsoever they bid you, these do," they extract that every inferior is to obey them in all things. And so these priests clamorously apply to themselves at their own pleasure whatsoever appeals to them out of Christ's Gospel, and without any ministry of love on their part to correspond. But what plainly calls for toil and worldly self-abnegation and the imitation of Christ, that they spurn away as something inapplicable to themselves, or make believe they hold it when they do not.

Hence, because Jesus said to Peter, "I will give unto thee the keys of the kingdom of heaven and whatsoever thou shalt bind on earth, etc.," this they lay hold of with great complacency for the exaltation of their own power. But what the Lord said to Peter, John 21 : 17, "Follow me and feed my sheep," this they flee from as poison. Likewise, what he said to his disciples, Matt. 18 : 18, "What things soever ye shall bind on earth shall be bound in heaven," they gratefully seize upon and glory in. But what he says, Matt.

10 : 9, "Get you no gold nor silver," they shun as hurtful.
In the same way what he said to his disciples, John 20 : 23,
"Receive ye the Holy Ghost. Whosesoever sins ye remit
they are remitted unto them; and whosesoever sins ye retain they are retained," very placidly they accept.   But what
he says in Matt. 11 : 29, "Learn of me for I am meek and
lowly of heart," even the gentleness and meekness, which prepare a place for the Holy Spirit, they do not admit to their
hearts.

Also what the Lord said to his disciples, Luke 10 : 16,
"He that heareth you heareth me," they seize upon as meaning obedience to themselves, but what the Lord says in Matt.
20 : 25, "Ye know that the rulers of the Gentiles do lord it
over them and their great ones exercise authority over them.
Not so shall it be among you, but, whosoever would become
great among you, shall be your minister, and whosoever
would be first among you shall be your servant: even as the
Son of Man came not to be ministered unto but to minister,"
—this most weighty saying they repudiate in word and deed
—in word, saying that they ought to rule, and in deed because
they do not wish to minister to the church after the custom
of Jesus Christ the Lord.

And that I may gather up briefly all that the Scripture
says, and especially the Gospel: what seems to indicate to
them that they ought to be rich, live delicately, be famous
in the world, and suffer no reproach for Christ, these sayings
they ruminate over, proclaim aloud and make known all too
extensively.   But whatever calls for the imitation of Christ,
as poverty, gentleness, humility, endurance, chastity, toil or
patience—these passages they suppress or gloss over at their
pleasure or expressly set aside as not pertaining to salvation.   And the devil, who is the worst of sophists, leads
them astray by their ignorance of the logical consequences,
arguing in this way: "Christ gave such authority to Peter
and the rest of the apostles, therefore also to you."   And

from this they draw the inference that it is lawful for them
to do whatsoever they please, and so, by reasoning of the
same kind, they are most blessed fathers together with Christ
in pronouncing judgment in the church and because they are
to be crowned later with an everlasting crown. But blessed
be Christ, the omniscient, who said these things to his apostles, knowing that the authority which was given to them
they would use according to his good pleasure in ministering
to his bride.

So far, therefore, as the power—authority—is concerned
in which the clergy glories it is to be noted, that power is
sometimes taken to mean lordship or real power, as in Romans 13 : 1: "Let every soul be in subjection to the higher
powers." Sometimes it is taken in an ambiguous sense to
mean assumed or simulated power, as Christ said to his cap-
tors sent by the power of the high priests, Luke 22 : 53:
"This is your hour and the power of darkness." And it is
said, Rev. 6 : 8: "Lo, a pale horse: and he that sat upon
him, his name was Death: and hell followed him, and there
was given unto him power over the four parts of the earth
to kill with sword, famine, and death, and by the wild beasts
of the earth." Also it is said, Rev. 13 : 4, that the "dragon
gave his authority—power—unto the beast, and they worshipped the beast saying, Who is like unto the beast? who
is able to war with him? . . .   And it was given unto him
to make war with the saints and to overcome them, and there
was given to him authority over every tribe and people and
every tongue and nation; and all that dwell on the earth
shall worship him, every one whose name hath not been written in the book of life and of the Lamb,[1] that hath been
slain." Who is this beast whom men worship out of fear of
his power? He who reads let him understand and resist assumed power of this kind and let him not fear, as they did,
because it was given to that beast to make war against the

[1] The Vulgate has *libro vitæ Agni*, the *Lamb's Book of Life*.

saints and to overcome by the death of this body—the saints who, dying for the law of Christ, finally overcome that beast. For to these very ones the Saviour said, "Fear not them which kill the body," Matt. 10 : 28, and "In the world ye shall have tribulation, but be of good cheer, I have overcome the world," John 16 : 33. Here Augustine, in his Com. on John [*Nic. Fathers*, 7 : 393], says: "In whom do they have good cheer and overcome except in Him? For he would not have overcome the world if the world overcame his members. Hence the apostle says: 'Thanks be to God which giveth us the victory,' and adds, 'through our Lord Jesus Christ,' who said to his disciples, 'Be of good cheer for I have overcome the world.'" Thus much Augustine. But they overcome the power of the dragon and the beast who have the power of predestination which is the chief of powers and of which John speaks: "To them gave he the power to become the sons of God," John 1 : 12. And to this power is added perfecting power, and that is the power which God gives to the blessed in the heavenly country to fully enjoy the Lord and every creature in Him.

Therefore, the true worshippers of Christ, wishing to obtain that power, ought to resist every assumed power which seeks to remove them from the imitation of Christ by force or craft, for, in thus resisting such power we do not resist the ordinance of God but the abuse of power. And such abuse, in respect to the power of the keys, the simoniacs[1]

[1] Huss constantly attacked the simony of the clergy and regarded his legal troubles as a result of these assaults. He wrote a special tract on the subject in Czech entitled, *The Traffic in Holy Things*, which he closed by exalting Christ as the only way, truth and life. In his *de sex Erroribus*, *Mon.*, 1 : 240–243, he also gave the subject elaborate treatment, quoting at length from the canon law and declaring that prelates guilty of it are in mortal sin, and so their acts invalid. He speaks there of the sale of baptisms, confirmations, chrism, the marrriage blessing, the mass and sepulture. Laymen also were guilty of it who abet or wink at the practise in their priests. He returned to this vice in almost all his writings. He speaks of Prague clerics selling consecrated oil at a higher price than common oil and charging thirty groschen for thirty masses, and says that if priests would attempt to say all the masses they as-

exercise who allege that they can either damn the deserving or loose those who are bound, and they do this because the obedience they falsely demand is refused them or for the sake of the gain they derive. Of such priests the Lord said: "They polluted me among my people for a handful of barley and a piece of bread that they might slay souls, which do not die, and make alive souls, which do not live, lying to my people which believes lies," Ezek. 13 : 19. On this passage Gregory comments, 11 : 3, Plerisque[1] [Friedberg, 1 : 667], and says: "Rightly does the prophet say they put souls to death which do not die and make alive souls which do not live. For, indeed, he puts to death one who does not die when he condemns the righteous, and he attempts to make alive him who does not live[2] when he seeks to loose the guilty from the sentence of death." This abuse of power they exercise who sell and buy the sacred orders, episcopates, canonries, and parishes—plebanias. They secure and sell simoniacally who make spoil out of the sacraments, living in pleasure, avarice, and luxury or who, by any other kind of criminality, defile the power of the priesthood. For even if they declare that they know God, they, nevertheless, deny Him by their deeds, Titus 1 : 16. Consequently, they do not believe in God, and so, as unbelieving children, they have unbelieving thoughts about the seven sacraments of the church and also about the keys, the ministries, censures, the customs, ceremonies, and sacred things of the church and likewise the worship of relics, indulgences, and sacred orders.

This is clear because such despise God's name. Hence it is said in Mal. 1 : 6, 10: "Unto you, O priests, that despise my name. And ye say, Wherein have we despised thy name? Ye offer polluted bread upon my altar. . . . Oh, that there were one among you that would shut the doors and kindle

sumed to say, saying fifteen a day, they would not have gotten through in fifteen years. One of Gregory VII's reform movements was to do away with clerical simony. Dante put simoniacal popes in hell, including Boniface VIII.

[1] Mistake for plerumque.   [2] Vivum, a mistake for victurum.

fire upon my altar in vain! I have no pleasure in you, saith the Lord of hosts, neither will I accept an offering at your hand." Behold how the Lord speaks to the wicked priests because they despise His name and offer polluted bread. Hence Gregory, 1 : 1, *Multi sec.* [Friedberg, 1 : 388], follows up his statement about the sacraments and power by saying: "So we defile the bread, that is, Christ's body, when we approach unworthily the altar, and with filthy lips drink his pure blood." And the apostle says: "He who despised Moses' law, died without any mercy under two or three witnesses. Of how much sorer punishment, think ye, shall he be judged worthy who hath trodden under foot the Son of God and accounted the blood of the covenant wherewith he was sanctified an unholy thing?" Heb. 10 : 28, 29.

In the second place, such crucify the Son of God. For the apostle says: "Crucifying to themselves afresh the Son of God, they put him to an open shame," Heb. 6 : 6. Thirdly, such deal wickedly with the law of Christ, of whom St. Jerome *in Sophoniam Proph.*, 1 : 1 [Com. on Zephaniah, Friedberg, 1 : 391], says: "The priests who minister in the eucharist and distribute the Lord's flesh to his people, deal wickedly with Christ's law in thinking that the words of the one who curses make the eucharist and not his life, and that such a solemn address is all that is necessary and not the merits of priests." Of these he says: "A priest who is assoiled by any stain of sin should not approach the table to offer sacrifices to the Lord." Fourthly, the persons spoken of above blaspheme the Lord's majesty. Hence we read: "Who walk after the flesh in the lusts of defilement and despise damnation," II Peter 2 : 10. Further on Peter says: "But these as creatures without reason to be taken and destroyed, railing in matters whereof they are ignorant." On this point St. Augustine, on Psalm 147 [*Nic. Fathers*, 8 : 665], says: "If thou dost exceed the due measure of nature by gluttonous immoderation and satest thyself with wine-bibbing, so often as thy tongue sounds the praises of God, so often thy life blasphemes." How, then, shall the avaricious, simoniacs, the self-indulgent and those guilty of other crimes think in goodness of heart about the Lord or about his sacraments when they, like infidels, despise the Lord's name, defile his bread, crucify to themselves the Son of God and put him to an open shame, deal wickedly with God's law and despise government and blaspheme?

It is also clear that to this class belong the pestiferous clergy who, in an infidel way, think of the seven sacraments of the church and of the keys and of other things belonging to Christ's law. It is also clear that the dictum of the doctors—whose leader at that time was Stephen Palecz, supported by Stanislaus, who led after them Peter of Znaim, John Heliæ, Andrew Broda, John Hildissen, Matthew the Monk, Herman the Hermit, George Boras, and Simon Vuenda—laid down as a statement of the matter of disagreement, is to be verified by the conduct of the clergy who were living in sin.[1] For, in the beginning of their writing, they say: "The matter of this disagreement is manifest from the lives of some of the clergy who are pestiferous." Because Christ's

---

[1] The document referred to (*Doc.*, 475 *sqq.*) was signed by eight doctors of the theological faculty of the university of Prague against the XLV Articles of Wyclif and seven other articles alleged to give Huss's views, such as that the priest does no more than announce the forgiveness of sins in the sacrament of penance. It was an attack upon Huss for the hostile position he had assumed to the sale of indulgences ordered by John XXIII, 1411. The disturbances which followed in Prague led the king, Wenzel, to call the eight magisters and Huss before him at his summer residence of Zebrak. There, after a meeting in the parish house at which Palecz read a paper charging Huss with disobedience to the university authorities, they appeared before the king. Huss offered to submit himself to the ordeal of fire provided that the others did and that the party not proving its case from Scripture should undergo it. The proposition was not accepted, the meeting seems to have come to naught, and the disturbances in Prague went on, and the three men were murdered to whom reference is made in a succeeding chapter. Huss made an elaborate Reply to the Eight Doctors, *Mon.*, 1 : 366–408, in which he goes into the scriptural authority limiting the papal power of indulgence and the priestly power of remission of sins. The eight doctors included the names given above with the exception of Boras and Vuenda. See *ad Stanisl., Mon.*, 1: 331.

priests preach against the offenses of pestiferous clerics, therefore has this disagreement arisen, for the reason that the clergy in imparting to the people the plague of criminal living and refusing to tolerate the preaching of those who preach against their plague, which is at variance with the Gospel and who seek to cure their infection by the Word of the Lord, has conspired together and desires in malice to suppress preaching. But the purpose of the said doctors was to prove that those who evangelize against the wickedness of the pestiferous clergy were heretical on the subject of the keys, which, with the help of the Lord, during the term of their lives, they will not prove.

CHAPTER XII

CHRIST THE TRUE ROMAN PONTIFF UPON WHOM SALVATION DEPENDS

To the honor of our Lord Jesus Christ, which honor and also Christ the aforesaid doctors nowhere mention in their writing, this conclusion is proved, namely, "to be subject to the Roman pontiff is necessary for salvation for every human being." [1] From this it is clear, that no one can be saved unless he is meritoriously subject to Jesus Christ. But Christ is the Roman pontiff, just as he is the head of the universal church and every particular church. Therefore the conclusion is a true one. The consequence is clear from the major premise. And the minor premise is clear from the things said above and from what is said in I Peter 2 : 25, "For ye were sometime going astray like sheep but are now returned unto the shepherd and bishop of your souls," and also from Heb. 7 : 22: "By so much also hath Jesus become the surety of a better covenant and they indeed have been made free, many in number, according to the law because that by death they are hindered from continuing. But this man, because he continueth forever, hath his priesthood unchangeable, wherefore also he is able to save to the uttermost, drawing near through himself [2] to the Lord and always living to intercede for us. For such a high priest became us holy, guileless, undefiled, separated from sinners and made higher than the heavens, who needeth not daily like those

---

[1] From Boniface VIII's bull *Unam sanctam*. The expression in the next sentence, "meritoriously," refers to the mediæval doctrine of merit in proportion to our good works.

[2] *Accedens* refers the drawing near to Christ. The Vulgate has the plural, *accidentes*, those who draw near through Christ.

priests, to offer up sacrifices first for his own sins and then
for the sins of the people, for this he did once for all when
he offered himself."

Truly this is the most holy and chief Roman pontiff, sitting at God's right hand and dwelling with us, for he said:
"And lo, I am with you all the days, even unto the consummation of the age," Matt. 28 : 20. For that person, Christ,
is everywhere present, since he is very God whose right it is
to be everywhere without limitation. He is the bishop, who
baptizes and takes away the sins of the world, John 1 : 29.
He is the one who joins in marriage so that no man may put
asunder: "What God hath joined together let not man put
asunder," Matt. 19 : 6. He is the one who makes us priests:
"He made us a kingdom and priests," Rev. 1 : 6. He performs the sacrament of the eucharist, saying: "This is my
body," Luke 22 : 19. This is he who confirms his faithful
ones: "I will give you a mouth of wisdom which all your
adversaries will not be able to withstand or gainsay," Luke
21 : 15. He it is who feeds his sheep by his word and example and by the food of his body. All these things, however, he does on his part indefectibly, because he is a holy
priest, guileless, undefiled, separated from sinners and made
higher than the heavens. He is the bishop holding supreme
guardianship over his flock, because he sleeps not nor is he,
that watches over Israel, weary. He is the pontiff who in
advance makes the way easy for us to the heavenly country.
He is the pope—*papa*—because he is the wonderful Prince
of Peace, the Father of the future age. For, indeed, such a
pontiff became us who, since he was in the form of God, did
not think it robbery to be equal with God but emptied himself, taking upon him the form of a servant, because he humbled himself by being made obedient unto death, even the
death of the cross. Wherefore God hath highly exalted
him and given him a name which is above every name,
that at the name of Jesus every knee should bow, of things

in heaven, of things on the earth, and things in hell [Phil. 2 : 6 *sqq.*].

To this the conclusion follows, namely: "To be subject to the Roman pontiff is necessary for salvation for every human being." But there is no other such pontiff except the Lord Jesus Christ himself, our pontiff. This is so because the humanity of Christ is not subject to any other pontiff as of necessity to salvation, inasmuch as God hath exalted him and given him a name which is to be the most worthy above every other name, that at the name of Jesus every knee should bow and every power bend in obedience to him "of things in heaven," that is, the angels; "things on the earth," that is, all men; and "of things in hell," that is, the devils. And it is also so because Christ's mother was a human being; John the Baptist also, Peter the apostle, and other saints now in heaven, and for none of these was it necessary for salvation to be subject to any other Roman pontiff besides Christ, seeing that they are already saved, persons whom no Roman pontiff can loose or bind. Therefore, Pope Clement extended his authority all too far when in his bull The Angels of Paradise, he commanded the angels to lead into the everlasting joys the soul of one who had died on a journey to Rome to secure indulgence, and who had been absolved from purgatory. For this pope wished that at his command the heavenly angels should bow their knees. And he added, "We wish that the pain of hell be not inflicted upon that soul in any degree," and so he commanded that the power or the knees of the spirits in hell should also bow at his command. Not so did the apostles presume, for John wished not to command but to worship at the feet of angels, as he said, Rev. 22 : 8: "I, John, fell down to worship before the feet of the angel, and he said to me, see thou do it not, for I am a fellow servant with thee and with thy brethren the prophets and with them that keep the words of the prophecy of this book. Worship God." See how great is this apostle and prophet, beloved of God, who without doubt excelled modern popes and notably Clement, who gave command to the angels. He did not wish to give any command to an angel but, falling down, wished to worship before his feet, and the holy angel forbade him, showing him that he ought to worship God.

But in view of Heb. 7 : 23, "many indeed are made priests according to the law," it is to be noted that every high priest of the old law prefigured Christ in all his legal acts. Therefore he is called, uniquely, the High Priest and Bishop of our souls, and for this reason that multitude of priests and their offices are fulfilled in Christ alone, as the apostle says in Heb. 7 and 9. And this is the reason why the apostles did not call themselves most holy popes, heads of the universal church, or universal pontiffs; but, having with them the High Priest even unto the consummation of the age, they called themselves servants of Christ, his companions in tribulation and ministers of the church. Hence this holy custom was observed in the time of St. Gregory, *Decretum, Dist.* 92 [Friedberg, 1 : 318]; and in the preface of his letter [*Nic. Fathers,* 2d Ser., 12 : 241] Gregory says: "See how, so far as I am concerned, I forbade that thou shouldst use that word of proud entitlement. Thou wert concerned to confer upon me the title of universal pope which I beg thy most sweet holiness not to do any more, for in this way would be taken away from thee and shown to another more authority than reason allows. I do not seek to be advanced with words— [titles]—but by my good life—*moribus.* Nor do I regard that to be an honor wherein I would know that my brethren had lost their honor. For mine is also the honor of the universal church; my honor is the solid stability of my brethren. Then am I honored, when the honor due is not denied to any single one of them, for if thy holiness entitles me universal pope, it denies that thou art this, because thy holiness professes that I am the whole—*universum.* But far be that from us! Away with words which puff up vanity[1] and wound love!" From the words of this holy pope the deduction is to be drawn that he may be easily puffed up who is called most holy father, though he perhaps lives in sin and is struck through with flattery or through ignorance lies.

Therefore, Gregory most notably says: "I desire not to be advanced with words but by a good life." Alas! not thus do modern pontiffs think who, destitute of good lives— morals—glory in a bare title, imagining to themselves that the name, Holiness, befits them in virtue of their office or ecclesiastical dignity. But if this reasoning held, then Judas would have had to be called holy apostle. But blessed be the Lord, who, in order to remove this cloak, said to his disciples: "Have I not chosen you and one of you is a devil?" John 6 : 70. This he said before Iscariot had betrayed his master.

Hence holy men, when they have been praised by men, have humbled themselves and have burdened their minds with fear, lest praise should cast them down from a merit still more worthy. Therefore, Peter, Christ's apostle, when he was called by messengers went humbly to the Gentile, Cornelius, and when he was on the way, Cornelius went to meet him, instructed by an angel of Peter's holiness, and worshipped at Peter's feet. And Peter, taught of God about Cornelius and assured through revelation of his blessedness, did not permit Cornelius to lie at his feet as do modern pontiffs in whom not a scintilla of holiness is seen. Nay, often they are conscious of their sin in allowing themselves to be reverenced and, on that account, make the more ostentation, and if the ostentatious title—*titulus pompositalis*—be omitted, they at once shake with anger.

---

[1] *Vanitatem*, Huss's text has wrongly *unitatem*, unity. This famous letter (see Mirbt, p. 77, for the full text), addressed to Eulogius, patriarch of Alexandria, by Gregory the Great, 598, is a strong testimony, constantly appealed to, against the exorbitant claims of the papacy. Six hundred years later, one of Gregory's successors, Innocent III, added to the other papal titles that of Vicar of God.

Wishing to put an end to this pride, the African council,[1] *Dist.* 99 [Friedberg, 1 : 350], says: "Let not the bishop of the first see be called the prince of priests or high priest or anything of this kind, but only bishop of the first see. And the Roman pontiff is not to be called universal bishop." Proscribed are all these things which proceed from ostentations, pride, flattery, avarice, and from the blind deception of the unlearned. Returning, therefore, to our most lowly High Priest, Jesus Christ, who bade him that was called to the wedding take the lowest place [Luke 14 : 9], let us confess to him according to his precept that we are unprofitable servants, Luke 17 : 10. For he said: "When ye shall have done all those things which are commanded you, say, We are unprofitable servants." For, when we have kept all his precepts, and shall have humbled our souls before this High Priest—knowing that it is possible that our pontiffs may be thieves and robbers—this Bishop of our souls will not fail us in things necessary to salvation, but will pasture, guard, and feed his sheep as a truly good Shepherd.

[1] Third council of Carthage, 397, which fixed the catholic canon of the O. T. and the canon of the N. T. as then accepted by all Western Christendom.

CHAPTER XIII

THE POPE NOT THE HEAD OF THE CHURCH BUT CHRIST'S VICAR

FURTHER, the aforesaid doctors lay down in their writing that "the pope is head of the Roman church and the college of cardinals the body, and that they are very successors and princes of the apostle Peter and the college of Christ's other apostles in ecclesiastical office for the purpose of discerning and defining all catholic and church matters, correcting and purging all errors in respect to them and, in all these matters, to have the care of all the churches and of all the faithful of Christ. For in order to govern the church throughout the whole world it is fitting there should always continue to be such manifest and true successors in the office of Peter, the prince of the apostles, and of the college of the other apostles of Christ. And such successors cannot be found or procured on the earth other than the pope, the existing head, and the college of cardinals, the existing body, of the aforesaid Roman church."

These follies, long drawn out, which, I think, proceeded for the most part from the brain of Stanislaus, overcome and terrified by the Roman curia, involve many points. And in regard to these, I note that in their writing the church is taken to mean all Christian pilgrims. They seem to admit this when they say that " the body of the clergy in the kingdom of Bohemia, not only with the whole body of clergy in the world but also with the whole body of Christendom, always feels and believes as the faith dictates, just as the Roman church does." Or, secondly, these doctors call the pope, together with his cardinals, alone the Roman church, when they say that they believe just as the Roman church believes and not otherwise, the pope being the head of this Roman church and the cardinals the body. In these ways only, so far as I can see, do the doctors designate the church in their writing.

I assume that the pope stands for that spiritual bishop who, in the highest way and in the most similar way, occupies the place of Christ, just as Peter did after the ascension. But if any person whatsoever is to be called pope—whom the Western church accepts as Roman bishop—appointed to decide as the final court ecclesiastical cases and to teach the faithful whatever he wishes, then there is an abuse of the term, because according to this view, it would be necessary in cases to concede that the most unlettered layman or a female, or a heretic and antichrist, may be pope. This is plain, for Constantine II, an unlettered layman, was suddenly ordained a priest and through ambition made pope and then was deposed and all the things which he ordained were declared invalid, about A. D. 707.[1] And the same is plain from the case of Gregory, who was unlettered and consecrated another in addition to himself. And as the people were displeased with the act, a third pope was superinduced. Then these quarrelling among themselves, the emperor came to Rome and elected another as sole pope.[2] As for a female,

[1] Constantine II, 767–768—not 707—was elected through the influence of his brother Toto, duke of Nepi. He was rushed through the various grades of ordination and then forced out of the papal chair by a military insurrection, thrown into prison, and blinded. Huss often cites his case. *Mon.*, 1 : 342, etc.

[2] Huss seems to refer to Gregory VI, 1045–1046 (see also Reply to Stanislaus, *Mon.*, 1 : 342), although a part of his statement cannot be verified. Gregory bought the papacy from the flagitious Benedict IX for one thousand or, according to another account, two thousand pounds silver. There were then three popes, Benedict IX, Sylvester III, and Gregory, all three elected by the Roman people. At the synod of Sutri, 1046, two of these popes were deposed and Gregory abdicated and, at the instance of the Emperor Henry III, the bishop of Bamberg was elected and took the name Clement II. Gregory was taken to Germany as a prisoner and died about 1048.

it is plain in the case of Agnes, who was called John Anglicus,[1] and of her Castrensis, 5·: 3,[2] writes: "A certain woman
sat in the papal chair two years and five months, following
Leo. She is said to have been a girl, called Agnes, of the
nation of Mainz, was led about by her paramour in a man's
dress in Athens and named John Anglicus. She made such
progress in different studies that, coming to Rome, she read
the trivium to an audience of great teachers. Finally, elected
pope, she was with child by her paramour, and, as she was
proceeding from St. Peter's to the Lateran, she had the pains
of labor in a narrow street between the Colosseum and St.
Clement's and gave birth to a child. Shortly afterward she
died there and was buried. For this reason it is said that
all the popes avoid this street. Therefore, she is not put
down in the catalogue of popes."

As for a heretic occupying the papal chair we have an instance in Liberius, of whom Castrensis writes, IV [Rolls Ser.,
5 : 158], that at Constantius's command he was exiled for

---

[1] This story of the female Pope Agnes (John VIII, about 855), to which Huss
refers again and again in his writings (*Doc.*, 59, 61; *Mon.*, 1 : 323, 324, 326, 336,
339, 343, 345, 347) as a proof that the papacy is not necessary to the being of the
church, was fully believed in his time. Gerson used it to prove that the church
may err in matters of fact, and a bust of Agnes was included among the busts
of the other popes in the cathedral of Siena in the beginning of the fifteenth
century. Dietrich of Nieheim names the very school in which she taught.
So far as the story can be traced, it was first told by Martin von Troppau—
Martinus Polonus—d. 1278, in his *Chronicles*. It is now discredited, and the
invention regarded as a satire upon the rule of meretricious women over worthless and wicked popes in the ninth and tenth centuries. See Mirbt, p. 97;
Döllinger: *Fables of the Middle Ages.*

[2] Castrensis or Cestrensis, a derivative of Chester—*castra*, the name by
which Ranulph Higden was often quoted, the author of the *Polychronicon or
Universal History*, in seven books, ed. by Babington and Lumby in Rolls Series,
1865 *sqq.*, 9 vols. The ed. gives the Latin text and also two Engl. translations,
one by Trevisa and the other by an unknown writer of the fifteenth century.
Nothing is known of the author except that he was a Benedictine monk of St.
Werburgh, Chester. He wrote probably after the middle of the fourteenth century. The historical part begins with Abraham and continues to the reign of
Edward III, 1312–1377. The work was widely circulated and the author gives
a list of the writers upon whom he has drawn. The quotation in regard to
Joan, vol. VI, 330, Cestrensis draws from Martinus Polonus.

three years because he wished [1] to favor the Arians. At
the counsel of the same Constantius, the Roman clergy ordained Felix pope who, during the sessions of a synod condemned and cast out two Arian presbyters, Ursacius and
Valens, and when this became known, Liberius was recalled
from exile, and being wearied by his long exile and exhilarated
by the reoccupation of the papal chair, he yielded to heretical depravity; and when Felix was cast down, Liberius
with violence held the church of Peter and Paul and St.
Lawrence so that the clergy and priests who favored Felix
were murdered in the church, and Felix was martyred, Liberius not preventing.

As for antichrist occupying the papal chair, it is evident that a pope living contrary to Christ, like any other
perverted person, is called by common consent antichrist.
In accordance with John 2 : 22, many are become antichrists. And the faithful will not dare to deny persistently
that it is possible for the man of sin to sit in the holy place.
Of him the Saviour prophesied when he said: "When ye see
the abomination of desolation, which is spoken of by Daniel,

[1] *Voluit*, that is, Constantius wished. The original has *noluit* "he would
not," referring to Liberius's refusal to consent to heresy. Cestrensis inter-
jects the statement, which Huss omits, that "Constantius recalled Liberius
from exile as one who treated the Arians more mildly." The implication is
that during his exile in Thrace Liberius yielded to heretical views, or perhaps
on his way back to Rome, where he remained very popular and whither he
was recalled by the emperor. The statement of the text represents the
view which prevailed during the Middle Ages. Felix's martyrdom was ascribed to his being cast into a hole where he died after languishing for seven
months. The history of Liberius and Felix is a matter of historical uncertainty.
Döllinger, *Fables of the Middle Ages*, Engl. translation, 183–209, pronounced
the mediæval view an invention of the sixth or seventh century, and rejected
the charge of heresy made against Liberius as well as the story of Felix's martyrdom. Liberius was pope 352–366 with an interim of three years. Felix
died a natural death, 365. It is difficult to exempt Liberius altogether from the
taint of heresy in spite of Sozomen's spirited denial of it. Athanasius implies
that he was a heretic and Jerome distinctly called him one. In a document,
whose genuineness is questioned, Hilary anathematized the unfortunate pontiff. Felix's name was included in the Breviary from which it has been ex-
punged and his bust was given a place in the Siena cathedral among other
popes.

standing in the holy place," Matt. 24 : 15. The apostle also says: "Let no man beguile you in any wise, for it will not be except the falling away come first and the man of sin be revealed, the son of perdition; he that opposeth and exalteth himself against all that is called God or is worshipped; so that he sitteth in the temple of God setting himself forth as God," II Thess. 2 : 3–4. And it is apparent from the *Chronicles* how the papal dignity has sunk.

For the emperor Constantine, about A. D. 301, thought and commanded that the highest bishop should be called by all pope and in his dotation that name also sprang up. The emperor Phocas likewise, about the year 600, at the instance of the clergy confirmed this same thing, as may be read in his *Annals*. Therefore, Castrensis, 4 : 14, describes how the excellency of the Roman empire helped the papacy of the Roman pontiff above others. He says: "The Nicene council conferred this prerogative on the Roman pontiff, that, just as Augustus had rank above other kings, so the Roman pontiff should be held as bishop, and the pope be called chief father—*principalis pater.*"[1] The origin, however, of this name and this excellency is to be found in the dotation of the church, as is indicated in the *Decretum*, 96, *Dist. Constant.*[2]

---

[1] Rolls Series, 5 : 140, Castrensis prefaces the words quoted by Huss with the statement that "in the early church there were only three patriarchs, corresponding to Abraham, Isaac, and Jacob, namely Antioch, Alexandria, and Rome. Peter constructed these three seats by his occupancy—sua sessione. Over two of them he himself was president and his disciple, Mark, occupied the third, Alexandria." Of course the Nicene council, 325, did no such thing but in its sixth canon makes the three bishops of Alexandria, Rome, and Antioch, each supreme in his own diocese. See Schaff, *Ch. Hist.*, III, 275.

[2] Constantine's donation was the reputed gift to Pope Sylvester of dominion over the city of Rome, Italy, and all the provinces, cities, and territories of the West. The gift, it was alleged, was made out of gratitude to Sylvester for having healed the emperor of leprosy and baptized him. In view of Sylvester's healing power, Constantine was assured of the divine power given to Peter and his successors. In addition, the emperor also acknowledged the Roman bishop as universal pope and his supremacy over Antioch, Alexandria, Jerusalem and Constantinople, called him the vicar of the Son of God, and as Huss notes, *Mon.*, 1 : 337, gave him the Lateran palace. This colossal fraud of the middle of the eighth century was a part of the Pseudo-Isidorian decretals, and

These things being noted, in order to remove ambiguity, I assume that the doctors in their writing designate by the Roman church that church of which the Saviour said to Peter: "On this rock I will build my church" (see Chapter VII). The holy writers and the Decretals speak of it as the Roman church, *Dist.* 21 : 3 [Friedberg, 1 : 70], 24 : 1, *capp.* 9, 14 [Friedberg, 1 : 969, 970]. And in the Clementines, *de Jurejurando* [Friedberg, 2 : 1147],[1] it is said: "The Romans, princes, professors of the orthodox faith, venerate with warm faith and pure devotion the holy Roman church, whose head is Christ, our Saviour, and the Roman pontiff, the Saviour's vicar."[2] And in the *Sextus* it is said: "Our alma mater, the church" [Friedberg, 2 : 1106], and in the *Extravagante* of Boniface VIII, "The holy Roman church." And the same is true of the other statements made in other places and alleged above.

In regard to these follies of the Unlearned—*indoctorum*—I find these points: (1) The pope is the head of the holy Roman church. (2) The college of cardinals is the body of the holy Roman church. (3) The pope is manifestly and truly

was more influential than anything else in building up the arrogant claims of the papacy. Dante denied the right of Constantine to grant secular power to the pope, but did not call in question the authenticity of Constantine's gift. He expressed himself in the lines:

> Ah, Constantine, of how much ill was cause
> Not thy conversion, but those rich domains
> Which the first wealthy pope received of thee.

The fraud was not shown up till the middle of the fifteenth century by Laurentius Valla, and a profound impression was made upon Luther in 1520 when he was informed of the fraudulent character of the document by von Hutten. Of course, Constantine was baptized by Eusebius of Nicomedia, and not till the very last year of his life and never had the leprosy. Huss fully believed the story and often refers to the donation as the beginning of papal wealth, pomp, and corruption. The text in Mirbt, pp. 81–87. Also Boehmer's art. in Herzog, XI, 1–7.

[1] The first of these decretals is by Gelasius, 495, and states that the "holy Roman catholic and apostolic church is placed at the head of the other churches not by virtue of the action of synods but by the appointment of Christ." The second is by Lucius, the third by Jerome writing to Pope Damasus.

[2] Clement V, 1314, the first of the Avignon popes. He declares that the "Roman church transferred the empire from the Greeks to the Germans."

the successor of the prince of the apostles, Peter. (4) Cardinals are manifest and true successors of the college of Christ's other apostles. (5) For the government of the church throughout the whole world, there should always be manifest and true successors of the same kind in the office of the prince of the apostles and in the office of Christ's other apostles. (6) Such successors are not to be found or procured on the earth, other than the pope, the existing head and the college of cardinals, the existing body of the church.

Against all these six points, the argument in brief runs thus: all truth in the religion of Christ is to be followed and only that is truth which is known by the bodily senses, or discovered by an infallible intelligence, or made known through revelation, or laid down in sacred Scripture. But none of these six points is truth known by the bodily senses or discovered by an infallible intelligence or known through revelation, or laid down in divine Scripture. Therefore, no one of these six points is truth in the religion of Jesus Christ which is to be followed. The major premise is seen in what St. Augustine says, *Enchiridion*, 4 [*Nic. Fathers*, 3 : 238]: "These things chiefly, yea almost exclusively, are to be followed in religion, and he who contradicts them is altogether a stranger to the name of Christ or he is a heretic. . . . These things are to be defended by the reason whether they start from the bodily senses or are discovered by the intelligence of the mind. But these things, which we have not been aware of through the bodily senses or been able to reach with the mind, nor now are able—these are beyond doubt to be believed on the testimony of those witnesses by whom the Scriptures, deservedly called divine, were written, because, assisted with divine help, they were able to see these things or to foresee them either through the bodily senses or through the mind." Thus much St. Augustine.

The minor premise, however, the doctors are unable to disprove unless one of these six points should be revealed to them by divine revelation. For neither by the bodily senses, nor by the reason, nor from sacred Scripture do these points appear. Yea, the doctors in making these points authoritative, so that they must be believed, are seen to be anathema by the authority of Augustine himself which they adduce in their writing. If any one venerate any other scriptures than those which the catholic church has received or has handed down to be held as authoritative, let him be anathema. This is clear because these doctors have offered their own writings as authoritative and to be believed and the catholic church has not received them for they are found neither in the divine law nor in the code of canons. Therefore, it follows that these doctors are themselves anathema, and it is clear that religious faith is not held by them so far as these points are concerned unless they prove them plainly or show them to be founded in sacred Scripture or in clear reasoning, for Augustine says, *Ep. ad Hieron.*, *Decretum*, *Dist.* 9 : 5 [Friedberg, 1 : 17]: "I have learned to give only to those writers, who are now called canonical, honor and regard, so that I would not dare to believe that any of them erred in writing. But other writers I will read [1] as far as they seem to excel by sanctity or true doctrine but I will not regard as true what they say because they have felt it to be true, but because they have been able to convince me by other writers, or by canonical or probable reasons, that they do not differ from the truth."

Inasmuch as these doctors are not writers of sacred Scripture—it being granted that they excel by their sanctity—the faithful are not, therefore, to think a thing is true because they feel it to be true unless by other writers of Scripture or for canonical or probable reasons they prove that these points do not deviate from the truth. Then, similarly, as to the point that the pope is always and uniformly to be regarded as the head of the Roman church, and that the

---

[1] *Legam.* The original has *lego*.

church is the bride of Christ built upon Christ "against which the gates of hell cannot prevail," we must argue thus: No pope is the most exalted person of the catholic church but Christ himself; therefore no pope is the head of the catholic church besides Christ. The conclusion is valid reasoning from description to the thing described. Inasmuch as the head of the church is the capital or chief person of the church, yea, inasmuch as the head is a name of dignity and of office—dignity in view of predestination, and office in view of the administration of the whole church—it follows that no one may reasonably assert of himself or of another without revelation that he is the head of a particular holy church, although if he live well he ought to hope that he is a member of the holy catholic church, the bride of Christ. Therefore, we should not contend in regard to the reality of the incumbency whether any one, whoever he may be, living with us is the head of a particular holy church but, on the ground of his works, we ought assume that, if he is a superior, ruling over a particular holy church, then he is the superior in that particular church, and this ought to be assumed of the Roman pontiff, unless his works gainsay it, for the Saviour said: "Beware of false prophets which come unto you in sheep's clothing but inwardly they are ravening wolves. By their fruits ye shall know them," Matt. 7 : 15. Also John 10 : 38: "Believe the works."

Likewise, it is not necessary to believe that every Roman pontiff whatsoever is the head of any particular holy church unless God has predestinated him. This is clear because otherwise the Christian faith would be perverted and a Christian would have to believe a lie. For the church was deceived in the case of Agnes, and for the sake of His own, and without doubt for the better, God permits that he who is chosen pope should not forthwith and without reverent hesitancy be regarded as holy or such as he assumes himself to be. Hence I could wish that the doctors would openly teach the people whether for the whole clergy that lived at that time and held Agnes to be a true pope, Agnes was really the head of the church; or, if the church was at that time without a head—*acephalous*[1]—with only a nominal pope in the church militant for two years and five months, the faithful for that reason ought not to think that it is not of the substance of the catholic faith to believe expressly [beyond a doubt] that Liberius, Joanna, Boniface, Clement, or Urban were predestinate or members of holy mother church—in view of the judgment given above.

In the same way, it is not of necessity to salvation for all Christians, living together, that they should believe expressly that any one is head of any church whatsoever unless his evangelical life and works plainly moved them to believe this. For it would be all too much presumption to affirm that we are heads of any particular church which perhaps might be a part of holy mother church. How, therefore, may any one of us without revelation presume to assert of himself or of another that he is the head, since it is said truly, Ecclesiasticus 9, that "no one knows, so far as predestination goes, whether one is worthy of love or hatred."

Likewise, if we examine in the light of the feeling and influence with which we influence inferiors and, on the other hand, examine by the mirror of Scripture, according to which we should regulate our whole life, then we would choose rather to be called servants and ministers of the church than its heads. For it is certain that if we do not fulfil the office of a head, we are not heads, as Augustine, *de decem chordis* [Migne's ed., 38 : 75–91], says: that a perverse husband is not the head of his wife, much less is a prelate of the church, who alone from God could have a dignity of this kind, the head of a particular church in case he fall away from Christ.[2]

---

[1] Huss uses the same Greek word a number of times as in his Replies to Palecz and Stanislaus, *Mon.*, 1 : 320, 347.

[2] Not an exact quotation. The inference is drawn by Huss. The Sermon on the Ten Strings, Psalms 144 : 9, has much to say on the relation of husband and wife on the basis of "Thou shalt not commit adultery."

Therefore, after Augustine has shown that a truly Christian wife ought to mourn over the fornication of her husband, not for carnal reasons, but out of love and for the chastity due to the man Christ—he says consequentially that Christ speaks in the hearts of good women, where the husband does not hear, and he goes on to say: "Mourn over the injuries done by thy husband, but do not imitate them that he may rather imitate you in that which is good. For in that wherein he does wrong, do not regard him as thy head but me, thy Lord." And he proves that this ought to be the case and says: "If he is the head in that wherein he does wrong and the body follow its head, they both go over the precipice. But that the Christian may not follow this bad head, let him keep himself to the head of the church, Christ, to whom he owes his chastity, to whom he yields his honor, no longer a single man but now a man wedded to his mother, the church." Blessed, therefore, be the head of the church, Christ, who cannot be separated from his bride which is his mystical body, as the popes have often been separated from the church by heresy.

But some of the aforesaid doctors say that the pope is the bodily head of the church militant and this head ought always to be here with the church, but in this sense Christ is not the bodily head. Here is meant that the same difficulty remains, namely, that they prove the first part of the statement. For it remains for them to prove that the pope is the head of holy church, a thing they have not proved. And, before that, it remains for them to prove that Christ is not the bodily head of the church militant, inasmuch as Christ is a bodily person, because the man who is the head of the church militant, who is Christ, is present through all time with his church unto the consummation of the age, in virtue of his divine personality. Similarly, he is present by grace, giving his body to the church to be eaten in a sacramental and spiritual way. Wherefore, is not that bridegroom, who is the head of the church, much more present with us than the pope, who is removed from us two thousand miles and incapable of influencing of himself our feeling or movements? Let it suffice, therefore, to say, that the pope may be the vicar of Christ and may be so to his profit, if he is a faithful minister predestinated unto the glory of the head, Jesus Christ.[1]

[1] The same thought is expressed in Reply to Palecz, *Mon.*, 1 : 321: "God gave Christ to be the head over the militant church, that he might preside over it most excellently without any hindrance of local distance . . . and pour into it, as the head pours into the body, movement, feeling and a gracious life whether there be no pope or a woman be pope."

CHAPTER XIV

WHEN THE CARDINALS ARE THE TRUE SUCCESSORS OF THE APOSTLES

THE second point is this: the college of cardinals is the body of the holy Roman church. This being so, then the college of the cardinals is the holy Roman church. The conclusion follows from Eph. 1 : 22: "He gave him to be head over the whole church, which is his body." And as the church, which is Christ's mystical body, cannot be damned, as when Christ said, "on this rock I will build my church and the gates of hell shall not prevail against it"—it follows, that the college of cardinals cannot be damned; and since this conclusion is false or, at least, for the doctors doubtful, it follows that in this particular point they have laid down as truth what is doctrinally false or doubtful. What is the fruit of teaching the worshippers of Christ in this way?

Likewise, the college of cardinals is either the true body of the holy Roman church or the pretended body. Not the second, according to the doctors. Therefore they must be the true body, and consequently that college is predestinated unto glory, and, as the doctors have not the revelation of predestination with reference to that college, it follows, that they ought not to have affirmed that the college is the body of the Roman church.

Again, the body of the holy Roman church is made up of all the predestinate, and the college by itself does not include all these. The first part of this statement appears from the words of the apostle, who spoke as the representative of the predestinate: "We being many are one body in Christ," Romans 12 : 5. And, showing the unity of the body, he does not make the college of the apostles the body of the church, I Cor. 12 : 28, but he says: "God hath set some in the church, first apostles, second prophets, thirdly teachers, then miracles, then gifts of healings," etc. And making a comparison of the body of the church with a man's natural body, he says, "For as there is one body and it has many members but all the members of the body being many are one body: so also is Christ," namely, he is one, because he is one person with his holy church, which is his body.

The second part of this statement, that all the predestinate are not that college, is evident of itself. Therefore, better would the doctors have said that Christ is the head of the holy Roman church, and each of the predestinate a member and that all together are the body, which is the church, than to have said that the pope is the head of the Roman church and the college of cardinals the body, for in this case they would have agreed with the apostles and with the saints quoted in Chapter I, especially with St. Augustine, *de doct. christ.* III [*Nic. Fathers*, 2 : 569], who says: "For, in truth, that is not the Lord's body which will not remain with him through eternity." [1] If, therefore, the college of cardinals will not remain through eternity, a thing which is hidden from me, how is it the body of the holy Roman church or of Christ? In a similar way, how is the pope with the aforesaid college the holy Roman church against which the gates of hell cannot prevail?

Therefore, we will speak more safely with St. Augustine who, *Commentary on Psalms*, 80 : 1 [*Nic. Fathers*, 7 : 386], says: "Finally by this testimony, the confession is made both of Christ and the vine that is the head and the body, king and people, shepherd and flock, and the whole mystery

---

[1] Augustine here, in reply to Tychonius, the Donatist, denies that the "body of the Lord" can be properly said to be "twofold." The full quotation is: "Twofold is not 'a suitable word, for that is really no part of the body of Christ which will not be with him in eternity.'" Hypocrites may be said to belong to the mixed church, but not to be of "the body of Christ."

of all Christians, Christ and the church." See, how the doctor of holy church shows us another holy church with its head than the one defined of the [eight] doctors who, without support of Scripture, say that the body of the holy Roman church is the college of cardinals, for which college it were well if its parts were members of the holy church of Jesus Christ. And we ought to think how St. Augustine himself feared to call Christ Lord-man, for the reason that this sense does not appear in Scripture; therefore much more ought we to fear to call any Christian head of the holy church militant, lest Christ perhaps be blasphemed, to whom this name is reserved by the Nicene council, *Trinitatis concilio*, as proper to him. How, then, do the doctors, without any Scripture proof, teach that the pope is head of holy church and the college its body? Since it is enough for the faithful Christian with inwrought faith and perseverance to believe the article of faith concerning the catholic church that it is the one totality of all the predestinate faithful who are to be saved by virtue of the merit of Christ—who is the head of the catholic church—it is not permissible for us expressly to descend to any particular vicar whom the Christian might recognize as the chief—*capitalis*. For many have been saved in Judea, Asia and Ethiopia who have believed in Christ, following the teaching of the apostles, and who did not expressly recognize Peter, nay, or expressly believe what concerns Peter, just as they did not hear anything about him.

The third point is this: the pope is the manifest and true successor of the prince of the apostles, and about this I have treated in Chapter VII near the close. It is, however, to be said again that the doctors do not prove this point. And, as the vicar ought to occupy the place of his superior from whom he has received vicarial power, therefore, occupying his place, he ought more directly to be conformed to him in his works or otherwise the power would be frustrated in him. From this, then, the argument is constructed: a man is the vicar of the person whose place he fills and from whom, in a legitimate way, he receives procuratorial power [delegated as with the Roman procurators]. But no one truly occupies the place of Christ, or Peter, unless he follows him in his life, for no other kind of following is more fitting; nor does any one otherwise receive procuratorial power. The requirements, therefore, of the vicarial office are conformity of life and authority from him who appoints. If, therefore, the pope is a most humble man, depending little upon mundane honors and the gain of this world, if he is a shepherd deriving his name from the pasturage of God's Word, of which pasturage the Lord said to Peter, "Pasture my sheep," John 21 : 17, if he pasture the sheep by the Word and the example of his virtues being made ensample of the flock with his whole heart, as Peter says, I Peter 5 : 3, if he is meek, patient, chaste, laboring anxiously and solicitously in the service of the church, esteeming all temporal things as dung—then, without doubt, is he the true vicar of Jesus Christ, manifest to God and men, so far as the judgment of the outward senses can determine. But, if he lives at discord with these virtues—for there is "no communion[1] between Christ and Belial," II Cor. 6 : 15, and, as Christ himself said, "He that is not with me is against," Matt. 12 : 30—how can he be the true and manifest vicar of Christ or of Peter and not rather the vicar of antichrist, seeing he resists Christ in morals and in life?

Therefore, when Peter was opposed to Christ in will and words and after Christ had promised him the keys, Christ called Peter Satan, that is, "adversary," and said: "Get thee behind me, Satan, thou art an offence to me, because thou savorest not the things that be of God but the things that be of men." If, therefore, Peter, chosen to be Christ's first vicar by Christ and deputed to serve the church in

[1] *Communicatio*. The Vulgate: *conventio*.

spiritual matters, was called by Christ Satan, Peter out of affectionate love having tried to dissuade him from submitting to the sentence of death, why should not another one, more opposed to Christ in his life, not be called Satan and consequently antichrist or antichrist's vicar or antichrist's chief minister? Hence, St. Bernard, *Com. on Canticles*, says: "Evil has gone out from thy elder judges, who seem to be ruling the poeple. Alas! alas! O Lord God, for they were the first to persecute thee who seemed to hold primacy in thy church and to rule the spiritual princedom. Likewise all friends are all foes, all clients are all adversaries, all servants are no peaceful men, all who seek the things which are their own, they are ministers of Christ and yet the servants of antichrist." See how plainly that holy man brings out that bad prelates are in pretence friends, servants, and ministers of Christ. But in fact they are the foes of Christ and the servants of antichrist.

Likewise, Augustine, Com. on John, also *Decretum*, 8 : 1 [*Nic. Fathers*, 7 : 446; Friedberg, 1 : 596], pointing out who are not true shepherds, but mercenaries, says: "There are some superiors in the church about whom the apostle Paul says: 'they seek their own things and not the things of Christ.' What is it, therefore, 'to seek one's own things'? Not to love Christ freely, not to seek God for His own sake,[1] to follow after temporal comforts, to heap up riches, to hanker after honors from men. When these are loved by the superior, and when God is served for such things, whoever he may be that serves, he is a mercenary and he does not count himself among the children." For about such the Lord also says: 'Verily, verily, I say unto you, they received their reward.' Hence the same Augustine says: "That just as Peter, the apostle, was the type of all good men and especially good bishops, so Judas represented all bad men, especially bad priests."

---

[1] *Propter se ipsum;* the original, *propter Deum.*

Therefore, commenting on John 12 : 8 [*Nic. Fathers*, 7 : 283], "The poor ye have always with you, but me ye have not always," he says: "What does he wish for himself? How is this to be understood,—'me ye have not always'? Do not fear. The words were spoken to Judas. Why, therefore, did Christ not say, 'thou hast,' but 'ye have'? Because there is not one Judas or one wicked person, but Judas represents the body of the wicked, just as Peter represents the body of the good." Further on he says: "In Peter's person the good in the church are represented; in Judas's person the evil in the church are represented. To them it was said: 'But me ye have not always.' What is this 'not always,' and what is this 'always'? If thou art good, if thou belongest to the body which Peter represents, then thou hast Christ both now and in the future—now, by faith; now, figuratively; now, by the sacrament of baptism; now, by the food and drink of the altar. Thou hast Christ now, and thou hast him always, because when thou goest hence thou wilt go to him who said to the thief: 'To-day thou shalt be with me in paradise.' But if thou livest wickedly, thou seemest now to have Christ because thou enterest into the church, signest thyself with the sign of Christ, art baptized with the baptism of Christ, dost mingle with the members of Christ—now thou hast Christ, but on account of wicked living thou wilt not always have him." Thus much Augustine, who shows that Peter's true vicars are the righteous and Judas Iscariot's vicars are the wicked, and especially wicked priests, hypocrites and blasphemers. And he shows the same when he comments upon Psalm 109: "Deus laudem meam ne tacueris." And Ambrose, 22 : 20 [Friedberg, 1 : 888], says: "Beware, my brethren, against lies.[1] . . . For it is a lie to say one is a Christian and not to do the works of Christ. It is a lie to profess oneself to be a

---

[1] Ambrose continues: "For all who love a lie are children of the devil. For a lie is found not only in false words but also in hypocritical works."

bishop, a priest, or a cleric, and to act at variance with this
order." Again, 2 : 1 [Friedberg, 1 : 438]. All prelates are
not to be esteemed as prelates. Not the name makes the
bishop, but the life. And, *Dist. IV sub rubrica*, under "He
is not truly a priest who is called a priest," Chrysostom also
says [*Dist.* 40 : 12; Friedberg, 1 : 147]: "There are many
priests and few priests."

From these and other sayings it is evident that no pope
is the manifest and true successor of Peter, the prince of the
apostles, if in morals he lives at variance with the principles
of Peter; and, if he is avaricious, then is he the vicar of Judas,
who loved the reward of iniquity and sold Jesus Christ. And
by the same kind of proof the cardinals are not the manifest
and true successors of the college of Christ's other apostles
unless the cardinals live after the manner of the apostles
and keep the commands and counsels of our Lord Jesus Christ.
For, if they climb up by another way than by the door of
our Lord Jesus Christ, then are they thieves and robbers,
just as the Saviour himself declared when of all such he said:
"All that came before me are thieves and robbers," John
10 : 8. Whosoever, therefore, say that they are Christ's true
and manifest vicars, knowing that they are living in sin, lie.
Therefore the apostle says: How "do they of the synagogue
of Satan say that they are Jews, and they are not, but lie"?
[Rev. 2 : 9.]

Hence, if the cardinals heap up to themselves ecclesiastical livings and barter with them and take money for their
sale either themselves or through others, and so devour and
consume in luxurious living the goods of the poor, and if
they do not do miracles or preach the Word of God to the
people or pray sincerely or fill the place of deacons—whom
the apostles appointed, Acts 6—by not performing their duties or living their lives—in how far, I ask, are they the vicars
of the apostles? In this that they heap up livings or, like
Gehazi, seize upon gifts, or because very early in the morn-

ing they come into the pope's presence clad in the most splendid apparel, and attended with the most sumptuous retinue of horsemen—thus attended, not on account of the distance of place or difficulty of the journey but to show their magnificence to the world and their contrariety to Christ and his apostles, who went about among the towns, cities, and castles clad in humble garb, on foot, preaching—*evangelizando*—the kingdom of God.[1]

Nor in this are they the true and manifest vicars of Christ that they permit themselves to be adored of men on bended knee or that they surround the pope with visitors from abroad, that while he sits on high, splendidly apparelled even down to his feet, yea and far beyond his chair, they with bended knee humbly seek the kisses of his blessed feet, as if the sanctity of this father, the pope, would descend even to the place where his foot is planted? But do they, themselves weak, receive from those feet health? For Christ suffered his feet to be kissed by a woman, but did not protrude them, as appears in Luke 7, because sincere contrition and the care and washing of Christ's feet, that is, of the poor, deletes the sins of pilgrims. But that kiss profits no part [of the body] unto salvation. For, he who kisses, moved by guilty greed or fear or flattery, or deceived by blind devotion, will be altogether chargeable with guilt, he bending his knees and approaching the pope's feet[2] more solicitously and reverentially than he would do before the sacrament

---

[1] In his *Postilla, Doc.*, 729 Huss said: "Jesus went about preaching on foot, and did not drive about in a splendid carriage as nowadays our priests drive. I, alas, also drive about . . . and I do not know whether it will be a sufficient excuse in the future that I have not been able to cover the long distances on foot and with sufficient speed."

[2] The emperor Caligula seems to have been the first Roman emperor to introduce the custom of kissing the foot from the East. The pope wears a red slipper, but when the custom of kissing his feet entered is not known. In the Address to the German Nobility Luther denounced the custom whereby 'a poor sinful man suffers his foot to be kissed by one who may be a hundred times better than he.' In chapter XXI Huss again refers to the custom of adoring the pope.

of the body of the Saviour. But in allowing himself to be kissed the pope is altogether guilty, because he cannot make himself equal to Christ so as to deserve such honor. And if he may equal Christ (though he will not quickly equal the apostles), yet should he not exceed in honors of this kind what they received, unto the increase of his merit, and by a similar confession, for the profit of the people doing honor. Therefore, they, like Christ, began to do good by excelling in good works and not by receiving kisses, given as unto God. For they despised mundane honors and for that reason forbade men to make genuflections in their presence. For they kept in memory Christ's words: "When thou art bidden to a marriage feast, sit not down in the chief seat, lest a more honorable man than thou be bidden of him, and he that bade thee and him shall come to thee and say, Friend, give this man place; and then thou shalt begin with shame to take the lowest place," Luke 14 : 8, 9.

But it is certain from the sayings of the saints that Christ is speaking of the spiritual and not the corporal vocation, place and meal, for by the wedding is intended the marriage of Christ and the church which will be fulfilled perpetually in the last supper. To this marriage feast many are called, and few are chosen, as Christ said, Matt. 22 : 14, but he sits in the lowest place who, with a good heart, esteems himself the least of the elect, just as did Christ's apostle, who saw into the secret things which it is not lawful for a man to utter and esteemed himself the least of the apostles. If, therefore, the pope esteems himself to be the most holy father, or consents to receive from his inferiors the address, "Most Holy Father," does he not in presumption choose the first place? Therefore, if he had humility, such as St. Gregory had, he would with all haste put a stop to this style of address or seek to put a stop to it. Not because he holds the place of Peter and because he holds the great dotation, is he most holy—*sanctissimus*—but if he follows Christ in humility, in waging warfare, in patience and toil, and out of the great bond of love, then is he holy. But far be it that he is most holy, because then he would be God almighty and consequently not the vicar of Jesus Christ. For Christ did not want the woman to kiss his feet after the resurrection—immortal and undoubtedly blessed—so that he keep from blasphemous presumption the miserable persons who, for the time, falsely assume that they are Christ's vicars. But the feet of Christ and those ascending with Christ are blessed and not the food of worms, a putrid member and a fetid sweat of mundane fluids. By these things we should be persuaded in regard to the fourth point—namely, that the cardinals are the manifest and true successors of the apostles, that it does not contain the truth. For by the fruits which it bears, is the tree known.

CHAPTER XV

THE CHURCH MAY BE RULED WITHOUT POPE AND CARDINALS

THE fifth point is this: "for the government of the church throughout the whole world, there ought always to be cardinals as the manifest and true successors in the office of Peter, the prince of the apostles, and of Christ's other apostles." Here that word "ought" does not mean opportuneness —*opportunitas*—on the side of God who rules the church, and who is able to rule the church scattered throughout the world, without such successors, nor does it mean fitness on the side of the church which can be properly ruled by holy priests, even if those twelve cardinals were removed; just as it was ruled for three hundred years and more after Christ's ascension, unless perhaps it be said that that word "ought" means necessity, a thing which the Saviour indicated when he said: "It must needs be that offences come, but woe to that man by whom the offence cometh," Matt. 18 : 7. For these words the Saviour spoke after his rebuke of his disciples who asked who was the greatest among them, when he commanded them, saying: "Verily I say unto you, except ye turn and become as little children, ye shall in no wise enter into the kingdom of heaven," Matt. 18 : 3. And, that they might not offend by pride those who believed in Christ, he added: "Whoso shall cause one of these little ones that believe on me to stumble, it is profitable for him that a great millstone should be hanged about his neck, and that he should be sunk in the depth of the sea," Matt. 18 : 6.

Commenting on these words, St. Gregory, Pastoral Rule I : 2 [*Nic. Fathers*, 2d Ser., 12 : 2], says: "Pastors, perverse in their lives, impugn in their morals what they preach in

words.   Therefore, it happens when a pastor walks along
steep places, the flock follows him to the precipice"; because,
when laymen have learned the sayings of prelates, they are
perverted by their works.   "Hence, it is written by the
prophet: 'Wicked priests are the cause of the people's down-
fall,' and of these the Lord said through the prophet: 'They
are made to be a stumbling-block of iniquity to the house
of Israel' [Hosea 5 : 8].   For indeed no one does more injury in
the church than he who acts perversely and yet has the name
and order of sanctity.   For no one dares to oppose and re-
fute such a delinquent, and his guilt is greatly extended, becoming an example, when the sinner is honored on account
of the reverence paid to his order.   For the unworthy would
flee the dangers of such a burden of guilt if they would carefully consider the meaning of the truth, namely, 'Whoso shall
cause one of these little ones who believe on me to stumble, it is profitable for him that a great millstone should be
hung about his neck, and he should be sunk in the depth of
the sea,' Matt. 18 : 6.   By 'a great millstone' is meant the
treadmill and sorrow of the secular life; and by the 'depth
of the sea' is meant utmost damnation.   He, therefore, who,
led along by the appearance of sanctity, destroys others
either by word or example, would truly be far better off if
his worldly acts under an external cloak bound such an one
to death, rather than that the ministries of his sacred office
performed in guilt should show to others that he was change-
able, because, doubtless, if he was the only one to fall, a
more tolerable pain of hell would torment him."

That Holy Pope knew the conditions and dangers incident to a prelate's life and especially incident to the position
of the Roman pontiff, inasmuch as his sin of commission and
omission would be a scandal to the wnole Christian people.
For it is said goodness in a pope is like salt for all, and
badness in him inures to the damnation of persons without
number, *Dist.* 40, *Si Papa* [Friedberg, 1 : 146].   If, therefore,

the pope and the cardinals by pompous equipages, resplendence of dress, exquisite and wonderful furnishings, by excessive anxiety to heap up benefices or money, and by the manifest ambition for honor in greater measure than secular laymen—if they offend those who believe in Christ—how is it that they always and necessarily continue to be essential " for the government of the universal church as manifest and true successors in the office of Peter and Christ's other apostles "? Never was the office of the apostles other than one of following Christ in good living and in teaching the church, baptizing men, healing the sick, casting out devils, offering up the sacrifice of Christ's body and everywhere exercising the power connected with their office for the perfecting of the church. If, therefore, the pope and his cardinals exercise that office, then the pope holds the office of Peter. But, if he with the cardinals falls away from it, who doubts that he falls away from the true vicariate of Christ and his apostles?

By the same method of proof the sixth point is set forth which is: " there are not to be found or given [by God] on earth other such successors than the pope, the present head, and the college of cardinals, the present body of the Roman church." On this point I note in the first place that Christ is a most sufficient head as he proved during three hundred years or more, when his church prospered and his law was most efficient for the closing of ecclesiastical cases, the end for which God gave his law. For Christ and his law did not fail for the governing of the church, seeing devoted priests ministered this law unto the people, who followed the judgment of holy doctors, which judgment they issued by the indwelling of the Holy Spirit as is clear from the cases of St. Augustine, St. Jerome, St. Gregory and St. Ambrose, who were given after the apostles' death to the church to teach her. Hence, it is not to be doubted that St. Augustine was more profitable to the church than many popes, and in matters of doctrine much more profitable than all the cardinals, from the first cardinals down to those now in office. For, in the government of the church, he knew the Scriptures of Christ better than they and also defined the nature of the catholic faith better by clearing the church of heretical errors and correcting them. Why, therefore, were those four doctors not true vicars of the apostles and their manifest successors, nay, even more true and reliable, so far as the people go, than any modern pope with his cardinals who shine before the people neither by virtue of a holy life nor by doctrine? Therefore, do I boldly assert that, if in any point these four doctors agree, the pope and his cardinals may not lawfully declare the opposite as the faith of the people. And the same is true of other saints, such as John Chrysostom, John of Damascus and Dionysius the Areopagite, who, taught by the Holy Spirit, illuminated the church of Christ by their knowledge and piety.

Against this point it is argued chiefly in this way: God is omnipotent, therefore, God may give other true successors of the apostles than are the pope and the cardinals. Therefore, other true successors of the apostles can be found or given who are not the pope or the cardinals. Hence that [sixth] point is false and the first consequence is proved. For, if God is not able to give other true successors, than are the pope and the cardinals, it follows that the power of Cæsar, a man and not God, in setting up the pope and cardinals limited God's power, a thing which is false. Hence the consequence is proven, for Constantine, the Cæsar, three hundred years after Christ, instituted the pope; because the Roman pontiff was an associate of other pontiffs until the donation of Cæsar by whose authority the pope began to rule as head. Hence the *Decretum, Dist.* 96 : 14 [Friedberg, 1 : 342 *sq.*],[1] which out of reverence we cannot deny, thus

---

[1] Huss's text gives the citation wrongly as *Dist.* 98. Huss quotes a small part of the spurious decretal of Pope Gelasius. The preceding decretal con-

speaks: "The emperor Constantine on the fourth day after his baptism conferred on the pontiff the grant—*privilegium* —of the Roman church that the pontiffs might have headship in all the earth, as judges over the king." In this grant, this among other things is read: "We have bestowed upon him power and ability and imperial honor, seeing that he is thus to hold the government over the four sees, Alexandria, Antioch, Jerusalem and Constantinople, and is the highest ruler over all priests in the whole world," etc. See how the institution and pre-eminence of the pope emanated from Cæsar's power, which, however, cannot limit God's power. For this reason later pontiffs, fearing that they might lose their pre-eminence, sought confirmation from other Cæsars, as the *Decretum, Dist.* 63 [Friedberg, 1 : 244], says: "I, Lewis, Roman emperor, Augustus, do decree and bestow by this our act of confirmation upon thee, blessed Peter, prince of the apostles, and through thee upon thy vicar, Lord Pascal, supreme pontiff, and upon thy successors forever, even as by our [your] predecessors ye have up to this time held in our [your] power and gift alone and controlled the Roman state."[1]

But there need be no anxiety over this grant of words when Cæsar says: "I, Lewis, concede unto thee, blessed Peter." Never did Peter, who at that time was already in possession of the kingdom of heaven, stand in need of civil possession over Rome, and never was Lewis greater than Peter and more truly in possession than Peter. Would that Peter, if it had been God's will, had said: I do not accept

tains the express assertion of Constantine's donation: "The emperor Constantine bestowed upon the apostolic see the crown and all royal authority in the city of Rome and in Italy and in the regions of the West."

[1] Huss's text departs from the original substituting *nostris* for *vestris*, and *nostra* for *vestra*, the original reading, "even as by your predecessors ye have held in your own power and gift and disposed of the city of Rome with its duchy and all the suburban regions and towns, its hilly territory, and its seacoast line and harbors and all cities, strongholds, walled towns and villas in the regions of Tuscany," etc. This pact between Lewis and Pascal, 817–824, is first found in Anselm of Lucca, d. 1073, and is deemed altogether spurious or at least largely interpolated.

thy grant because, when I was Roman bishop, I had already forsaken all and did not crave from Nero dominion over Rome; nor do I stand in need of it.   And I see that it greatly hurts my descendants, for it hinders them in the preaching of the Gospel and in salutary prayer and in the performance of God's counsels and commandments and makes many of them proud and arrogant.   Since, therefore, the good—*optimus*—God is able to take away the grant—*privilegium*—made by those emperors and to bring His church back to a state where pontiffs are on a parity, even as it was before the donation—it follows, that God is able to give to His church other true successors than the pope and the cardinals that they may minister even as did the holy apostles.

But against this the objection is brought: "The pope has this very appointment from the Lord," as the *Decretum* states, *Dist.* 22 [Friedberg, 1 : 73], where Pope Anacletus says: "The holy Roman church obtained the primacy not from the apostles but from the Lord himself."   From this it follows, that the pope was not appointed to his high office by the emperor or man but immediately by God.   And this is clear [22] 2, 3 from the submission rendered by kings and also from the testimony of doctors where they treat of the pope's authority.

As for the first statement, it is to be laid down that that pope, Anacletus, understood by the holy Roman church not the basilica of stone or wood, but St. Peter and St. Paul, and the other saints who dwelt in that place.   For this reason, in this same decretal, he says, that Peter and Paul were associates in the city of Rome, wherefore it is said figuratively that he obtained the primacy.

In regard to the second statement it is to be laid down that he is speaking about the primacy over men from God's standpoint, by virtue of the primacy of virtues and in view of the edification of the church and not about a primacy of temporal riches or human glory—a primacy which the apostles of Christ spurned. It is thus clear how weak the argumentation is: namely, the Roman church obtained the primacy not from the apostles, but from the Lord himself. For this reason every Roman pontiff ought to have pre-eminence in the matter of mundane glory and have secular rule, when, in fact, it ought rather to follow from the *Decretum* that the Roman pontiff is charged with serving the people not by ruling for his own ends, or suspending the people, but by praying efficiently for the people, as according to the *Decretum* [Friedberg, 1 : 74] Paul did, Romans 1 : 8. He says: "A prayer may be poured out for all to the Lord of all the saints, and in these words Paul, most blessed, promised the Romans over his own signature, 'God is my witness whom I serve in my spirit, in the Gospel of his Son, how unceasingly I make mention of you always in my prayers.'" From this decretal it is seen that Pope Anacletus did not intend to affirm that he himself was to have civil rule over all others or hold a primacy of government over all other persons of the church militant. Because, in thus seeking his own glory he would show most clearly the mark of antichrist. John 5 : 41 *sqq.* Yea, even Boniface VIII, in his bull *Unam sanctam*, did not dare expressly to affirm this, for then he alone would have borne witness that he was the most holy man and, in this case, the faithful as well as unbelievers might appositely object against him: "Thou bearest witness of thyself; thy witness is not true" [John 5 : 31].

Therefore, the Roman pontiffs have become involved in this difficulty by reason of the dotation and exaltation derived from Cæsar, because, when the emperor asks them, whether, in the matter of government, they excel all mortals living, in power, primacy and dignity, they have to admit it to be so, for otherwise, as they say, no one is under obligation to believe that they are popes. But Peter and Paul did not make any such statement about themselves, for they did not have any power given them by Cæsar. For this reason, Paul truly and humbly made this confession concerning himself: "I am least of all the apostles, who am not worthy to be called an apostle," I Cor. 15 : 9. On this account, therefore, the Roman pontiff would not make such a profession if the imperial dignity were not in the way. Wherefore, the conclusion holds that from God direct and not from a man—who is not God—or from a mere man, does the pope hold the excellency of his rank. But he should make himself deserving of that rank by an humble demeanor and without pomp. And if Cæsar's dignity exalts the pope in the eyes of the world when he is without humility and a holy life, how can this exaltation fit in with the life and glory of Christ, when antichrist is exalted in the same worldly way?

As for the second point—the subjection of the kingdoms—it is said that at first it was rendered without the pope's seeking, but arose out of fear of the emperor's command, according to which all peoples did not owe subjection to him, that he should have secular rule over them, and therefore that subjection does not argue for the necessity that a Roman pontiff and his cardinals govern until the end of time.

Thirdly, concerning the testimony of the doctors who treat of the pope's power, it is alleged, that all who thus magnify the pope's power and say that he can do without guilt whatsoever he wills and that nobody has the right to ask why he does this or that—all these are mendacious rhetoricians, leading the people of our Lord Jesus Christ astray. Nor ought such to be believed except as their words are founded in Scripture. For thus the great doctor, Augustine, often asserted of himself that he ought to be believed only so far as he had grounded himself in Scripture. It is evident, that God may give other successors of the apostles than the pope and the cardinals, just as he was able to give others in the place of the pontiffs of the old law, the scribes and the Pharisees with their traditions. And to these, who did not

keep God's law, the Lord said: "I say unto you, the kingdom of heaven shall be taken away from you and shall be
given to a nation bringing forth the fruits thereof," Matt.
21 : 43. These words the Saviour spoke to the priests when
they alone bore sentence against themselves in that they said:
"He will miserably destroy those wicked men and will let out
the vineyard to other husbandmen who shall render him the
fruits in their seasons." How, therefore, is the hand of the
Lord shortened that He is not able to cast out the pope and
the cardinals and appoint others in their places who, though
they have no titles, will build up the church as the Lord did
with the apostles?

Likewise all bishops of Christ's church, who follow Christ
in their lives, they are true vicars of the apostles and they
are not pope or cardinals. Therefore, other true successors
of the apostles can be found and given besides the pope and
the cardinals. The consequence is given with the minor
premise, and the first part of it is clear from *Decretum*, 21,
in novo [Friedberg, 1 : 69, 70], where Pope Anacletus says
that "the rest of the apostles, by reason of an equal fellowship [with Christ], received with Peter honor and authority."
And later on he says: "When they were deceased, bishops
arose in their places." And here the Gloss says, *Argumentum,*
that "every bishop is equal in apostolic power by virtue of
his ordination and the ground of his consecration." The same
is clear from *Decretum*, 24 : 1, *Loquitur ad Petrum* [Fried-
berg, 1 : 971], where Cyprian, the bishop and martyr, says
that "after his resurrection Christ conferred on all the apostles equal power." This also appears from what Jerome
says, *Dist.* 95, *Olim* [Friedberg, 1 : 332]: "The same person
formerly was both presbyter and bishop, before rivalries had
been started by the insinuation of the devil, and before it
was said amongst the people, 'I am of Paul and I of Apollos.'"

Likewise, all archbishops, patriarchs and bishops, at the
council of Pisa who recognized, determined and condemned

Pope Gregory XII, as a heretic,[1] these were and now are true successors of the apostles, and these are other persons than the pope and cardinals. Hence the sixth point is false. The consequence follows together with the part spoken of above. And the doctors did not dare to deny the first part.

Likewise, it should be evangelical wisdom that all priests are consecrated and guided directly by the one and only pontiff, our Lord Jesus Christ. For this was so at the time of the apostles, when the church grew, and this statement accords with Scripture. Therefore, God is able to bring his church back to its pristine state by taking away the government from the pope and cardinals. And so it stands that others besides these may be vicars of the apostles.

Likewise the designation of the power and the office, "minister of the church," is indicated lest he wander away, into forbidden ground, but no other one is indicated save the one whom Christ appointed. For, since Christ is almighty, omniscient, and all-merciful, it is clear that reason requires that he ordain finally and unchangeably, and more especially in view of the fact that in the primitive church the harvest was larger, and God ordained more copiously different kinds of ministers as laborers in the harvest. But then he only ordained deacons and presbyters and the presbyter and the bishop was the same person, as says Jerome and as appears from Paul's epistles to Timothy and Titus. From these Jerome draws the conclusion in his letter to the

---

[1] Gregory XII, Angelo Correr, fourth and last pope of the Roman line, 1406–1415, and contemporary with Benedict XIII, of the Avignon line, was together with Benedict deposed as a schismatic and heretic by the council of Pisa, June, 1409. He still claimed to be pope till 1415, when he resigned his office to the council of Constance. He died 1417. Bohemia was true to the Roman obedience till King Wenzel acknowledged the council of Pisa and the pope it elected, Alexander V. Gregory and his two predecessors had seemed to favor Wenzel's rival for the imperial crown—Ruprecht. The archbishop of Prague, Zbynek, continued to acknowledge Gregory until the fall of 1409, and Huss's alleged indorsement of Wenzel's action and acknowledgment of Alexander was one of the immediate causes of the archbishop's strained relations with Huss.

presbyter Evagrius, *Dist.* 93, *Legimus* [Friedberg, 1 : 328], when he says: "What does the bishop do, except ordain, that the presbyter does not do? Nor is the church of the city of Rome one thing, and the church of the whole world another. And the church of Gaul and of Britain and Africa and Persia and the Orient and India and all the barbarous nations adore one Christ and observe one rule of truth. If authority is sought, the world is greater than the city. Wherever there may be a bishop, either at Rome, Constantinople or Alexandria, the bishop is of the same merit and of the same priesthood. The power of riches and the lowliness of poverty make[1] the bishop either higher or lower. Besides," he says, "all are successors of the apostles." So we see that the pope and his cardinals are not the only successors of Christ.

The same is made to appear by Bede who, commenting on Luke 10 : 1 [*Com. on Luke*, Migne's ed., 92 : 461], "The Lord hath appointed seventy-two others," says: "There is no one who doubts that just as the twelve apostles prefigured the class of bishops, so these seventy-two the class of presbyters and bore the mark of the second order of the priesthood."[2] From the things already said it is shown that others than the pope and cardinals may be given and found as true successors of the apostles. Inasmuch, therefore, as by Christ's appointment in the days of the apostles, two orders of the clergy sufficed for his church, that is, the deacon and the priest, as the saints say, and also the *Decretum*, 93, *Dominus Noster* [Friedberg, 1 : 329], where it runs: "The Lord chose apostles, disciples, bishops and presbyters,

---

[1] Huss's text omits *non* and also Rhegium and other cities of whose bishops Jerome makes mention.

[2] The number, seventy-two, is given by some MSS. and in the Vulgate. Bede goes on to say that in the first period of the church, as the Scriptures bear witness, the terms bishop and presbyter were used interchangeably. The Venerable Bede, d. 735, the first English scholar, wrote commentaries, and on many subjects, but is more particularly known by his *Eccles. History*, a history of England from the time of Cæsar to 731. Huss as well as Wyclif quote Bede frequently.

and the apostles appointed for themselves after the Lord's ascension deacons to be ministers of their episcopate and of the church,"[1]—why should it be wondered at if God almighty, putting the pope and his cardinals to death and giving them also eternal life—in case they merit it—should allow His church throughout the whole world to wage war with these same orders now as originally, namely, without the cardinals, and should ordain that the church should be ruled again as she was ruled by His own indestructible law, by giving bishops and priests who, by evangelizing and prayer and the exemplification of good lives, would diligently feed Christ's sheep. For this office alone was given to Peter by Christ, as appears in John 21.

Hence Augustine notes, *Ep.* 141, *ad Paulinum* [Migne's ed., xxxiii : 635], how in the apostolic passage, Eph. 4 : 11, the office of pastor and the office of teacher are joined. "Pastors," he says, "and teachers whom thou hast appointed to discern above all the truth, are, I think, the same, and not the pastors one and the teachers another. And so, as he had spoken previously of pastors, he added teachers that pastors might understand that teaching—*doctrina*—belonged to their office. And, therefore, he did not say, 'some pastors and some teachers'—the form of speech used in the former part of the preceding verse—but 'some pastors and teachers,' as if one office were embraced under the two words: 'some,' he said, 'pastors and teachers.'"

Hence, if that which is superfluous be taken away, it would appear what pope, cardinal or bishop would remain a true shepherd out of the treasury of the Lord, and perhaps more would be found useless thieves and robbers rather than true vicars of the Lord Jesus Christ.

But against what has been said the objection is brought,

---

[1] Cyprian's text, which Huss is quoting, runs thus: "The deacons should remember how the Lord chose the apostles, that is, the bishops and presbyters, but after the Lord's ascension, the apostles appointed them as ministers of their episcopate and the church."

that, if the pope and cardinals are not the true and manifest successors of the apostles, then for the same reason others are not, inasmuch as the power of discrimination cannot be based upon the fact that they may be clad in sheep's clothing, and yet may be inwardly ravening wolves, as stated, Matt. 7 : 15.   Here it becomes us to consider the two sects of the clergy, namely, the clergy of Christ and the clergy of antichrist.   Christ's clergy rests in its head, Christ, and in his laws; but antichrist's clergy leans wholly or chiefly on human laws and the laws of antichrist, and yet it is clothed upon like the clergy of Christ and the church with the design that the people may be led astray by its simulation.   And so it is fitting that these two things which are so contrary to each other obey two contrary heads with their laws.   The outward evidence teaches the class to which the members belong. Indeed, it is established that the clergy of the church falls away[1] into two parts and for this reason laymen cannot help but waver who are borne along by those who are so different from Christ in opinion and in life.

But these parts may be commonly best discerned from the fact that the clergy of antichrist is zealously intent upon human traditions and rights which savor of pride and the greed of this world, and that it wishes to live ostentatiously and in pleasure and in a way contrary to Christ, wholly neglecting the imitation of the Lord Jesus Christ in its living. But Christ's clergy labors diligently for Christ's laws and his rights, whereby spiritual good is acquired that it may be shown, and it flees pride and the pleasure of this world, and seeks to live in conformity with Christ, giving itself up most zealously, following the Lord Jesus Christ.   Nor is it right for the faithful to doubt that this part is the true clergy, and the other part is the false.   And although in the absence of revelation, the pilgrim is not able clearly and with cer-

---

[1] *Claudicat*, literally limps or falters; DuCange derives it from *claudeo* and *claudo*.

tainty to determine who the holy pastor really is, nevertheless we ought to decide by his works, which are conformed to Christ's law, that he is such a pastor.

If, however, the pilgrim sees him living at variance with Christ, to what other judgment can he come than that he is antichrist's vicar, for Christ says: "Ye shall know them by their fruits," Matt. 7 : 16, and "He that is not with me is against me," Matt. 12 : 30. Here the *Glossa ordinaria* says: "He that is not with me"—that is, does works dissimilar to mine—"he is against me." If, therefore, a prelate is proud, lives in luxury, follows after greed, is impatient, does not feed the sheep, but oppresses and scatters them, is he not antichrist? Hence men may easily recognize the wicked by their outward works which are contrary to Christ; but the good cannot be so known because hypocrisy may lurk in them.

CHAPTER XVI

THE LAW OF GOD THE STANDARD OF ECCLESIASTICAL JUDGMENTS

FURTHER, the aforementioned doctors lay down that " certain of the Bohemian clergy, leaning too little on the pope and the college of cardinals, do not want to agree to this, wishing to have holy Scripture for the only judge in such matters, which Scripture they interpret and wish to have interpreted according to their own heads, not caring for the interpretation accepted by the community of wise men in the church nor heeding the holy Scripture recorded in Deut. 17 : 8–12: 'If thou seest that there is a matter in judgment too uncertain and hard for thee, between blood and blood, between plea and plea, between leprous and nonleprous, and perceivest that the words of the judges do not agree within thy gates; then arise and get thee up unto the place which the Lord thy God shall choose and thou shalt come unto the priests, the Levites, and unto the judge which shall be in those days, and thou shalt inquire from them and they shall pronounce for thee a sentence of truth. And thou shalt do according to whatever they may say who preside in that place which Jehovah hath chosen; and they shall teach thee according to his law and thou shalt observe their sentence, nor shalt thou turn aside from the sentence to the right hand or to the left. And the man that doth presumptuously, not willing to obey the priest's jurisdiction who at that time standeth to minister before thy God, and to obey the sentence of the judge, even that man shall die: and thou shalt put away the evil from Israel. And all the people shall hear and fear and do no more presumptuously.'[1] It is certain that for all the faithful the Roman church is the place which the Lord has chosen, the place where the Lord has placed the primacy of the whole church, and the high priest who occupies the primacy, and is set over that place, is the pope, the true and manifest successor of Peter. And the cardinals are the priests of the tribe of Levi who are joined with the lord pope in the administration of the priestly office, to whom in cases of doubt and difficulty recourse must be had in matters, catholic and ecclesiastical, the judgment of God being followed.

"Hence Jerome, *Ep. ad papam* [Letter to Damasus, Friedberg, 1 : 970], speaking of the same thing, says: 'This is the faith, most blessed pope,[2] which we have learned in the catholic church and which we have always held, and, if anything less proper or anything indiscreet has been placed in her, we desire that it be corrected by thee, who holdest Peter's seat and faith. And if this, our confession, approves itself to the judgment of thy apostleship—whosoever may wish to charge me with guilt—he will prove himself to be inexperienced or malevolent, or perchance not a catholic but a heretic.'"

This exposition, so far as the principles go, I think flowed chiefly from the head of Stephen Palecz, for by it he attempts first to arouse the pope and the cardinals against the party opposed to him, when he says: "Certain of the clergy of Bohemia, leaning too little on the pope and the cardinals, do not wish to agree to this": namely, that the pope is the head of the Roman church and the cardinals its body, the true and manifest vicars of Christ. However, in regard to this too little dependence, I say that, so far as their vanity, greed and illegal commands go, the pope with the cardinals ought to be depended upon little. For so the Saviour put little dependence upon the savorless salt, which was good for noth-

---

[1] The translation follows the Vulgate which Huss gives exactly.

[2] *Beatissime papa.* Huss has *beatissimi papæ.* Damasus, pope 366–384, is said to have called upon Jerome to make his Vulgate translation.

ing except to be trodden under foot of man, Matt. 5 : 13,[1] and he added: "Nor is it fit for the dunghill," Luke 14 : 35. And Judas Iscariot he depended upon little, for he called him a devil and the son of perdition, John 6 : 71; 17 : 12. Peter he also called Satan, when Peter opposed him, Matt. 16 : 22.

Later on that doctor heaps together many lies against us. The first lie is that we wish to have the holy Scriptures alone for our judge in such matters. And in this statement he affirms that we would not wish to have for our judge God, the apostles, the holy doctors, or the universal church. But he draws this lie from a certain disputation in which we were engaged, when it was said that he would offer Scripture for his statements and for the reason that we would not agree to the positions of our opponents. The doctor, however, ought to know that neither with him nor with any of his adherents do we agree in matters of faith unless they ground themselves in Scripture or reason. But revelation I do not expect from them, and if it did perchance come to them, we would feel that it taught otherwise than the Scripture teaches.

The second lie that he ascribes to us is that we interpret holy Scripture according to our heads, that is—as he himself and the other doctors allege—that we expound holy Scripture according to our erroneous understanding or according to our pleasure, and in this he charges upon us the arrogance of wisdom and also heresy, but mendaciously, because, with God's help, we do not intend to explain Scripture otherwise than the Holy Spirit requires and than it is explained by the holy doctors to whom the Holy Spirit gave understanding. And I could wish that that doctor and all his colleagues might show which Scripture it is which we expound ill. Hence, he is the more to be suspected of lying

---

[1] In his Reply to Palecz, *Mon.*, 1 : 352, Huss says Christians must judge by the effects or fruits whether the pope and cardinals are the salt of the earth and the light of the world.

when he adds, "And they wish to interpret," because if he is not a knower of hearts how does he dare to say that we wish to expound Scripture otherwise than we ought? But this statement is vented forth because we do not follow his pleasure and the pleasure of his colleague Stanislaus, and stand with them who deem themselves, with the doctors agreeing with them, the wise in the church. And even much more are they to be suspected of lying for they have not dared to charge us with not giving heed to the interpretation of the holy doctors.

But they add the biggest lie of all when they speak without applying the holy Scripture as written in Deut. 17 : 8–12. For this these doctors ought to know that we turn to sacred Scripture and affirm that it is the true Word of God, which also confirms our judgment. For that diligent expounder of Scripture, Nicholas of Lyra, on Deut. 17, says: "The opinion of no man, whatever his authority may be, is to be held if it plainly contains falsehood or error, and this appears by the promise made in the text, 'They shall pronounce for thee a sentence of truth,' and 'they shall teach thee according to His law.' From this it appears that, if they said what was false or plainly fell away from God's law they were not to be heard." Thus much Lyra. And what has been said is confirmed by that word of the Lord: "Thou shalt not follow the multitude to do evil; neither shalt thou acquiesce in the judgment of the many to depart from the truth," Ex. 23 : 2. On this Lyra says that in the Hebrew it runs: "Thou shalt not fall away after the rabbins—that is, teachers or the great men—to commit sin." And further on, he says: "As you are not to fall away from the truth on account of the larger number who sit in judgment, and fall away from the truth, so you are not to fall away on account of those who have greater authority in giving judgment." Thus much Lyra.[1]

[1] Nicholas of Lyra, born in France, d. Paris, 1340, member of the Franciscan order, a notable exegete, who knew Hebrew and in his *Postillæ* gave a running

Certainly I confide in this expounder, so far as this opinion goes, more than in all the aforesaid doctors. For Lyra aptly draws from Scripture (1) that the opinion of no man, whatever his authority may be—and consequently the opinion of no pope—is to be held if it plainly contains falsehood or error. It seems to me to be certain that Palecz and Stanislaus are so afraid of the pope and the cardinals that they would not dare publicly to avow this holy saying. (2) Lyra declares that God's law is the standard according to which individual judges and especially ecclesiastical judges ought to pronounce sentence and not otherwise. For this law shows what ought to be accepted as true. Hence he says that this appears from the words: "They shall pronounce for thee a sentence of truth." And the words follow: "They shall teach thee according to His law." O doctors, why do you not hold to this Scripture? You were asked and for God's sake publicly besought in the convocation of the university to pronounce a sentence of truth according to God's law, whether the bulls for the raising of the cross obligated the scholars of the university to give of the goods collected by God subsidies to the pope against Ladislaus and against his allies at the pope's command.[1] And you responded that you did not

comment on all the books of the Bible. He was much used by the Reformers, especially Luther, so that it was said: "If Lyra had not harped, Luther would not have danced." Lyra quotes Raschi at length on the O. T.

[1] Ladislaus, king of Naples, by occupying the city of Rome, called forth against himself the severest papal censures from John XXIII. John's two bulls calling for a crusade against the refractory prince promised full forgiveness from "guilt and punishment" to all who went to the holy war or helped others to go. Three places were set up in Prague where the pardons were sold. Huss lifted his voice and used his pen against the crusade as Wyclif had done against the crusade preached by Henry de Spenser. Palecz and seven other members of the theological faculty of the university, that is, the Eight Doctors, took sides against Huss and defended John's bulls. Huss took the ground that the pope has no right to forgive sins unless he surely knows that God in these cases has forgiven, that the pope does no more than announce God's decisions, and that, instead of calling upon Christians to make war against Christians, he ought to imitate Christ, who did not call down fire upon his enemies, and with tears and prayers seek to overcome opposition to the church. Huss, in his Reply to Palecz, *Mon.*, 1 : 330, says that Palecz was at first opposed to

wish to instruct them [the convocation] nor pronounce judgment upon the pope's bulls, and interpret them. But in
corners you have written differently, and especially have I
heard Palecz say about the articles which were handed to
him by the pope's legates that they contained plain errors
evident to the eye, which articles, nevertheless, were taken
from the bull and were handed out to the preachers by these
legates as the first deputies under the authority of the pope
to be promulgated. Hence, as I have heard, the preacher,
Master Briccius, in their lecture-room said to those masters
that he would rather die than announce those articles. But
when Palecz receded and was followed by others, Briccius
also receded, for letters from the lord king frightened them,
which letters the legates used for their financial support—
subsidium.

(3) Lyra deduces from the aforesaid Scripture of the
Lord that if judges say what is false or plainly fall away
from God's law they are not to be heard, because God said,
as I have quoted: "Thou shalt not follow the multitude to
do evil; neither shalt thou acquiesce in the judgment of the
many to depart from the truth" [Ex. 23 : 2]. How, therefore, can we be bound contrary to that most holy mandate
of God to follow the multitude which the doctors gathered
together and led to the city hall that they might overcome
by fright those whom they were not able to overcome by
Scripture or reason? The priests, scribes and Pharisees did
not dare to go into the prætorium and accuse Jesus for fear
of being polluted. But these, when the scribes and Pharisees and elders of the people were assembled, gladly went
in and one of them, named Palecz, read, while all listened,
the words of Deut. 17 : 8–12: "But that man that doeth
presumptuously, not willing to obey the judge's decree, even

the sale of the indulgences and declared the pope's bull to his legates was full
of evident errors. For the bulls and Huss's treatise, *Mon.*, 1 : 212–235, see
Schaff: *John Huss*, p. 111 *sq.*, 116–122.

that man shall die." He did not fear to incur irregularity, and if perchance he had been with the Jews in accusing Christ, perhaps he would have said: "His blood be upon us and upon our children; for we have a law and by that law he ought to die." Pilate was not, therefore, excused because he heard the high priests and the magistrates, scribes and elders of the people, for God said: "Thou shalt not follow the multitude to do evil," etc. Here Lyra says the Hebrew is, "Thou shalt not fall away after the rabbins," that is, the teachers or great men, "to commit sin"—whoever the great men and teachers in the city hall were who condemned and decreed many things which down to this day they have not shown should be condemned at their pleasure.

And according to the purpose of the doctors, in the Scripture quoted, some might Judaize and say that under the rule of Caiaphas, the high priest, or Annas, who then presided in the holy place which the Lord had chosen, and by Pilate's decree the judge, Jesus Christ, was justly condemned, a thing which is against what Paul says: "They that dwell in Jerusalem and their rulers, because they knew not him or the voices of the prophets which are read every Sabbath, fulfilled them by condemning him. And though they found no cause of death in him, yet asked they of Pilate that they might slay him," Acts 13 : 27, 28. And it is clear that, in condemning Christ, the high priest was present, the priests of the house of Levi were present, and Pilate, the judge, was present in the place which the Lord had chosen; and these persons Christ Jesus did not wish to obey in the evil they were doing, although he obeyed God, his Father, and Pilate, submitting to death meekly. Did, therefore, the high priest, followed by the priests, the Levites, the magistrates and elders of the people, Pilate and the soldiers, yea, and by the crowd shouting, "Crucify Him, crucify Him!" did they justly condemn Christ the Lord? Yea, truly, because

not love but hate, not truth but lying, urged them on and
ignorance of God's law led them astray, did they err gravely.

Equally, there may be a leading astray in the case of the
pope and cardinals, our doctors themselves being included,
that they should condemn some truth or other. For if the
apostles, chosen by Christ, who received the Holy Spirit,
fell into heresy, as St. Augustine and Bede affirm, how is
it that the pope and cardinals have received greater gifts of
the Spirit, making it impossible for them to stray off in the
same degree or even in a larger degree? And it is not a matter of doubt that obedience should be rendered to pope and
cardinals so long as they teach the truth according to God's
law, as the authority says: "They shall pronounce for thee
a sentence of truth, and thou shalt do whatsoever they say
and whatsoever they teach thee according to His law." But
if the rabbins, that is, the teachers or great men, as Lyra says,
or popes or cardinals charge or admonish anything besides
the truth, even though the whole Roman curia is on their
side, the faithful is not to obey when he knows the truth,
for God says: "Thou shalt not follow after the multitude
to do evil."[1] Daniel, Nicodemus and the thief on the cross
put this principle into practise, who would not fall in with
the crowds in condemning the truth, as the Scripture states.
For Daniel condemned as naught the sentence of the elders
of the children of Israel by liberating Susanna and pronouncing against the senior elders from whom the iniquity started,
Daniel 13.[2] Nicodemus in the council of the Pharisees and

---

[1] In his treatises against John XXIII's bulls, *Mon.*, 215–235, Huss asserts
the fallibility of popes and that they are not always to be obeyed. Popes
do not know whether they themselves are among the predestinate, not to
speak of others. Many popes who gave indulgences are lost.

[2] The *History of Susanna*, Lange: *Apocrypha*, 456 *sq.* This apocryphal
work gives the story of the attempt on the virtue of a beautiful married woman,
Susanna, by two elders of Israel. Rejecting their proposal rather than incur
God's condemnation, she was nevertheless accused by her would-be seducers
and sentenced to death. Daniel then intervened, proved the charges false,
and Susanna's accusers were put to death.

priests, when they had sent the servants to bring Jesus, wishing to put him to death, and when they said to the servants, "Hath any of the rulers believed on him or of the Pharisees? But this multitude that knoweth not the law are accursed "— then Nicodemus said to them: "Doth our law judge a man, except it first hear from himself and know what he doeth?" John 7 : 47–51. O blessed Nicodemus, thou didst accord such force to God's law; thou didst bear witness to the law that it should be the judge of man.

See, how inconvenient the statements of our doctors are when they pronounce the sentence that we wish to have the law as judge—a judge which judges most justly and does not judge otherwise than does God, the most just judge. Thou sayest, "Doth our law judge a man, except it first hear from him and know what he doeth?" as if he would say, No, because it judges justly. To that judge Christ referred the priests, Pharisees, scribes and Jews, who accused him of sin because he kept not the Sabbath day, and called God his Father, saying: "Ye search the Scriptures. These are they which bear witness of me," John 5 : 39. Did not, therefore, Christ wish the Scriptures to judge the Jews which believed not on Christ? Certainly, he wished it. In proportion, therefore, as the doctors wish that the Scriptures be not the judge, in that proportion they wish themselves to be believed that whatever they condemn should be condemned and that whatever they approve should be approved. For this they asked and begged in the city hall; for this they sought the signatures of the magisters who gainsaid their opinions. But the counsel of the Pharisees, scribes and priests has come to naught, because the faithful who gainsaid them were not willing to agree without hearing the proof from the law, which holds wrapped up in itself all truth that is to be believed. If the pontiffs, Pharisees, priests and elders of the people had known this law they would not have condemned Christ—but they did condemn and blaspheme. More learned than they was the thief, who, hanging on the cross, bare witness to Christ, saying: "This man hath done nothing amiss," Luke 23 : 41.

And, so far as the chief purpose of the doctors goes, who intend that the pope ought to be the judge of all cases and that whoso does not obey him ought to die the death of the body, these doctors ought to be reverenced for their apish and cruel comparison [that is, to those who put Christ to death], especially as our Lord Jesus Christ, priest of both Testaments, neither wished to pronounce civil judgment nor to condemn the disobedient to bodily death. For, so far as the first goes, he said: "Man, who made me a judge or divider over you?" Luke 12 : 14. And so far as the second, he said to the woman taken in adultery, whom the Pharisees pronounced worthy of death according to the law: "Neither do I condemn thee; go thy way; from henceforth sin no more," John 8 : 11.

But, perhaps it may be said by the doctors that this is not to the point, that the law says: "He who does presumptuously, not willing to obey the rule of the priest." See, I will give a case in form—for, Christ said: "If thy brother sin against thee, go show him his fault between thee and him alone: if he hear thee, thou hast gained thy brother, but if he hear thee not, take with thee one or two, that at the mouth of two witnesses or three every word may be established; and if he refuse to hear them, tell it to the church: and if he refuse to hear the church let him be unto thee as the gentile and the publican," Matt. 18 : 15–17. See, to whom the supreme lord of the law and the supreme pontiff speaks? Certainly to Peter, the future Roman pontiff, next after himself, that he might kindly correct the erring and convince the disobedient person before witnesses, and if he remained hardened in disobedience he spoke to the church, that is, he announced to the multitude, not to put to death the perverse and disobedient with corporal death, but to avoid him as a publican and gentile. What ground, therefore, is there for the argument from comparison [with those who put Christ to death]? Under the old law the disobedient person was to be put to death, therefore, also under the law of grace. Even Christ's disciples have been deceived by this argument from comparison, for after the manner of Elijah the prophet, they wanted the Samaritans who refused to receive Christ to be consumed by fire from heaven, saying: "Lord, wilt thou that we bid fire to come down from heaven and consume them?" That most good priest and best of masters reproved them, for the words follow that he, turning around, rebuked them, saying: "Ye know not what spirit ye are of, for the Son of Man came not to destroy souls but to save them," Luke 9 : 54–56.

This good Gospel the doctors did not turn to and so they have joined to their statements this sanguinary corollary— *sanguinolentum corollarium*[1]—and say: "If any of the clergy be found in Bohemia acting contrary to these premises or a single one of them, such an one is to be corrected by ecclesiastical censure and, if he refuses to be corrected, he is to be turned over to the secular tribunal." For a certainty in this

[1] This is one of the rare protests before the Reformation against the bloody practice of putting heretics to death. In his Reply to Eight Doctors, *Mon.*, 1 : 382 *sqq.*, Huss takes up again at length the treatment of heresy. The definite position taken by the church was that they should be put out of the world. The laws of Frederick II ordered death by burning for all heretics and the church well knew that when it turned a heretic over to the civil power, though its sentence asked for mercy, the death penalty would follow. In fact, as Vacandard has shown, the ecclesiastical court sometimes actually pronounced the death penalty and carried it out, and popes and other ecclesiastics demanded on pain of excommunication the summary treatment by the civil authorities of persons condemned by the church. See Schaff: *John Huss*. It would have been well if Calvin and Beza had made the same distinction between the Old Testament and the New which Huss makes in the preceding paragraph. In this case, they would not have justified the execution of heretics upon the basis of the examples given in the Old Testament. A strong passage in Huss's treatise against indulgences, *Mon.*, 1 : 223, runs: "The Saviour taught Peter and in him his vicars and pontiffs in their necessities to flee to God in prayer and not to money or physical battle." For a more elaborate treatment of putting heretics to death, etc., see *ad octo Doctores*, *Mon.*, 1 : 393 *sqq.*, 399 *sqq.*

they follow the pontiffs, scribes and Pharisees who, when Christ refused to obey them in all things, said: "It is not lawful for us to put any man to death," and then delivered him over to the secular tribunal. Are they not murderers? Truly they are worse murderers than Pilate. The Saviour bore witness and said to Pilate: "He who delivered me to thee hath the greater sin." These are they to whom Peter spoke when he said: "Ye denied the Holy and Righteous One and asked for a murderer to be granted unto you and killed the Prince of Life," Acts 3 : 14.

Then the doctors add: "It is fixed for every one of the faithful that the Roman church is the place which the Lord hath chosen, where the Lord placed the headship of the whole church. And the high priest who presides there is the pope, the true and manifest successor of Peter, and the cardinals are the priests of the tribe of Levi." In this statement, the doctors heap together many things that they do not prove. For when did they prove that it is fixed for every one of the faithful to accept that legal loaf of theirs?—*brodium* —[see DuCange, *Glossarium*, vol. 1]. For many of their party are without doubt among the faithful and know nothing about Rome, the pope, and the cardinals, and especially whether the pope is the true successor of Peter, and the cardinals the priests of the order of Levi. But these doctors call the church perhaps that place of which the Saviour prophesied when he said: "When ye see the abomination of desolation standing in the holy place (let him that heareth understand)" Matt. 24 : 15. Or the doctors call the Roman church a place, the basilica of St. Peter, or the apostolical dignity, for in these two senses "the place" in their statement may be understood, for there the Lord located the chief government—*principatus*—of the whole church because he wanted the apostles Peter and Paul to undergo their chief sufferings there, men who were appointed to be the spiritual rulers over the whole church and in whom, after Christ's

death, the spiritual government of the church chiefly in-
hered. And in this church not the pope but Christ is the
chief ruler who presides over that place, that is, the basilica
or apostolic dignity, and he rules the church which is his
bride. But, if in the pope is discovered a life at variance
with Christ, lived in pride, greed, restless impatience, ambition, and in the flaunting of power and giving preponderance
to his own law over the law of Christ—then is seen the abomination of the desolation of Christ's virtues standing in the
holy place, where it ought not to stand, as Christ said, Mark
13 : 14. Wherefore, if faithful souls should observe anywhere the spiritual state of the church set up, where one head
of a family[1] was accustomed to preside over his house, who
graciously received all his servants whom he had invited,
took care of them by warming them, and defended them
by helping them, but if in that same house he should find
that one presides over a condition altogether the opposite,
it would not be wondered at if many were confounded, just
as though a traveller wished to be entertained by a true
head of a household, a man of large hospitality, goodness
and good nature, and of an altogether virtuous life, and
afterward should find a monstrous wild beast which was
wont to tyrannize over the guests by giving them cold comfort and by craft, cruelty and avarice and betrayal—the
traveller, entering the house and seeing such an one sitting
in the chair of the good head of the household, would wonder, be troubled and not a little confounded at his looks.
So the abomination of desolation may be understood in accord with Zech. 11 : 15: "Take unto thee yet again the instruments of a foolish shepherd, for I will raise up a shepherd in the land which will not visit those which are cut
off, neither seek those which are scattered nor heal that
which is broken nor feed that which is sound; but he will
eat the flesh of the fat sheep and will tear their hoofs in

[1] This is taken from Gregory the Great, Migne, 76 : 1154.

pieces. Woe to the shepherd and idol[1] that leaveth the flock!" If, therefore, this description of "the idol" and this forsaking of the flock fit the pope, how could the saying of the doctors be true of any possible pope in the future, that he is the high priest, the true and manifest successor of Peter, presiding over the church which is the bride of Christ? For it does not follow,—he is the idol [worthless shepherd] who forsakes the flock; therefore, he is the high priest, the true and manifest successor of Peter. And it also does not follow,— he is the pseudo-Christ, therefore, he is the true and manifest Christ; for the true Christ said: "If any one shall say to you, Lo here is Christ or there! believe it not, for there shall arise pseudo-Christs and pseudo-prophets." Let, therefore, the faithful beware lest, moved by flattery, they call the pseudo-Christs most holy and the worthless shepherd high priest and true successor of St. Peter, the apostle. For, in so calling Agnes most holy father and high priest, presiding over the whole church—Agnes who gave birth to a child— they are deceived.

Then, to turn to the saying of Jerome, "This is the faith, O most blessed pope," *Decr.* 24 : 1 [Friedberg, 1 : 970], it is said that presumably he spoke of the apostolic works of Pope Damasus as he wrote to St. Augustine in letters addressing him "Augustine, our lord and most holy and blessed pope."[2] And so likewise the saints are reported to have spoken of prelates when they saw them straying away from the steps of Christ, and said they were to be condemned or were members of the devil. But, woe to them who see the pope doing works directly at variance with Christ and yet call him most holy father, for it is written, "Woe unto them that call evil good and good evil," Isaiah 5 : 20, for by their lying flattery they deceive both themselves and him. For, again,

---

[1] *Pastor et idolum.* So the Vulgate. The Rev. Vs. has "worthless shepherd."

[2] Augustine's Letters [*Nic. Fathers*, 1: 272, 324, 545].

it is written: "O my people, they that call thee blessed, they deceive thee, and destroy the way of thy paths. The Lord standeth to judge," Isaiah 3 : 12. For, if those learned in the law would boldly speak the truth about the pope and the cardinals and not flatter them out of fear or in hope of promotion to benefices, then the popes might at times recognize themselves and not allow themselves to be venerated as gods. But, because both parties sin in hypocritically rejoicing over honors and beatification [allowing themselves to be called and treated as blessed], and are tickled over such lying adulation, so necessarily both parties shall be hurled down. For the prophet says, Isaiah 9 : 16: "They that bless this people and lead them astray and they that are blessed will be hurled down." And who these are, the prophet shows in the verses immediately preceding: "The Lord will destroy in one day from Israel head and tail, crooked and refractory. The elder and honorable man, he is the head and the prophet who teaches lies, he is the tail." Lo, the one prophet expounds the head and the tail. Let him, therefore, that will, take note that he is called honorable and elder father whom they call head. And with probability it may be said of every pope, from the first one to the last, who lives at variance with Christ and whom they have called or will call head and holy father—that he is that honorable and elder one, because this succession began a long time ago. But the tail, which by flattery or false show or by vain excuses covers the works of that elder father, and the prophet who teaches lies, represent the learned clergy which teaches that the pope is neither God nor man but a mixed God or an earthly God and also teaches that the pope is able to give me another's good and that I will be safe, because the pope is able to depose a bishop without cause, is able to dispense at variance with the apostles' teaching, at variance with his oath, his vow and with natural law, and no one has a right to say to him, Why doest thou this?

For he himself may lawfully say: "Thus I will, thus I command; let my will be the reason." And so he is impeccable; and he cannot commit simony because all things are his. Therefore, he may do with his as he pleases, for he is able even to command angels and to save men or damn them as he chooses, and, what is more, he is able to bend not only the pope but the subject people and those who will not bow themselves in flattery and in a worldly way before him as the head and the honorable one and bend their knees to him. For the pope, the people and themselves also they lead astray into wrong paths by sowing such lies. And it· is about them, as is probable, that Christ spoke the words: "There shall arise pseudo-Christs and pseudo-prophets and shall show great signs and wonders so as to lead astray if possible even the elect," Matt. 24 : 24.

But, returning to the statement of St. Jerome, it is said that "it was, presumably, of his good works that he spoke in addressing that pope" [Damasus]. But whether St. Jerome had a revelation with regard to this pope's predestination and the righteousness of his works is unknown. In the second place, it is said that St. Jerome addressed the pope in this way, secure about the faith of which he wrote, because in that letter he wrote expressly what is contained in Scripture and in the symbols of the church, as appears to one who wishes to read the letter. And hence he says: "This is the faith which we have learned in the catholic church, and which we have always held." It is clear how the conditional element in St. Jerome's statement is to be understood. For, if that confession of his was confirmed by the judgment of that pope, whosoever might impugn it would be a heretic. For presumably he said and affirmed nothing by revelation or certitude of the faith he was setting forth which the pope would not confirm except it were true, and he would not change anything rightly held in the church long before. But it would be insane to believe that a conclusion is to be drawn from this concerning every Roman pope, for it is certain that many of them

have ratified errors and heresies, for they were heretics themselves.

Hence the text, *Dist.* 24, *in nomine Domini* [Friedberg,
1 : 78], describes how the pope laments because that [apos-
tolical] seat has often been smitten with the frequent din[1]
of simoniacal heresy.   Therefore, wishing to provide a remedy for the future, he [Nicolas II] decreed that, at the pope's
death, the cardinals, the religious, clerics and laymen, shall
meet together for the election of a suitable pope from the
bosom of that church or from the bosom of some other, wherever the most fit might happen to be found, and that the
privilege of the emperor, Henry, should always be honored,
namely, that he and his successors shall have the right to
be present at the pope's election.[2]   But a true pope being
elected, he shall have before his consecration, following the
example of St. Gregory, power to dispose of the goods of the
church, and every one who should hinder this ordinance he
might anathematize as a most wicked antichrist.   Here the
Glossa ordinaria says, that at this point is plainly touched
upon what is read in the *Chronicles*, how Benedict, who suc-
ceeded Stephen, was ejected from the pontifical office, and
for a money consideration John, bishop of Sabina, was made
pope, to whom the name Sylvester was given.   But he in
turn was cast down and Benedict restored, and Benedict was
again ejected and the papacy given to John, archpriest at
the Latin Gate, on whom was imposed the name Gregory.
And he was cast down by the emperor Henry and transferred beyond the mountains; and these things all happened
in a single year.   On account of these things that privilege
was given to Henry.[3]   Thus much the *Glossa* of the *Decretum.*

[1] *Tunsionibus;* probably from *tundo,* to beat, to thump. I do not find the
word in DuCange.

[2] The decree of Nicolas II, 1059, confining election of the pope to the college of cardinals. The rule was soon after set aside in the case of the election
of Gregory VII, 1073. The emperor, Henry III, at Sutri, 1046, dictated the
election of his chaplain as Clement II. For Nicolas's edict, Mirbt, p. 110.

[3] The reference here is to the synod of Sutri, 1046, when Henry III was
present, having come south to Rome to rid the church of the scandal of having

And, as is gathered from the *Chronicles* of Martin, Castrensis and Rudolph,[1] (1) Pope Boniface was presiding at Rome A. D. 420, and Eulalius having been ordained in opposition to him and the church being divided on the question, both by the command of Honorius Augustus left the city; and, Eulalius being condemned, Boniface, who had previously been ordained, was by the command of Augustus restored to the apostolic seat.[2]

(2) A. D. 493 Laurentius was ordained over against Pope Symmachus by a dissident faction.[3]

(3) A. D. 768 the schismatic pope Constantine was deprived of his eyes, and Stephen was made pope. The latter assembled a synod at Rome and reordained those who had been ordained by the schismatic Constantine.[4]

(4) A. D. 873 Pope Anastasius invaded the præsulate as against Benedict.[5]

three contemporary popes and to receive the imperial crown. As before said, Benedict IX, a dissolute fellow, was opposed by an antipope, Sylvester III, elected by the Romans, and, wishing to marry, sold the papacy to Gregory VI. All three were disposed of at Sutri and Clement II elected.

[1] Martinus Polonus, d. 1278, whose work, *de Imperatoribus et Pontificibus*, was one of the most esteemed chronicles of the later M. A. Rudolph is Radulphus Glaber, a monk of Cluny, about 1050, who wrote *Historia sui temporis*, Migne, vol. 142. Castrensis was Ranulph of Higden.

[2] After the death of Zosimus, Eulalius was chosen pope by a part of the clergy and consecrated 418. The day before the consecration Boniface I was elected by another part of the clergy. Honorius recognized Boniface and expelled Eulalius, who died 423, a year after Boniface, refusing to stand again for election to the papal chair.

[3] Symmachus, 498–514. Both were consecrated, one in the Lateran and Laurentius in the S. Maria Magg. Laurentius at first submitted and was made bishop of Nocera, Campania, but his party pressed his case, and it was not till four years had passed that, forced by the decrees of synods and the attitude of Theodoric, he withdrew permanently from Rome.

[4] Stephen III, 768–772. The antipope Constantine II, the creature of his brother, Duke Toto, was deposed by a Lateran synod, 769, which also enacted a rule against the election of laymen to the papal chair. Constantine's eyes were put out, as Huss has said before.

[5] Benedict III, 855–858. Anastasius had resisted Benedict's predecessor, Leo IV, and, receiving the support of the imperial legates, forced his way into the Lateran and had Benedict torn from his throne. The clergy and people of Rome were against him and he was obliged to withdraw. Of his end there is no credible account.

(5) A. D. 907 Pope Leo presided, and against him rose up Christophorus.[1]

(6) A. D. 968 a synod of bishops was collected from all Italy, and Pope John was disgraced for nefarious crimes, and, because he excused himself and delayed to come, another, Leo, up to that time a layman, was made pope by a unanimous election and with the emperor's consent. And so Leo performed ordinations and did other acts which were apostolic. Not long afterward the Romans, proving faithless to the emperor, received Pope John. He assembled a synod and deposed Leo and set aside his acts, and it was decreed by Leo that the synod was not to be called a synod but a brothel because it favored adultery. Whoever, therefore, were condemned by his decree were commanded to present his proscription of them in a writing containing these things, "My father had nothing for himself, gave nothing to me," and so these remained deposed from those positions which they had who had not been ordained by Leo. This Pope John was found lying with a man's wife, was struck through during the commission of adultery, and died without the Lord's viaticum.[2]

(7) It happened that the Romans—violating the oath which they had made to the emperor never to elect a pope without his consent or the consent of his son Otto—made Benedict pope. But the emperor, besieging Rome, so afflicted the Romans that they promised to receive Leo as pope, and so Benedict was dismissed.[3]

[1] Leo V, 903, pope, died in prison. Christophorus was deposed by Leo and seems to have been murdered.

[2] John XII, one of the dissolute popes, 955–964, was condemned by a Roman synod for perjury, murder, sacrilege and almost every crime and his place filled by the election of Leo VIII, but John was received again by the Roman people. While the emperor Otto was on his way to Rome to settle matters, John, as Huss says, was put to death while he was in the act of adultery, an act worthy of Marozia, whose grandson he was.

[3] Benedict V, 964–966. Leo VIII, at Otto I's instance, was elected pope. After Otto's departure from Rome, John XII entered the city and expelled Leo. John died 964, and the Romans elected Benedict V. The emperor set

(8) A. D. 1047 Benedict, who got into the papacy by simony, an illiterate man, had another consecrated pope with himself to perform the ecclesiastical duties for him—namely, Sylvester; and, as this did not please many, a third was brought in who was to fill the places of the other two.

(9) A. D. 1046, when at Rome one pope was contending against two and two against one over the papacy, King Henry proceeded to Rome against them; and when they were deposed, Clement was chosen to preside. By him Henry was consecrated emperor, and the Romans swore never again to elect a pope without the emperor's consent. Then was constituted the law, III *Reg.*, 2, that, following the example of Solomon, the king in case of necessity is bound to depose the pontiff. Then King Henry humbly received at the hands of Clement consecration, and thereafter without such confirmation no other was to be regarded as emperor. But why was this necessary in accordance with the law of God, since, prior to the institution of the cardinals, it was held that the pope was elected by the people of Rome?[1]

(10) A. D. 1068, while two were contending at Rome for the papacy and Alexander, after he had established his innocence against the charge of simony, was received and Cadalus, bishop of Parma, condemned. Hence, it was said: "Cadalus, in Parma, was made by me bow and arms. Cadalus died; Parma was made a ruin."[2]

(11) A. D. 1083 Henry broke into the city of Rome and placed Wibert in the apostolic chair. Hildebrand departed to Beneventum, where he remained till his death.[3]

him aside and restored Leo VIII, Benedict being placed under charge of the archbishop of Hamburg and dying in Germany.

[1] The three popes disposed of at Sutri, 1046.

[2] Alexander II, 1061–1073, gave offense by being elected by the cardinals and entering upon the papacy without the emperor's confirmation. Agnes, the queen regent and mother of Henry IV, called a synod, which elected Cadalus, of Parma, known as Honorius II. The latter died 1072.

[3] This is the famous Wibert of Ravenna, Clement III, who was elected antipope at the instance of Henry IV against Henry's opponent, Gregory VII.

(12) A. D. 1087 Desiderius, called also Victor, was made pope against Clement.[1]

(13) A. D. 1091 there were, it is said, two, who were called Roman pontiffs, at discord one with the other and drawing about the church of God, divided between themselves, Urban, who first had been bishop of Ostia, and Clement, called Wibert, who had been bishop of Ravenna.

(14) A. D. 1130, when Innocent was ruling as pope, Peter Leoni thrust himself in and was called Anacletus, and Innocent passed over into France.[2] Hence it is said:

"Peter has Rome, Gregory the whole world."

(15) A. D. 1189 Pope Albert ruled, against whom Octavian thrust himself in, but he died in schism, and so also Guido of Crema; but John, who had thrust himself in, was reconciled.[3]

And so within a centenary of years from the time of the dotation of the church a notable contention occurred between popes; and in our times there was begun the two-headed schism between Urban VI, who lived at Rome, and Robert of Geneva, who held his seat in Avignon; and this two-headed split lasted between their successors until A. D. 1409. In that year both popes were condemned at the council of Pisa as heretics, namely Gregory and Benedict, and Alexander, of the Franciscan order, was elected pope.[4] And when

---

Wibert, "the usurper of the holy see," was the only one of his enemies that Gregory refused to forgive on his death-bed. Henry was crowned emperor by Wibert in St. Peter's. Hildebrand died 1085 at Salerno, not at Beneventum.

[1] Victor III, 1087, was the legitimate pope as against Wibert.

[2] Anacletus II, antipope 1130–1138, the son of a Jew of Rome and elected by the majority of the cardinals. Innocent II, 1130–1143, elected by a minority had the support of Bernard and the emperor. Anacletus's last supporter was Roger of Sicily. See Schaff, *Ch. Hist.*, V, part 1, 94 *sq.*

[3] Albert was antipope at the time of Pascal II; Octavian, Victor IV, under Alexander III in the days of Barbarossa, and Guido at Victor's death, 1164, elected antipope under the name of Pascal III.

[4] At the death of Gregory XI, the Avignon pope, in Rome, 1378, Urban VI, an Italian, was made pope under circumstances the most sensational. See Schaff, *Ch. Hist.*, V, part 2, 117 *sqq.* This election was followed by the election

he died there remained three to contend for the papacy,
Pope John XXIII, Gregory in Sicily and Benedict in Spain.
But from what moving cause this diabolical strife originally
came, even the blind can discern, namely, from the dotation.
Hence, St. Jerome, in his *Lives of the Fathers*, wrote: "As
the church increased in possessions, she decreased in virtues." And what is set down as a probability by the *Chronicles* seems clear, as narrated by Castrensis, 4 : 86, who describes how, 'at the time of the dotation of the church, an
angelic voice[1] was heard in the air, saying, that day poison
was infused in the holy church of God. For, however it
came to be, this is true: either a good angel or a devil uttered
the voice, because it is certain that demons, who rejoice when
they do evil, are bound to serve God and to be messengers
of the truth, and it becomes God by the mammon of iniquity
to announce in advance to the people their danger.' From
these things the faithful are able to form a judgment whether
any one, by the mere fact that he is called pope, is indeed
the chief pontiff of the church and the most blessed father,
and in matters of the faith learned above all worshippers of
Christ, and whether he is the head of God's holy church.

of the notorious French cardinal, Robert of Geneva, by the Avignonese cardinals, and the papal schism followed, lasting 1378-1417, with one pope at
Rome and another at Avignon. The council of Pisa, 1409, attempted to bring
the schism to an end by the election of Peter Philargi, cardinal of Milan, Alexander V, who appears prominently in the history of Huss. He lived only a year
after his election, and was followed by John XXIII, who was deposed by the
council of Constance, 1415. After receiving the resignation of Gregory XII, of
the Roman line, and deposing Benedict XIII, the last of the Avignon popes,
the council, 1417, finally terminated the schism by the election of Martin V.

[1] Rolls Series, 5 : 130. Trevisa's translation runs: "The olde enemy cryde
openliche in the ayer." Castrensis quotes Jerome's words as given by Huss,
and he adds that "when Constantine was baptized of Sylvester, he opened
the prisons, destroyed the temples of the idols, built new and restored old
churches, endowing them with spiritual privileges and immunities and assigned
one-tenth of all his possessions to the churches and, at the repairing of St.
Peter's, turned the first spade of earth and carried ten baskets full of earth
on his shoulders," etc.

CHAPTER XVII

HUSS'S RESISTANCE TO PAPAL AUTHORITY

FURTHER, as for the principal thing according to which they believe all their sayings to be necessary or true, the afore-mentioned doctors lay down that " obedience is due to the apostolic see and to prelates from inferiors in all things whatsoever, where the purely good is not prohibited or the purely evil commanded, but also in that which is intermediate, which, in view of the mode, place, time or person, may be either good or bad in accordance with the Saviour's statement, Matt. 23 : 2: 'Whatsoever they bid you, these do and observe.' " And they add the following from Bernard's Letter to Adam the Monk [Migne's ed., 182 : 95], which begins thus: "'If thou remain in love, the law for obedience is fixed as in the tree of the knowledge of good and evil which was in the midst of paradise.' In such things certainly it is not right to submit our interpretation to the opinion of the magisters, and in such things neither the command nor the prohibition of prelates is in any wise to be spurned."

And they add: "But some of the clergy in the kingdom of Bohemia refuse to agree to this, endeavoring, as much as in them lies, to lead the faithful people to disobedience towards prelates and to irreverence towards the papal, episcopal, sacerdotal and clerical dignities, not giving attention to that which St. Augustine says in the words (Sermon 8): 'If thou hast fasted, hast made prayer night and day, if thou hast been in ashes or begging, if thou hast done nothing else except what is prescribed for thee in the law and thou hast been wise in thine own sight and not obedient to

thy father—understand, not bodily father, but spiritual—
thou hast lost all virtues. Therefore obedience is worth
more than all the other moral virtues.'"

By the combination of the above sayings the doctors
mix up the false with the true, flattery with fear, and these
three things are involved in these words: "Certain of the
clergy"—here having in mind our party—"refuse to agree
to this, endeavoring as much as in them lies to lead the faithful people to disobedience." See what a false lie this is, by
which they indicate that we are become seducers of the
people, when it is (1) not the purpose of our side to seduce the
people from real obedience, but that the people may be one,
governed harmoniously by the law of Christ. (2) The purpose of our side is that the rules of antichrist shall not
seduce or separate the people from Christ, but that the law
of Christ shall honestly rule in connection with the customs
of the people so far as they are approved by God's law. (3)
The purpose of our side is that the clergy live honestly according to the doctrine of Jesus Christ, laying aside pomp,
avarice and luxury. (4) Our side wishes and preaches that
the church militant, in its different parts which God has
ordained, be honestly commingled, namely, of Christ's priests
those who administer his law in purity, and from the world
the nobles who press for the observance of the ordinances of
Christ and the common people, both these parts serving in
accordance with Christ's law. Therefore, let the doctors bestow this wrong on our side. But the flattery which they
show to prelates and the fear with which they would affright
our side are involved in the words: "endeavouring to lead
the faithful people to disobedience towards prelates, and irreverence towards the papal, episcopal, sacerdotal and clerical dignities." Blessed be Christ Jesus that they have not
dared to lay on us the calumny of disobedience to Jesus
Christ—or perhaps they have forgotten to do so, for to serve
him is to reign, and obedience rendered to him avails so much

that it is of no advantage to obey any one except in so far as such obedience is obedience to our God.

Wherefore, as to that saying of the doctors, "that obedience is due to the apostolic see of the Roman church and to prelates by inferiors in all things," etc. [we proceed as follows]:

As for obedience, this is to be said: It is to be noted that obedience first is to be understood by analogy or in a very general sense, as is the loyalty of any created thing whatsoever, in respect to the divine will which all created things obey, without resistance—*repugnantia*—even as a stone obeys by falling or tending downwards, or fire by rising and the sun by illuminating, and so in regard to all other created things. Or else obedience is rendered with resistance, as the devil or a damned man who obeys by suffering because he must. And in this way the saints speak when they say that all things obey their Creator, and man alone, the sinner, does not obey; that is, the sinner does not submit to the rule of the Creator without resistance on the part of his will. But obedience, so far as it is an act of virtue or is virtue, is thus described by some, namely, obedience is the subjection of our own will to the will and judgment of a superior in things lawful and honest—or obedience is the disposition to follow voluntarily a superior's command in things lawful and honest.

The first kind is exhibited in acts, the second in the disposition. And from these definitions, it follows that there is no such thing as obedience in the case of things unlawful. And so obedience is correlated to that which is good, disobedience to that which is evil. But the first definition seems to me to be wanting in this, that obedience is a more general thing than submission, since obedience is becoming in God and submission is not, for God obeyed a man's voice, for it is said, Joshua 10 : 14: "There was no day like to it before or after, that God hearkened unto the voice of a man and fought for Israel." Nevertheless God, the Trinity, was not subject to man, or under a man as a lesser to a greater. Nor is all obedience to the will of a superior, for Christ was subject to his parents, Luke 2 : 51. And it is certain that, as among others born of women a greater than John the Baptist hath not arisen, so Christ was infinitely greater than Joseph or Mary.

Therefore, as Christ did nothing but what he ought to have done, it is plain that the greater ought to be subject to the lesser, that is, be obedient to him; for whatever the fountain of religion, as the chief of all, may teach, that is to be held. Hence Christ, who was of a twofold nature, was obedient in a twofold sense, for (1) he obeyed God, his Father, in all things, as being on the side of his humanity less than the Father, for he himself said: "The Father is greater than I," John 14 : 28. And (2) he was obedient to his parents as to the lesser. And he was also obedient to others and endured willingly at their hands, and he is obedient to true and holy Christians, supplying their need and filling up their desires. And it is clear that the conclusion does not follow: because one obeys another, therefore he is less than the other. Similarly, it does not follow that, because one serves another, therefore he is less than the other. For Christ obeyed another man and served him, wherefore he said, Isaiah 43 : 24: "Thou hast made me to serve in thy sins, thou hast put upon me toil in thy iniquities. I am he that blotteth out thy iniquities for my own sake, and I will not remember thy sins. Put me in remembrance that we may be judged together." He also said: "The Son of Man came not to be ministered unto but to minister," Matt. 20 : 28. And the apostle was speaking of him when he said: "Christ emptied himself, taking the form of a servant," Phil. 2 : 7. And it is also said, John 13 : 4: "He girded himself with a towel, poured water in a basin and washed his disciples' feet." Hence he is not falsely but truly a bishop, a servant of the servants of God,[1] not only a Roman bishop but, in a general way he is the bishop of all the churches. He is himself the bishop of Prague. But, as he is a servant or minister not by the compulsion of civil law, because a life where activities are moved by compulsion did not befit him, so he is the bishop of souls, not of secular riches or possessions, for he as bishop, lowly and meek, mounted the foal of an ass, as is attested by Zech. 9 : 9. And he said: "Foxes have holes, and the birds of heaven have nests, but the Son of Man hath not where to lay his head," Matt. 8 : 20. Why was this? The apostle gives the reason when he says: "Ye know the grace of our Lord Jesus Christ, who[2] for our sakes became poor, that we through his poverty might be made rich," II Cor. 8 : 9.

The second definition of obedience is also defective, as is seen from what has already been said, because it states that obedience is the disposition to follow the command of a superior. For all obedience is not with respect to a superior to whom the obedience is rendered, or with respect to a command. For sometimes obedience is with respect to an inferior, as has been said already. And obedience is also related to counsel, as when a man obeys the counsels of God, which he is not under obligation to obey under any pain of mortal sin. Obedience is also related to entreaty, as when God obeyed at Joshua's entreaty, bidding the sun stand still over Gibeon and not be moved towards its setting. Hence Jerome, *Ep.* 113, says: "God sometimes seems to obey the prayers of the saints." And it is clear that obedience is sometimes a fulfilment of a command, sometimes of a counsel, and sometimes of an entreaty, which is neither a command nor a counsel. And sometimes it is the result of persuasion, the way in which the devil persuaded Christ, Matt. 4 : 5, to go with him to

---

[1] A title used by Gregory the Great in his letters, and common in Huss's time; Boniface's bull *Unam sanctam* opens in that way: "Bon., bishop, the servant of the servants of God."

[2] *Qui.* Vulgate: *quoniam*, because.

the holy city and to a very high mountain, and Christ in a most virtuous way consented to this and fulfilled the devil's will. And so in view of this distinction, it is to be said that to obey is to truly fulfil another's will, and for this reason obedience always involves the relation of one to another. But this is not the case with other virtues, as for example, continence and temperance.

From these things it is gathered that obedience, like humility, is of three kinds: namely, of the greater to the less—which is the highest form of obedience;—of an equal to an equal—which is the intermediate form;—and of the less to the greater—which is the lowest form. To the last the first definition of obedience applies—namely, that obedience is the subjection of one's own will to the will of a superior in things lawful and right. And it may be defined thus: obedience is an act of the will of a rational creature by virtue of which he voluntarily and intelligently submits himself to his superior: and such obedience is related to what is good, just as disobedience is related to what is evil. In both cases, however, it pertains to the rational creature and his subjection. And secondly, it refers fundamentally to activity, suffering, silence or any other activity of this sort to which the command is directed.

Hence, as all sin is disobedience and as disobedience is related to sin, and as every good man obeys God, so every sinner is disobedient. But obedience may be in the understanding and the will—in the understanding, which discerns that obedience ought to be rendered in given cases; and in the will, which yields consent to him who commands. But its results are shown in certain powers within and in an external effect. And, because there is found in Scripture good obedience and evil disobedience, it is clear what the good is; and of the evil it was said to Adam, Gen. 3 : 17: "Because thou hast hearkened unto the voice of thy wife rather than unto my voice, cursed is the ground for thy sake." It is also said, "Why do ye also transgress the commandments of God, because of your traditions," Matt. 15 : 3, and, "We must obey God rather than men," Acts 5 : 29.

Hence, whenever obedience is rendered to man rather than God, as Adam obeyed Eve, then it is always evil obedience, so that every one obeying evilly is disobedient to God; and so it is that the same man may be obedient and disobedient, with respect to the different persons commanding or to different commands. And it does not follow that, because a beloved man[1] is disobedient, therefore he is not obedient, but it does follow that the man is not obedient to him with respect to whom he is disobedient or with respect to whose commands he is disobedient. And it is clear that to obey in one's brotherhood [religious community] is to fulfil the will of the one giving commands, and this is well, as when a man or a created spirit living in grace fulfils the lawful will of the one giving commands. But to obey is bad when either living in sin one fulfils the will of a superior as to a given command, as when one who lives in luxury, fasts from respect to the command; or, secondly, when one fulfils a bad command against God. In view of these things it is clear that it is impossible for a rational creature to be virtuous morally unless he is obedient to his God.

And so it must be known that, according to St. Thomas [Aquinas] 2 : 104, *art.* 5 [Migne's ed., 3 : 798],[2] obedience is threefold, namely, sufficient, perfect and unreasoning. Sufficient obedience is that which obeys only in those things where the obligation is of natural law and does not go be-

---

[1] " Beloved man," literally, *Sortes*, an abbreviation for Socrates and a general term common with writers in the Middle Ages for a person dear to us. Huss uses it in his *de Corpore*, Flajshans, ed., p. 22, and very frequently in his *Com. on the Lombard's Sentences*. "This human species is Sortes [Socrates], this Plato," p. 47. "Sortes and Plato are one and the same thing, *res*—and so do not really—*realiter*—differ," p. 54. "The body of Christ is not in the sacrament as Sortes is in a definite place and only in one place at one time," p. 566, etc.

[2] The distinction is taken from Th. Aquinas. Huss gives in his own language the substance of Thomas's treatment.

yond the limits of its own station. That is sufficient obedience by which any one obeys in those things to which he is expressly obligated, and examples of this there are in holy Scripture. For children are bound to obey their parents, according to the apostle where he says: "Children, obey your parents in all things," Col. 3 : 20. This is to be understood only to apply to those things which concern the outer course of life and household care, as Thomas says. Similarly, servants are bound to obey their masters: "Obey your masters according to the flesh in all things," Col. 3 : 22, and, "Servants, be in subjection to your masters in all fear, not only to the good and gentle, but also to the froward," I Peter 2 : 18. These texts are to be understood only of those things which apply to servile acts lawful to be performed, as Thomas also says. Wives are held to obey their husbands according to the words of the apostle, as above, and also of Peter [I Peter 3 : 1]: "Wives, be in subjection to your husbands in the Lord." This is to be understood only of those things which pertain to external marital conduct so far as such conduct is lawful.

Similarly, all Christians are bound to obey the secular power, each in his own rank, as the apostle says, Titus 3 : 1: "Put them in mind to be in subjection to rulers and powers," and, Romans 13 : 1, "Let every soul be subject unto the higher powers." Here the apostle proves that every man is in duty bound to obey his superiors, both in secular and spiritual affairs, because God's servants are ordained, the good to be guided, purged and to praise; but the evil to be corrected, punished and to wrath, because there is no power but of God, and he that resisteth the power resisteth the ordinance of God. With this Thomas agrees, 2 : 14, *art.* 6 [Migne's ed., 3 : 798]. And all this subjection or obedience is understood among those ranks over which the superiors have lawful authority, and in those cases when they command righteous commands and not otherwise. The

Glossa ordinaria also agrees in its comment on the words:
"the powers that be are ordained of God" [Romans 13 : 1].
The Master of Sentences also agrees, 2 : 44 [Migne's ed., p.
246].

Perfect obedience is that whereby the person obeying
places all his willing and not willing—*velle et nolle*—in the
will of his prelate, to do the acts commanded, so long as the
command does not gainsay the divine will or good morals
or the necessities of life, and so long as it does not conflict
with the commands and counsels of the Lord Jesus Christ.
And because obedience appertains to commands and counsels, the difference is to be noted between a command and an
evangelical counsel, so far as they may be distinguished as
opposites.[1]

A precept or command is a general teaching of God, obligating every man under pain of mortal sin—namely, in cases
in which he has fallen away from the command. Hence the
saints who for a period of their life lived hypocritically sinned
mortally for that period. So also the damned, by persistent false living sin persistently in hell.

A counsel is a special teaching of God, obligating under
pain only of venial sin and for the period of this life. And
so the doctors say that precepts are for the imperfect, obligating them for the reason that they are servants. But

[1] Huss is making the distinction between the mandates of the Scriptures—
præcepta—such as the duties enjoined by the Ten Commandments and the
evangelical counsels or counsels of perfection, *evangelica consilia*. He takes
it up in his *Com. on the Lombard*, pp. 482, 488 *sqq.* The counsels are voluntary
poverty, voluntary chastity and absolute obedience to the earthly ecclesiastical superior, as to an abbot or a bishop. Origen made the distinction in the
third century and based it on two kinds of morality. The mandates are for all
Christians and must be kept in order to salvation; the counsels of perfection
for the higher Christians or saints. By observing the counsels of perfection one
secures a higher grade of merit and a higher place in heaven. I Cor. 7 : 25
and Christ's words to the rich man are taken to justify the distinction. The
Protestant Reformers set it aside as unscriptural and tending to place those
who take the three vows above all ordinary mortals who follow Christ in the
usual daily avocations of life. Thomas Aquinas sets it forth at length, *Summa*,
1 : 2 *sq.*, 108 *sqq.* [Migne's ed., 2 : 894 *sqq.*].

counsels are for the perfect which obligate above what is commonly required by reason and everywhere and always under pain of mortal sin. And that they may shun the occasion of sin, counsels advise them as friends. Hence, if a saint should make a divine counsel an occasion of falling from his height into mortal sin—that would be by the breaking of the first command and not by a refusal to obey the divine counsel. But in the heavenly country where the danger and occasion of sin do not exist, the counsel is not spoken of in this way. For in the heavenly country there is no voluntary poverty nor is there any savor of indigence. This Christ counselled when he said, Matt. 19 : 21: "If thou wilt be perfect, go and sell all[1] that thou hast."

The second obedience is by co-operative submission to a superior, of which it is said, "If any one would come after me, let him deny himself," Luke 9 : 23, as does the beloved disciple. And in heaven there is no struggling against chastity, of which it is said: "There are eunuchs who have made themselves eunuchs for the kingdom of heaven's sake," Matt. 19 : 12. Nor is there found there any retaliation against adversaries, of which it is said: "Do good to them which hate you," Matt. 5 : 44. Nor is there any patient endurance of those who smite violently, of which it is said: "Whosoever shall smite thee on the right cheek, turn to him the other also," Matt. 5 : 39. Nor are there any supererogatory works of mercy there, about which it is said, "Give to every one that asketh of thee," Luke 6 : 30; nor any refraining from words and oaths, of which it is written: "For every idle word which men shall speak they shall give account in the day of judgment," Matt. 12 : 36, and, "I say unto you, swear not at all," Matt. 5 : 33. Nor will there be left the occasion to commit sin, of which it is said: "If thine eye cause thee to stumble, or foot, or hand, pluck it out and cut it off and cast it from thee," Matt. 5 : 29. Nor will there be any easement of ac-

---

[1] *Omnia* is not given in the Vulgate.

tivity, lest by defect of pure purpose we fall into hypocrisy, of
which it is said: "Take heed that ye do not your alms to
be seen of men," Matt. 6 : 1.   Nor will there be any example
of conforming one's works to one's words such as Christ spoke
of: "The Pharisees say and do not," Matt. 23 : 3.   And so he
counselled the hypocrite to "first cast out the beam out of
his own eye," Luke 6 : 42.   Nor will there be there the care of
this world, choking out the Word, of which it is said: "Be
not anxious, saying what shall we eat," etc., Matt. 6 : 31.
Nor will there be any reproving of the brother, of which it
is said: "If thy brother sin against thee, go and rebuke him
between thyself and him alone," Matt. 18 : 15.   All these
twelve counsels, in their primary form, they will not hold
it necessary to put into practice, but they will observe them
in a secondary sense and form, as eternal commands, which
are healthful in the way unto life.

And would that the clergy, and especially the religious
who value the counsels of men, and that all others who depend on human counsel might hearken unto these counsels
of the heavenly physician, for undoubtedly they are pre-
servatives against possible sins, purgatives for sins already
committed, and conservatives of health already attained.
Therefore, all pilgrims are obligated to keep these counsels
or some of them, as occasion demands, on the pain of venial
sin.   And in order to pronounce judgment in these cases the
best judge will be cautious in regard to himself when he is
watching out that he may not fall into sin by failure to observe any one of these twelve—that he does not act quickly,
lest he contemn a divine counsel.

And it is to be noted that the twelfth counsel, namely,
the rebuke of a brother, sometimes is a counsel when it concerns venial offences, and sometimes a command when it
concerns the rebuke of mortal sins.   And this second kind
of rebuke it belongs to every one to exercise, and it is always obligatory, but not on all occasions, for, as to place

and time, rebuke should be made when it seems likely to be useful.

Up to this point it is to be noted that human obedience is threefold—spiritual, secular and ecclesiastical—spiritual, which is due purely according to God's law, and under this kind of obedience Christ and the apostles lived and each Christian should live. Secular obedience is obedience due according to the secular code. Ecclesiastical obedience is obedience according to the regulations of the priests of the church aside from the express authority of Scripture. The first kind of obedience always excludes what is of itself evil, both on the part of the person giving the command and on the part of the person obeying. For he who commands according to God's law and he who obeys act rightly, and of both it is said: "Thou shalt do whatsoever the priests the Levites have taught, according to all I have taught them," Deut. 29 [Deut. 24 : 8].

Here it is affirmed that he who commands ought only to command things in agreement with the law, and the person obeying ought to the same extent to obey them and never act contrary to the will of God Almighty. On this I have in another place quoted Augustine, Gregory, Jerome, Chrysostom, Isidore, Bernard and Bede, as well as the Scripture and the canons. These for the sake of brevity I will pass. Only let the saying of Isidore be given, 11 : 3 [Friedberg, 1 : 672]: "He who presides, if he command anything or say anything otherwise than in accordance to God's will or what is plainly commanded in Holy Scripture, he shall be regarded as a false witness of God, or as committing sacrilege."

CHAPTER XVIII

THE APOSTOLIC SEE, OR CATHEDRA PETRI

Now that certain statements have been made about obedience, I want to return to the statement of the doctors, in which it appears that "obedience is to be rendered by inferiors to the apostolic see[1] of the Roman church, and to the prelates in all things whatsoever, where that which is purely good is not forbidden and that which is not purely evil is commanded, but also in that which is intermediate," etc.

And here consideration must be had of the apostolic see, about which many, and especially the canonists, predicate many things, who, nevertheless, are ignorant what the apostolic see is. For some think that it really is a seat of wood or stone in which the pope is wont to sit bodily. Others think that it is the Roman curia; others that it is the seat of St. Peter, in which he sat bodily; others that it is Rome; others that it is the pope's power; others still that it is the church or basilica of St. Peter. But it is to be noted that apostolic is derived from apostle, and apostle means one sent from God. The Saviour, whom God sent, said, John 3 : 34: "I speak the words of God." Hence, he also said to his disciples that "as the Father sent me, so also send I you," John 20 : 21—namely, to bear testimony to the truth, to preach the word of salvation, and, by life and teaching, to show the way of blessedness to the people.

Hence, every priest who is not seeking his own glory but

[1] The word "see" comes from *sedes*, a seat, and was interchangeable with the Greek word *thronos*, seat, and Latin *cathedra*, chair.

the honor of God, the prosperity of the church and the salvation of the people, and who does God's will and uncovers the wiles of antichrist, preaching the law of Christ—he has the marks which show that God sent him.

As to "glory," Christ said: "I receive not glory from men," John 5 : 41, and, "I seek not mine own glory," John 8 : 50. As to the second thing, he said: "I came in my Father's name and ye received me not. If another would come in his own name, him ye will receive," John 5 : 43. In regard to the third thing, Christ said: "I am come down from heaven not to do mine own will but the will of him that sent me," John 6 : 38. Christ so did because he sought the prosperity of the church and the people's salvation. As for the fourth thing, he said: "The world hateth me, because I testify of it that its works are evil," John 7 : 7. And finally Christ shows that he was sent from God to do the works of the Father: "If I do not the works of my Father, believe me not; but if I do them, though ye believe not me, believe the works," John 10 : 37.

And it is clear that the righteous conduct of a priest and his fruitful labor in Christ's Word show to the people that he is sent from God, because he does the works of the Father. Nor should a man be pope, bishop, priest or deacon unless he be so sent of God, and hence the apostle says: "How shall they preach unless they be sent?" Romans 10 : 15. Therefore, St. Augustine, *Quæstiones Orosii*, 65, thus answers the question of Orosius how we may know who are sent by God: "Recognize that one as sent by God whom the praise of a few men or rather their flattery did not choose, but him whom the best life and morals and examination have approved to the judgment of apostolic priests or all the people— the man who does not hanker after pre-eminence, who does not give money as the price of the episcopal honor. For he who hastens to secure pre-eminence, as one of the Fathers finely expresses it, 'Let him know that it does not profit

him to be a bishop, who desires pre-eminence.'" Thus
much Augustine.

It being understood by general consent what an apostle
is, we can understand what "apostolic" means. For apostolic means keeping the way of an apostle. Just as, therefore, a true Christian is one who follows Christ in his life,
so a truly apostolic man is the priest who follows the teaching of the apostles, living the life of an apostle and teaching
his doctrine. Hence, any pope is to be called apostolic so
far as he teaches the doctrine of the apostles and follows
them in works. But, if he puts the teaching of the apostles
aside, teaching in word or works what is contrary, then he
is properly called pseudo-apostolic or an apostate. Hence
Dist. 97 [79 : 9, Friedberg, 1 : 278]: If any one shall be en-
throned in the papal seat on account of money or human
favor or by the help of a popular or military uprising, without a harmonious and canonical election, he is not to be
considered apostolic but apostate. Since, therefore, the error
is greater in an active election when those electing are forced
by the devil to elect an individual whom God condemns—a
thing manifestly certain from his works and his neglect of
the spiritual office, that he is at variance with the life of the
apostles—much more does it follow that such an individual
is to be deemed not apostolic but an apostate.

Therefore, in view of these statements, the apostolic seat
may be called the life of the priest who efficiently maintains
the life of an apostle, just as the seat of an apostle is the
life of an apostle. Hence Chrysostom, *Hom.* 25, says [*Nic.
Fathers*, 10 : 395]: "That virtue of any apostle whereby he
may have been more perfect than the rest, that is his throne.
But all the virtues of Christ together are, as it were, one seat,
because he was equally perfect in all the virtues, and he
alone." See how well that saint perceives that the individual
life of each of Christ's apostles is his seat in which he reposes
by reason of his merits and for which reason he now sits in

the glory of Jesus Christ, as it is said: "Ye also shall sit upon twelve seats," Matt. 19 : 28. Here Augustine understands by seats the location of the apostles and of all holy predestinated prelates which, since it is in blessedness, cannot cease to be or suffer destruction at the hand of tyrants. But the Twelve—*duodenarius*—which is the whole number, does not indicate those twelve apostles man for man, for Iscariot ruled at that time and Paul was yet to become a part of the number.

But the seat of Christ's majesty is to be understood as the location of the eternal kingdom from which none can be removed. And that seat of Christ is his seat intrinsically, but his external seat in which he reposes, dwells and resides by grace is all the saints, just as, on the other hand, the seats of Satan in which Satan reposes, dwells and resides are all the wicked. Hence it is said: "To the angel which is in the church of Pergamos write, One like unto the Son of Man who hath a sharp two-edged sword saith, I know where thou dwellest, even where Satan's seat is," Rev. 2 : 12, 13. Here the Gloss says: "Understand, this means the places where Satan reposes." And, "Thou holdest fast my name and didst not deny my faith [even in the days of Antipas who was killed] among you, where Satan dwelleth." But as to the principal proposition, the apostolic see is the same as the cathedra—seat—of Moses, of which the Saviour said: "The scribes and Pharisees sit in Moses' cathedra," Matt. 23 : 2. But Moses' cathedra was not Moses nor an old stone or wooden seat on which Moses sat as a presiding judge. Nor is it the synagogue, but that cathedra is the authority to teach and judge the people. And this is shown by Christ's words, when he said, "in Moses' cathedra." And the words follow, "Whatsoever they say," that is, teach by the authority and doctrine of Moses, "that do." Therefore the apostolic see is the authority to teach and judge according to Christ's law, which the apostles taught, and in which men, wise and fearing the Lord, ought to sit, men in whom is the truth and who hate covetousness. For so Ex. 18 : 15 has it: "And Moses said to his father-in-law, Jethro, The people come unto me seeking the sentence of God, and when any act of false dealing has occurred they come unto me that I may judge between them and show them God's statutes and his laws." Here is meant the authority to pronounce judgment and to teach God's laws. And Jethro said to Moses: "Provide out of all the people able men who fear God, in whom is the truth and who hate covetousness, and Moses did so." At this place Lyra says: "Able to judge by reason of wisdom and experience. On this account another translation has 'wise' where we have 'able men who fear God' more than men 'in whom is the truth,' that is, the truth of life, of doctrine and righteousness, and men 'who hate covetousness,' because covetous men are easily turned away from righteousness by gifts." So much Lyra.

Would that that cathedra now had such men. And where are they to be found? Certainly in the Roman curia, where they preside over the cathedra of St. Peter, that is, sit in the authority of the apostles, which is the authority to pronounce judgment in spiritual things and teach the law of the Lord Jesus Christ, provided covetousness, unrighteousness and pride are kept out and holy living flourishes. The Saviour himself testified, saying: "Scribes and Pharisees sit in Moses' cathedra. Therefore all things whatsoever they bid you, these do and observe, but do not ye after their works, for they say and do not," Matt. 23 : 2, 3. Here certainly a life lacking the works of the law is referred to. For "they bind heavy burdens and grievous to be borne and lay them on men's shoulders." Certainly unreasonable doctrine and unrighteousness are here referred to. "But they themselves will not move them with their finger." Certainly an easy-going life! "All their works they do to be seen

of men"—certainly vainglory! "For they make broad their
phylacteries" in bulls distributed throughout the whole world,
as if they were pre-eminent in keeping God's law.   Here
is hypocrisy.   They enlarge the fringes with which they
cover their asses.[1] They love the chief places at feasts, seeking pleasure and honor of men, and "the chief cathedras
—seats—in the synagogues," that is, accumulations of church
livings, for this one wants to be a cardinal, this one a patriarch, this one an archbishop.   "And they love salutations
in the market-places," with genuflexions—that is, in public—
"and to be called of men, Rabbin" [Matt. 23 : 4 *sqq.*], that is,
our Master, and to rule the whole church of Christ.

Therefore, they also call the Roman curia the mistress
and teacher of churches. And granting the possibility of this,
these persons are seats not of Christ but of Satan, sitting
in view of their own life in the cathedra of pestilence. And
of this the Psalmist, speaking of Christ, said: "Blessed is
the man that walketh not in the counsel of the ungodly,
nor standeth in the way of sinners, nor sitteth in the cathedra of pestilence," Psalm 1 : 1.   Here Augustine says [*Com.
on Psalms, Nic. Fathers*, 8 : 1]: "This is to be understood of
our Lord Jesus Christ, the Lord-man, who does not sit in
the cathedra of pestilence. He did not desire an earthly
kingdom with its pride, which is rightly understood to be the
cathedra of pestilence, because there is hardly a single one
who is wanting in the love of dominion and does not hanker
after glory. The pestilence is a disease widely pervasive
and involving all or nearly all people. More amply, however, the cathedra stands for pernicious doctrine whose words
work as doth a cancer." Thus much Augustine, who calls
the cathedra of pestilence the lust of dominion and pernicious doctrine, a cathedra in which the elders of the church
sit, wishing to exercise secular dominion and teaching men
to keep their doctrines more carefully than the commandments of God.

[1] *Quibus operiunt mulas.*

In the cathedra, however, that is, in the authority and in the teaching of the law, he verily sits who teaches the law and keeps the commandments of the law. Hence Augustine says on Psalm 1 : 3: "'And his delight is in the law of the Lord.' It is one thing to be in the law and another to be under the law; he who is in the law acts and does according to the law; he who is under the law is acted upon according to the law." See how clear the exposition of this holy man is. Whoso, therefore, "does and teaches, he shall be great in the kingdom of heaven," says the Saviour, Matt. 5 : 19. Truly, therefore, he sits in the cathedra of Moses or Peter who lives well and teaches well in the authority of Scripture, who adds nothing extraneous to the law, nor seeks gain or profit from the cathedra.

On the other hand, he sits ill in the cathedra who either teaches ill or lives ill, or who teaches good things and lives ill, or who neither teaches good things nor lives well. And such, alas, are many who seek the things that are their own and not the things of Jesus Christ. Of these our Saviour said: "The scribes and Pharisees sit in Moses' cathedra, for they say and do not." And a little later he says: "Woe unto you scribes and Pharisees, who shut up the kingdom of heaven against men, for ye enter not in yourselves, neither suffer ye them that are entering in to enter," Matt. 23 : 13.

And see the other part. "Ye have made void the commandment of God because of your tradition. Ye hypocrites, well did Isaiah prophesy of you, saying, This people honoreth me with their lips, but their heart is far from me. But in vain do they worship me, teaching the doctrines and commandments of men," Matt. 15 : 6. They, therefore, sit ill in the cathedra of Moses and Peter, or of Christ, who teach good things and do them not. Worse are those who neither teach nor do. Worst are those who prevent the teaching of good things. And still worst of all are they who live ill, forbid the teaching of good things and teach their own things.

All such are thieves and robbers, as said the Shepherd truly, "As many as came before me are thieves and robbers," for all such, the aforesaid, came to the sheepfold apart from Christ, ascended to the cathedra by some other way, sought the things that are their own and so they are to be called hirelings, not shepherds. Therefore, the Saviour, showing who is an hireling and not a shepherd, said: "An hireling, and he who is not the shepherd and whose own the sheep are not, beholdeth the wolf coming, and leaveth the sheep, and fleeth away, and the wolf snatcheth and scattereth the sheep," John 10 : 12. Here Augustine, Homilies on John [*Nic. Fathers*, 7 : 257–259], says: "An hireling here does not bear a good character, yet he is useful in some respects, and he is not called an hireling, unless he receives the reward from the one guiding him. Who is, therefore, that hireling who is at once both guilty and necessary? Here, brethren, let the Lord himself give us light that we may understand who is the hireling and that we be not ourselves hirelings. What is, therefore, an hireling? There are in the church certain officials of whom Paul says that they seek their own and not the things of Jesus Christ. What is it, then, to seek one's own? They who seek their own are those that do not love Christ freely, do not seek God for God's sake, who pursue after temporal goods, coveting lucre and hankering after honors from men. When these things are loved by a superior, and when he serves God for the sake of these things, whoever he may be, he is an hireling; let him not count himself among the children. For of such the Lord says: 'Verily I say unto you, they have received their reward.'" Thus far Augustine. But because men of this kind sit in the cathedra, Augustine, after interposing some things, says at the same place: "But take note how the hirelings are necessary. Many, forsooth, in the church who pursue after worldly comforts nevertheless preach Christ and through them Christ's voice is heard, and the sheep follow not the

hirelings but the voice of the Shepherd at the call of the hireling. Listen to the hirelings as they are set forth by the
Lord himself. 'Scribes,' he said, 'and Pharisees sit in Moses'
seat. Whatsoever they bid you, those things do, but whatsoever they do, do not ye.' What else did he say except
hear the voice of the shepherd when the hireling calls? For,
sitting in Moses' seat, they teach God's law; therefore God
teaches through them. But, if they seek to teach their own
things, hear them not, do them not, for certainly such people
seek their own things and not the things of Jesus Christ.
No hireling, however, has dared to say to the people of God:
'I seek thy things and not the things of Jesus Christ.'" Thus
much Augustine. At the close of this homily he uses these
words: "See, how the hireling is said to flee when he seeth
the wolf. Why? Because he careth not for the sheep.
Why does he not care for the sheep? Because he is an hireling. What is an hireling? He is one that seeketh temporal
gain, but will not dwell in the house forever." Thus much
Augustine, who shows that there are now hirelings in the
church and they sit in the cathedras, that is, in the authority
of teaching God's law.

And again Augustine, on the words, "Simon Peter drew
in the net full of great fishes," John 21 : 11 [*Nic. Fathers*,
7 : 443], says, "He is least who breaks in deeds what he
teaches in words."; and further on: "Finally, to show that
those least ones are reprobates, who teach in words, speaking good things, which they break by living ill, and that
they will not be as the least in the life eternal and will not
even be there, after Christ had said, 'he shall be called least
in the kingdom of heaven,' Christ added: 'for I say unto you
except your righteousness shall exceed the righteousness of
the scribes and Pharisees, ye shall not enter the kingdom of
heaven.' These certainly are the scribes and Pharisees who
sit in Moses' seat, and of these Christ said: 'Whatsoever they
bid you, do, but whatsoever they do, do not ye, for they

say and do not, they teach in words and break in their lives.'"
Similarly, it is said, Psalm 119 : 2: "Blessed are they that keep
his testimonies, that seek him with a whole heart."

From what has just been said it is clear that the cathedra of Moses or the apostolic seat is the authority to teach
God's law, that is, the family of holy popes or of bishops
succeeding the apostles, which family, as it chiefly thinks of
God's honor, so it chiefly takes care for it and most profitably looks out for the holy church and most helpfully for
both superior and subject—not by preferring the unworthy,
not in putting aside the more fit, not in confirming without
examination an ecclesiastical office to any one for gain or blood
relationship or private personal tie.

And, further, it is clear, as concerning the apostolic commands, as said the lord of Lincoln[1] in the following reply to
the letters of the Roman pontiff about preferring a certain
relative to a stall in Lincoln church: "The apostolic commands I fully obey with filial affection, devotedly and reverently.   Indeed, I oppose and resist those who oppose
themselves to the apostolic commands, myself zealous for
the paternal honor.   To do both I consider myself held by
reason of my sonship and out of regard to the divine com-

---

[1] Robert Grosseteste, the famous bishop of Lincoln, 1235–1253, was one of
the chief English ecclesiastics of the Middle Ages.   He was a scholar and pa-
tron of learning as well as a vigorous and independent episcopal administrator.
The letters, quoted here and further on, are found in Luard's ed., Rolls Series,
1864, pp. 435, 437.   Grosseteste made bold protest against Innocent IV's
appointment of his nephew, Fred. of Lavagna to a stall at Lincoln.   It was
one of the boldest protests made against the custom of appointing Italians to
rich English livings.   Matthew Paris referred to the papal exactions upon
England as "bloodsucking extortion."   Shakespeare expressed a wide-spread
feeling, *King John*, 3 : 1:

> "That no Italian priest
> Shall tithe or toil in our dominions."

Although Grosseteste on more than one occasion resisted the pope, he did
not at one time deny the pope's right to "dispose freely of all ecclesiastical
benefices," as he wrote, 1238 to the papal legate Otho, Luard's ed., p. 145.
But in the letter from which Huss quotes, he said: "I disobey, I resist, I rebel."
Huss knew of Grosseteste through Wyclif's quotations, but, as is also probable,
at first hand, as Grosseteste's MSS. are in the Prague library.

mandment. Indeed, apostolic commands are not and cannot be other than apostolic teachings and teachings of our Lord Jesus Christ himself, the teacher of the apostles." Thus far he of Lincoln. Therefore, Christ's faithful disciple ought to consider how a command emanates from the pope, whether it is the express command of any apostle or of Christ's law or whether it has its foundation in Christ's law, and this being known to be the case, he ought to obey a command of this kind reverently and humbly. But, if he truly knows that a pope's command is at variance with Christ's command or counsel or tends to any hurt of the church, then he ought boldly to resist it lest he become a partaker in crime by consent.

For this reason, trusting in the Lord and in Christ Jesus, who mightily and wisely protects the professors of his truth and rewards them with the prize of never-ending glory, I withstood the bull of Alexander V, which Lord Zbynek, archbishop of Prague, secured, 1409, and in which he commands that there should be no more preaching or sermons to the people by any priest whatsoever—even though he might be fortified with an apostolic instrument taking precedence of such a mandate or by any other written instrument[1]—except in cathedrals, parochial or cloistral churches or in their cemeteries. This mandate, being contrary to the words and deeds of Christ and his apostles, is not apostolic, for Christ preached to the people on the sea, in the desert, in the fields and houses, in synagogues, in villages and on the streets, and taught his disciples, saying: "Go ye into all the world

---

[1] Alexander V's bull, dated Dec. 20, 1409, was in answer to protests sent by the part of the Prague clergy hostile to Huss against the spread of Wyclif's views in Bohemia. Alexander called upon Zbynek to be solicitous to clear his diocese of errors and bade him appoint a commission to detect and summon heretics. Huss's text in regard to the prohibition of preaching in chapels is taken word for word from Alexander's bull. Palacky, *Doc.*, 347 *sqq.* Bethlehem chapel was one of the privileged chapels which had papal sanction for popular preaching in the Bohemian tongue. Zbynek, at first favorable to Huss, was archbishop of Prague, 1403-1411. See Schaff, *Life of John Huss*.

and preach the Gospel to every creature," Mark 16 : 15. And
these, going forth, preached everywhere, that is, in every
place where the people were willing to listen, God working
with them. Therefore, this command is to the hurt of the
church, and binds the Word of God, that it should not run
freely. And, in the third place, it is prejudicial to the chapels
which are erected and have with reason been confirmed by
diocesans, and have been furnished with privileges by the
apostolic see for the preaching of God's Word in them. For
no advantage whatever can be seen to accrue from that
command, but it is a fallacious and faithless irony, because the places set apart for divine worship and furnished
with privileges for the preaching of the divine Word are deprived of their lawful liberties on account of some personal
feeling or of some injurious appeal or some importunity, or
on account of some temporal good. Hence, I appealed from
that command of Alexander to Alexander himself, better informed.[1] And while I was prosecuting the appeal, that lord
pope suddenly died. And, no audience being allowed me in
the Roman curia, the Lord Zbynek, archbishop of Prague
secured papers aggravating the censure against me, from
which, A. D. 1410, I appealed to Pope John XXIII, and he
during two years did not grant audience to my legal advo-
cates and solicitors.[2] In the meantime I was weighed down
still more by ecclesiastical proceedings.[3] When, therefore,
my appeal from one pope to his successor did not profit me
and to appeal from the pope to a council involves long waiting and because it is of uncertain advantage to beg for grace
in the matter of a grievance and censure, therefore I appealed

[1] Huss claimed that Alexander had been misinformed by Zbynek and the
Prague clergy in regard to the conditions in Prague.

[2] John of Jesenicz, Huss's chief legal advocate, remained faithful till Huss's
death, and after it. He presented Huss's case at Rome and Bologna, was cast
into prison and afterwards escaped and returned to Prague. See Schaff, *Life
of John Huss*, 140 *sq*.

[3] The reference is to the aggravated excommunication issued by the curia
against Huss, 1412, in view of his contumacy.

finally to the head of the church, Jesus Christ.[1] For he is superior to any pope whatever in deciding a case: he cannot err, nor to a suppliant, rightfully begging, can he deny justice, nor is he able in view of his law to condemn a man who in the sight of his law is without demerit.

Besides, I withstood in the matter of the indulgences issued or announced A. D. 1412 through the bulls of Pope John XXIII, about which I have said enough in another place.[2] For the pope cannot command anything lawfully except what makes for the destruction of evil and for the edification of the church—a thing which ought to be universally held. To this the apostle bore witness when he said: "The weapons of our warfare are not of the flesh, but mighty before God to the destruction of strongholds, by which we cast down counsels,[3] casting down every high thing which exalted itself against the knowledge of God," II Cor. 10 : 4, 5. And again he says: "That I may not deal sharply according to the authority which the Lord gave me for building up and not for destruction," II Cor. 13 : 10. Hence, he of Lincoln in his letters to the pope thus writes: "The apostolic see to which is given authority by the holiest of the holies, Jesus Christ, the apostle bearing witness, for building up and not for casting down, cannot commit schism." And further on he says: "For this reason your Discretion cannot ordain anything hard against me, because all my words and all my actions are not a gainsaying or a rebellion, but a filial honoring due to the father and mother, that is, Christ and the church, because it is the keeping of a divine command. But, recalling in brief, I say that the sanctity of the apostolic see

---

[1] Huss repeatedly refers to the appeal he made to Christ, now putting it on the simple ground of the right of a Christian to do so and now citing the case of Paul who appealed to the higher power, Cæsar. See Letter, *Doc.*, 73; *Mon.*, 1 : 325–392, etc., as well as later in this treatise.

[2] Huss's treatises against Papal Indulgences for the crusade against Ladislaus, king of Naples, *Mon.*, 1 : 215–237.

[3] Huss has *quibus consilia demolimur*, the Vulgate simply *consilia destruentes*.

can do nothing except for the building up and not for destroying, for this is the plenitude of power to be able to do all things to build up. These things, however, which they call provisions, are not adapted to build up, but clearly to destroy. Therefore, the most blessed apostolic see is not able to make these provisions."[1] These things by him of Lincoln, who appealed from Pope Innocent to the tribunal of Christ.

For this reason Castrensis, VII, tells how when Robert of Lincoln was dead, a voice was heard in the papal curia, Come, wretch, to thy judgment. And the pope was found the next morning dead as if pierced in the side by the point of a staff. And he of Lincoln, although noted for striking miracles, is nevertheless not admitted to a place in the list of the saints.[2]

And it is clear that the pope may err, and the more grievously because, in a given case, he may sin more abundantly, intensely and irresistibly [than others], as said Bernard in his book addressed to Pope Eugenius:[3] "More abundantly if the sin extends to all Christendom, more intensely if his act concerns the cure of souls and involves the withdrawal of spiritual benefits, and more irresistibly if no one dares to gainsay him, now in view of his alliance with the secular arms, now in view of the cloaked censures which he fulmi-

[1] A provision is the gift of a spiritual office or living by pope or bishop. The theory was that all the livings in Christendom were in the pope's hands for bestowment, a theory receiving its full statement from Clement IV, 1265. See Schaff, *Ch. Hist.*, V, part 2, 83 *sqq.* The Avignon popes, 1305-1377, appointed two and sometimes three successors with right to succeed living incumbents of ecclesiastical positions. A collation is equivalent to a provision.

[2] The full quotation runs, Rolls Series, 8 : 242: "Robert was summoned to the curia and excommunicated, but he appealed from Innocent's tribunal to the bar of Christ. Hence it happened after his death, Robert appeared to that pope in the night while he was lying in bed, himself clad as a bishop and said, Arise, wretch, and come to thy judgment. And straightway he pierced him with his pastoral staff in the left side unto the heart, and so the pope's bed was found in the morning full of blood and the pope was dead." Variations were given of this popular story. Matthew Paris, who has unbounded admiration for Grosseteste, reports that on the night of his death strange bells were heard.

[3] Quoted in chapter IX by its title, *de Consideratione.*

nates against the children of obedience, now in view of promotions and ecclesiastical dignities which he provides for his accomplices. Hence, as the papal office, when it profits the church, is the most deserving, so, when the papal office is perverted in that man who abuses his office, if it do injury to the church, is most undeserving. The evidence of a pope's defect is if he put aside the law and a devout profession of the Gospel and give heed to human tradition." It was on this subject that Bernard was reasoning with Eugenius.

This is the first mark. The second is when the pope and ecclesiastical superiors abandon the manner of life Christ followed and are involved in a secular way in things of the world. The third mark is when the pope advances the traffickers of this world in the ministry of Christ and gives himself up chiefly to the continued pursuit of the secular life so that the poor churches are oppressed. The fourth mark is when, by his own command or through the appointment of incapable persons in the pastoral cure, he deprives souls that are to be saved of the Word of God. Hence he of Lincoln, thinking over this, would not admit one of the pope's relatives to a stall in Lincoln, giving in this matter, among other things, a probable reason [for his conduct]. "After the sin of Lucifer," he said,"—and the case will be the same in the end of time with the son of perdition, antichrist, whom the Lord Jesus will destroy with the breath of his mouth— there is not, neither can there be, another class so adverse to or at variance with the apostolic and evangelical doctrine, so hateful and detestable to the Lord Jesus Christ himself, and so abominated by him and so pernicious to the human family as the class which kills and destroys by depriving and defrauding of pastoral ministries souls which are to be made alive and saved by the office and ministry of the pastoral cure. And this sin they are known from the very clearest testimonies of holy Scripture to commit who, entrusted with the power of the pastoral cure, satisfy their own fleshly pleasuring with the milk and wool of Christ's sheep, and do not minister the things due from the pastoral office for the working out of the eternal salvation of Christ's sheep. For the non-performance of pastoral ministries is, by Scripture testimony, the killing and perdition of Christ's sheep. And that these two classes of sins, although they are distinguished, are the very worst, and every other class of sin inestimably excels them, is clear from this that, although distinct and dissimilar, they are directly contrary to the very best things. For that is the worst which is contrary to what is best, etc. And because, in good things, the cause of the good is better than the thing caused; and, in evil things, the cause of the evil is worse than the thing caused—it is clear how those who introduce into the church of Christ those worst murderers of godlikeness and divinity among Christ's sheep are still worse than those worst murderers themselves, and more like Lucifer and antichrist than they. And in this gradation of badness those do more abundantly excel who, in view of the greater and the diviner power given them for edification and not for scattering the sheep, are the more held by the church of God in duty bound to exclude and exterminate those worst murderers." Thus much he of Lincoln.

He wished briefly to establish that the killing and driving to perdition of Christ's sheep are the two worst sins, although they may be distinguished, even as the making alive of the sheep by grace and their glorification are the two best things for the sheep, although different, and to them the killing and the destroying are opposites. And as killing is the opposite of making alive and murder of glorification, it follows that by as much as these two sins are more serious by so much are they opposed to the good things which are more excellent. And, as God of himself is the cause of these good things, it follows that by as much as the killers and murderers of the sheep are worse than others, by so much are the killing and murdering of the sheep the worse sins. And it is clear that those who kill souls are the worst servants of antichrist and Satan.

In view of these things it is to be held that to rebel against an erring pope is to obey Christ the Lord, because in making his provisions he chiefly makes those which savor of personal affection. Therefore, I call the world to witness that the papal distribution of benefices sows in the church hirelings all too widely. On the part of the popes, it gives them occasion to exalt their vicarial power, to put an excessive value on the world's dignity and to make an extravagant show of a fantastic sanctity. But these doctors, who are looking for temporal remuneration from the pope or servilely fear his power,[1] and also are saying that he has mysterious power and is impeccable and inerrant and that he may do lawfully whatsoever pleases him—these doctors are pseudo-prophets and pseudo-apostles of antichrist.

From the things already said, it is clear that the apostolic seat is the authority to judge and teach Christ's law, or secondly, as has been said, it is the family of holy popes who are successors to Christ. In this sense the apostolic seat is understood, Dist. 22 [Friedberg, 1 : 74], where Pope Anacletus says: "This apostolic seat has been established as the head and hinge by the Lord and not by another; and just as a gate is ruled by the hinge, so by the authority of the holy apostolic seat all the other churches are ruled, subject to the government of the Lord." That pope intended that he himself should be the head and hinge, the head in presiding and the hinge in ruling, but he has a weak enough argument for proving his purpose. For he argues from things that are alike, when he says: "As a gate is ruled by its hinge, so by the authority of the holy apostolic see all the churches are ruled." It would have been sufficient to argue that the pope and cardinals rule themselves well.

[1] Huss frequently ascribes the changed attitude of Palecz and Stanislaus to the fear of ecclesiastical penalties, Doc., 53, 466, etc.

For as by one hinge only one door is ruled, so it would be a good thing if by their doctrine and authority they were ruled well themselves, so that afterwards other churches should be well ruled. For in what manner do they rule our church of Prague except by distributing benefices to the covetous and collecting monies? But what has become of teaching and the other ministrations of power?

Thirdly, the seat is conceived of as power, and in this way it is conceived in *Dist. Inferior.* [21 : 4, Friedberg, 1 : 70], where Pope Nicolas says, "an inferior seat is not competent to absolve a superior," and he draws the conclusion but unfittingly enough from Isaiah 10 : 15, "Shall the axe boast itself against him that heweth? Shall the saw magnify itself against him that wieldeth it?" when he says: "Seeing these things are set forth in divine Scripture, we have shown more clearly than the sun that no one who is of lesser authority is competent to condemn by his judgments one who is of greater power, or subject him by definitions of his own." See how he here calls the inferior seat the man of lesser authority and the superior seat the man of greater authority. But how is the seat to be understood? This Pelagius [a mistake for Gelasius] answers, when he says: *Dist.* 21 [Friedberg, 1 : 70]: "The first seat of the apostle Peter is the Roman church, which has neither spot nor wrinkle nor any such thing." See how the seat of Peter is here called the Roman church. But by this is it verified, that it is "without spot and wrinkle"? Since neither is the pope that seat nor that church, nor is the pope in conjunction with the cardinals, for they are not "without spot." Nor is that seat the stone church. Of a truth, I am not able otherwise to think of that seat except as it is all those who imitate the life of Peter, measured finally by the law of Christ. For these will be "without spot and wrinkle" in the heavenly country. But whether this is the meaning of that pope or not, I do not know.

Hence Augustine, Com. on Psalm 122 : 5 [*Nic. Fathers,* 7 : 594], "The seats sat in judgment," speaks thus of the thing in question: "How did those seats sit in judgment? Wonderful enigma, wonderful question, if seat does not mean what the Greeks call throne! The Greeks call chairs thrones, as something honorable. Therefore, my brethren, it is not wonderful if men sit on seats, on chairs, but that the seats themselves sit, how are we to understand this? As if some one were to say, let the cathedras sit here, or the chairs sit here; to sit in a chair, to sit in seats, they sat in cathedras. The seats themselves do not sit. What, therefore, is the meaning of this, that the seats sat for judgment? Surely ye are accustomed to hear what the Lord said: 'Heaven is my throne and the earth is the footstool of my feet.' But in Latin the whole is said to be: 'Heaven is my seat [or seats].' Who are these but the righteous? Who are the heavens but the righteous? What church? The churches are many and yet they are one. So, therefore, it is also with the righteous. The righteous are heaven that they may be the heavens. On these God sits, and the things pertaining to them God judges. And not without reason was it said that 'the heavens declare the glory of God.'

"The apostles, however, are made heaven. Whence are they made heaven? Because they are made righteous. How is the sinner made earth, to whom it is said, 'Thou art earth and unto earth thou shalt go'? Even so those who have been made righteous are made heaven. They have borne God; for their sakes God has made wonderful lights to shine, thundered terrors, rained consolations. Therefore the righteous were heaven and 'declared the glory of God.' Now that ye may know that these are the heavens spoken of, it is said in the same Psalm, 'Their sound is gone out through all the earth, and their words unto the ends of the world.' You ask, Whose sound? and you will find, the sound of the heavens. If, therefore, heaven is God's seat and the apostles are heaven, then they are themselves made God's seat; they are God's throne. In another place it is said: 'The soul of the righteous man is the throne of wisdom.' This is a great thing which is said, namely, in the soul of the righteous man wisdom sits as on its throne and from there it judges whatever it judges. Therefore, there will be thrones of wisdom, and so the Lord said to them: 'Ye shall sit on twelve thrones, judging the twelve tribes of Israel.' So also they will sit on twelve seats; and they are themselves the seats of God. Of them, indeed, it was said: 'For there the seats sat.' How will the seats sit there? And who are the seats of whom it is said, 'The soul of the righteous man is the seat of wisdom'? And who are the seats of heaven? The heavens. Who are the heavens? Heaven. What is heaven, of which the Lord says, 'Heaven is my seat'? The righteous themselves are the seats, and have seats; and in that Jerusalem the seats will sit. For what purpose? 'For judgment, ye shall sit,' he says, 'on twelve seats, judging the twelve tribes of Israel.' Judging whom? Those who are below on the earth. Who will judge? Those who are made heaven." Thus much Augustine, showing from Scripture that the righteous are God's seats and they it is who will judge.

Fourthly, seat is understood of the place in which any apostle remains for a given period, ruling the people according to Christ's law, and, in this sense, Jerusalem was not the bare city, but with its people it was the seat of James the apostle who, elected by the apostles, was there constituted by the Lord its first bishop. And Antioch was the first seat of the apostle Peter, and so Pope Marcellus says, 24 : 1 [Friedberg, 1 : 970]: "We beseech you brethren that ye teach and think nothing else than what was taught by St. Peter the apostle and the remaining apostles and Fathers." And further on: "His seat, that is, Peter's, was the primary one among you, and it was afterwards, at God's bidding, transferred to Rome, over which we, with divine grace supporting us, preside this very day. But if your Antiochian seat, which originally was the first, gave way to the Roman seat, there is none which is not subject to its bestowal—*ditione.*" See how very finely this pope begins and how very confusedly he ends. In the first place, he asks and begs that the priests of Antioch teach nothing else than what they received from Peter and from other apostles and holy Fathers. O that all clerics had done this! Then he says, that the seat of Peter was the primary one among them, that is, the first place of his residence, in which as bishop he taught Christ's law. And this is true. But when he says, "Afterwards it was transferred to Rome," that is, Peter's seat—I certainly do not know what that seat was that was transferred; for no church, no locality, no people were transferred. If it be said, it was the authority of Peter to teach the law, then that authority was at one and the same time in Antioch and in Rome. What then was transferred unless it was Peter, when he came from Antioch to Rome? But Pope Marcellus did not preside over Peter, nor is Peter now the Roman seat. What, therefore, does this expression 'Over which,' mean, when he says, "Over which we preside." Certainly this pope speaks confusedly. For after the dotation, the Roman bishop then living intended that the Roman church by the authority of Cæsar should be called first, that is, the more worthy seat over which he himself presides, and so he intended that the priests of Antioch should be subject to himself. If Peter affected this superiority while he dwelt in Rome, I do not know. But I do know that in his letters he wished that they should follow in the steps of Jesus Christ. And I will pass by the way in which many popes and canonists speak obscurely about the apostolic see. I will, however, not say that the city of Rome is the apostolic seat, so necessary that without it the church of Jesus Christ could not stand. For, if by a possibility Rome, like Sodom, were destroyed, the Christian church would be still standing. And it is not true that, wherever the pope is, there is Rome. Howbeit, it is true that, wherever the pope shall be so long as he is here on the earth, there Peter's authority abides with the pope, so long as the pope does not depart from the law of our Lord Jesus Christ. So much I have wanted to say about the apostolic seat for the present.

CHAPTER XIX

WHEN ECCLESIASTICAL SUPERIORS ARE TO BE OBEYED

IT having been stated what the apostolic seat is, it is now to be stated in what cases obedience is to be rendered to this apostolic seat. And the aforesaid doctors say, that "it is to be obeyed by inferiors in all things—when the absolutely good is not forbidden or the absolutely evil is not" commanded [but the intermediate also][1] which in place, way, time or person may be either good or bad.

This they prove by four pertinent witnesses, the Saviour, Bernard, Augustine and Jerome. And because the doctors took the distinction from Bernard, *Ep. ad Adam monachum* [Migne's ed., 182 : 95 *sq.*], about the absolutely good and the absolutely evil, so it is to be noted that after St. Bernard shows that no one is to be obeyed in that which is evil and concludes, saying: "Therefore, to do evil, even when any one whosoever commands, certainly is not obedience but rather disobedience. This deserves soberly to be said, that some things are absolutely good, some absolutely evil, and in these latter no man owes obedience, just as the former are not to be left undone, even when forbidden. Nor are the latter to be performed, even though they be enjoined. Further, between these two are the things that are intermediate, which may be good or evil according to the place, time, mode or person involved. And in these things the law of obedience is fixed as in the tree of knowledge of good and evil, which was in the

---

[1] The printed text of the original ed. as well as of the reprint omits the words in brackets and " not " before commanded.

midst of Paradise. In these things, certainly, it is not right to prefer our thoughts to the sentence of the teachers. In these things neither the command of prelates nor their prohibition is to be in all cases spurned." And further on, Bernard says: "Faith, hope and love are absolutely good, and other things of this kind; and they may not be either forbidden or not kept. Absolutely evil are sacrilege, adultery, theft, and such like, which certainly may neither be properly enjoined nor done, and they may not be improperly not [1] forbidden and not done. For no one's prohibition is valid to set aside precepts, and no one's commandments are valid to prejudice in favor of things forbidden.

"Then there are the things intermediate, which indeed of themselves are not known to be either good or evil. They may, however, indifferently be either good or bad; they may be commanded or forbidden, but under no circumstances are they to be obeyed by inferiors, when they are evil. Among these are, by way of example, fasting, vigils, reading and such like. But it should be known that certain things intermediate go beyond the reason of things impure or evil. For since marriage may occur or not occur, but when once entered into it is not permissible to undo it, what, therefore, before marriage was permitted to be, as a thing indifferent, obtains in those already married the force of the absolutely good. Likewise, it is a matter indifferent for a secular man to possess private property, because he has the option of not possessing. But for a monk, because he is not permitted to have possessions, to possess goods is an absolute evil." Thus much Bernard.

Also it is to be noted that, so far as the sense of those speaking about human actions goes, a certain work is called neutral among them which, in its primary intent, cannot be said to be a good of morals or an evil of vice, as, for example, to build or to weave. But works are called good or evil

---

[1] Huss has improperly inserted this "not" which is not found in Migne.

by the standard of their class—*de genere*—which words designate from a moral standpoint the substance or nature of a good work or an evil. Nevertheless, they do not involve the circumstances which of themselves fix the natures of such acts as in the class of virtue or vice, as, for example, giving alms or putting a man to death. For both of these can become good or evil according to the diversity of their causes or the purpose of the doer. For to give alms for vainglory is evil, just as to kill a man by the authority of God, lest he infect the church, is good.[1] But of another kind are collective works, which from a moral standpoint are called purely good or bad, such as committing adultery and thieving, which are of vice, and loving God and our neighbor heartily, which are virtuous. Briefly, as one act is purely good, such as loving God with the heart, so another act is purely evil, as is hating God.

Likewise, a thing is good generically which, as it were, disposes a man to judge and discover that it is good more than to judge that it is evil, as fasting and giving alms. A thing is evil generically which, as it were, disposes a man to judge and discover what may be evil rather than what may be good. Howbeit, the thing may be well done, as the putting a man to death. But a neutral work is such a work which does not dispose a man to judge and discover what is good rather than what is evil, as weaving, eating, ploughing, or running.

Hence, a work absolutely good holds the first rank, a work generically good [that is, judged by its class], as it were, the middle rank, and a neutral work the lowest rank. Examples of these three are loving God, fasting, and weaving. The same applies to their opposites, for a work purely evil, as is hating God; a work generically evil is putting a man to death. But the third or neutral work is not counted as evil, for if it were it would not be neutral. For the name

---

[1] The special authority of God is essential. See Introduction.

neutral is used because it does not dispose to virtue more than to vice, or the contrary.

Further, it is to be noted that there is an immediate distinction between human works, because whether they are virtuous or vicious is manifest, for, if a man is vicious and does something, then he acts viciously; and if he is virtuous and does something, then he acts virtuously, for just as vice, which is called crime or mortal sin, infects the acts of the whole man, so virtue gives life to all the acts of a virtuous man, in so far as that, living in grace, he is said to be meritorious and pray even in sleeping or in doing anything whatsoever, as the holy doctors say, especially St. Augustine, Gregory, Jerome and others. And this statement is founded in the words of Jesus Christ our Saviour: "If thine eye be single, thy whole body shall be full of light," that is, if thy purpose be good and in grace unto the doing of good works, then "thy whole body," that is, the sum of all thy works, "will be full of light," because they are pure in the sight of God. "But if thine eye be evil," that is, thy purpose be bad, tainted and incriminate with vice, "thy whole body," that is, the sum of thy works, "will be full of darkness," that is, will be vicious. Hence, the doctor of the Gentiles, the apostle Paul, teaches thus: "Do all to the glory of God," II Cor. 10 : 31, and, "Let all your things be done in love," I Cor. 16 : 14. Therefore, the whole mode of living in love is virtuous, and the whole mode of a man's living without love is vicious.

From this it is clear that, as no one may be neutral, so far as virtue and vice go, since it must needs be that one is in the grace of Almighty God or outside it, so no conduct of any man may be neutral. In the case of virtuous commands, therefore, the superior is to be obeyed, but of vicious commands he is to be boldly withstood. These things having been stated [Chapter XVII, on Obedience], every one of Christ's faithful ought truly to be on his guard lest he believe that if the Roman pontiff or a prelate commands any-thing whatsoever, it is to be done as though it were a mandate of God, and that the prelate cannot err, even as Jesus Christ cannot.

Secondly, let him hold in regard to the commands in God's law, how some are commanded us in a mixed way and others distinctly. In a mixed way the commands are commanded which we ought to do every day and meritoriously, after the manner of which Augustine says, that all truth is contained in the Scriptures. But a work that is commanded, for which there is no reason or utility to the church of Christ, is not contained explicitly or implicitly in the Scriptures. And if such be commanded by pope or other prelate, the inferior is not bound to perform it, lest, in so doing, he offend against the liberty of the Lord's law. For we ought to receive as of faith that God commands us to do nothing except what is meritorious for us and reasonable, and consequently profitable to salvation.

The conclusion should be this: Subjects are bound to obey willingly and cheerfully virtuous, yea, and hard superiors, when they command us to do the mandates of the Lord Jesus Christ. This conclusion is evident, for Christ says, "The scribes and Pharisees sit in Moses' seat. All things, therefore, whatsoever they bid you, these do," Matt. 23 : 1, that is, all my commandments. Here Augustine, Com. on John, 20 [*Nic. Fathers*, 7 : 443], says: "In sitting in Moses' seat, they teach God's law. Therefore God teaches through them. But, if they wish to teach their own things, do not hear them, do not do them." And on this subject Christ also said, "He that heareth you, heareth me, and he that despiseth you," etc., Luke 10 : 16, consequently, also, God the Father; because such persons are not obeyed as men, but as ministers of God, who is to be obeyed above all.

Therefore, no one should obey man in anything, even the least thing, that opposes itself to the divine commands, which St. Bernard calls divine counsels. For Peter says: "We must obey God rather than men," Acts 5 : 29. Hence, as we are commanded to obey our superiors in things lawful and honorable, with the circumstances taken into consideration, so we are commanded to resist them to the face when they walk contrary to the divine counsels or commandments. For Paul, teaching that we should be his imitators, I Cor. 4 : 16, withstood Peter to the face for a light offence, Gal. 2 : 11. But much more are we bound to obey Paul and every writer of divine Scripture rather than the Roman pontiff, when it comes to matters indifferent or neutral. And as we are not bound to follow any apostle, except in so far as he follows Jesus Christ, so it is evident by the limitation laid down by the apostle that we are bound to obey no prelate who has lived since the apostles, except as he commands or counsels Christ's counsels or commands. And so the holy apostle, I Cor. 4, 11, when he counsels that they be his imitators immediately announces the manner of such imitation, when he says, "even as I also am a follower of Christ." Therefore, the wise inferior ought to examine into the commands of a superior when he seems to deviate from Christ's law, or his rule. For no superior is above correction. Hence, Christ often commanded us to be watchful in our works: "I say unto you all, watch," Mark 13 : 36. And the apostle said: "Beloved, do not believe every spirit, but prove the spirits whether they be of God, for many false prophets are gone out into the world," I John 4 : 1. The Saviour also said: "Many false prophets shall arise[1] and lead many astray," Matt. 24 : 5.

And in this connection, St. Bernard speaks very finely in his Letter to Adam the Monk [Migne, 182 : 100 *sq.*],[2] when he rebukes him because he had unwisely obeyed his abbot

---

[1] *Surgent;* Vulgate has *venient.*
[2] Adam, monk of Morimond, a Cistercian abbey in the diocese of Langres, whose abbot was Arnold. The letter is dated, in Migne, 1125.

contrary to the rule of his vow. Hence, he exclaims, but in a playful mood: "O most obedient of monks, whom of all the words of the elders not a single iota escapes, he does not heed of what nature the command is which is commanded, satisfied if he only obeys, and this obedience is without delay! If this ought to be so, let it now be scratched out from the book of the Gospel, where it is written, 'Be ye wise as serpents'; and let that be sufficient which follows: 'simple as doves.' And I do not say that the commandments of superiors are to be examined and judged by inferiors when nothing is found to be commanded[1] at variance with the divine appointments, but I assert prudence to be necessary, by which it may be determined whether anything is at variance; and also liberty to be necessary, with which we may honestly spurn commands." Further, he says: "I have nothing to enquire. Let him see to it, who has commanded.[2] Say, I ask, whether, if the sword were put in thy hands, he would order thee to be struck in the neck, wouldst thou consent?[3] Would it not be reputed to others as homicide, since thou couldst have prevented it? Come, therefore, see to it lest, perhaps, under the pretext of obedience, thou fall into something more grave." Thus much Bernard, who adduces many testimonies from Scripture and concludes: "Thou, therefore, in the face of all these things and other numberless testimonies of the truth to this same purport, dost thou think any one whosoever ought to be obeyed? Hateful perversity, this virtue of obedience, which always wars against the truth, and is girded about against the truth!" Thus much Bernard.

Therefore, this same Bernard in his sermon on the Lord's advent lays down five conditions of right obedience; the first, when the work is a holy work, for it is not permissible

---

[1] Huss's text leaves out the *juberi*, Migne.

[2] Migne has *quid jusserit*.

[3] Migne adds: "If he had been ready by thy act to be thrown into the fire or water, wouldst thou have obeyed and done it?"

to obey contrary to God; the second, when the work is voluntary; the third, when it is pure from the standpoint of a holy purpose, in accordance with the Saviour's teaching, when he said: "If thine eye is single, thy whole body shall be full of light," Matt. 6 : 22. The fourth condition is when the work is judicious, because neither defect nor excess infects it, and the fifth, when it is permanently persevered in, as an obligation, even to the end. From this it is clear that an inferior, recognizing a superior's injudicious command, that it is known or should be known as fitted to hurt the church, by drawing away from the worship of God and the profit of souls unto salvation,—he ought to resist that superior. For such resistance is true obedience done not only to God in view of the law of fraternal correction but also to the superior himself, for no superior has the right to command anything except what is good. Since, therefore, an inferior is obligated, for obedience's sake, to do that which is generically good and commanded by the superior, it follows that he is obeying in so resisting him, as he ought; for he thereby does what is good, and turns away from what is evil. Hence, it is clear that a subject, in obeying his prelate in that which is evil, is not excused from sin, for the Saviour says: "If the blind guide[1] the blind, both fall into the pit," Matt. 15 : 14.

This means that if a "blind man," that is, an ignorant or bad prelate, guides "a blind man," that is, an ignorant or bad subject, by commanding him to do something, they both fall into the pit of error. Hence, Christ aptly says to his disciples in regard to the scribes and Pharisees—who taught that it is a sin to eat bread with unwashen hands, when it is nevertheless not a sin:—"Let them alone, they are blind leaders of the blind." What does "let them alone" mean? The Gloss says, "Leave them to their own will; they are blind," that is, they are obscured by traditions.

And this rule of Christ the very brute animals observe,

---

[1] *Præbit ducatum.*   Vulgate: *præstet ducatum.*

for the horse or the ass, discerning the hole in front of them and urged on by spurs, avoid the ditch so far as they can, as is clear from the case of the ass, which discerned the angel forbidding, lest it go the way Balaam wanted to go [Num. 22 : 22], and, with a man's voice, admonished the prophet's unwisdom. Hence, Bernard says ironically in his letter to the monk Adam: "Thou, that most obedient son, thou, that most devoted disciple—as for that thy father and teacher, whom neither by an instant of time nor a turn of the foot, as they say, thou didst suffer to be removed from thee as long as he lived—after him not with blind eyes, but after the manner of Balaam, with open eyes, thou didst not hesitate to fall down into the pit!" So much Bernard.

From these truths, however, it follows further that clerical inferiors, and much more laics, may sit in judgment on the works of their superiors. From this it follows that the judgment by discreet and hidden arbitrament in the court of conscience is one thing, and the judgment in virtue of the empowered jurisdiction in the court of the church is another. By the first way the inferior ought chiefly to examine and judge himself, as it is written: "If we would judge[1] ourselves, we would not be judged," I Cor. 11 : 31. And again, in the same way, he ought to judge all things pertaining to his salvation as it is written: "He that is spiritual judgeth all things," I Cor. 2 : 15. The laic also ought to examine and judge the works of his superior, as the apostle judged the works of Peter, when he corrected him and said: "When I saw that they walked not uprightly according to the truth of the Gospel, I said unto Cephas before them all, If thou, who art a Jew, livest as do the Gentiles and not as do the Jews, how compellest thou the Gentiles to walk as do the Jews?" Gal. 2 : 14. Secondly, the laic ought to examine and judge his superior for the purpose of fleeing, for Christ said: "Beware of false prophets which come unto you in sheep's

---

[1] *Judicaremus;* the Vulgate *dijudicaremus.*

clothing, but inwardly they are ravening wolves," Matt. 7 : 15. Thirdly, he ought to examine and judge that the superior may attend to spiritual offices and bodily nourishment or other good works to be done. For not otherwise should clergymen ever be chosen by laics as their curates and confessors and the dispensers of their alms.

Therefore, it is lawful for the rich of this world with diligent scrutiny to examine by what and what kind of superiors they shall administer their alms and in what way they shall administer them, guarding against rapacious wolves, because according to the apostle, in Acts 20 : 29, and according to Chrysostom, *in Imperfecto*, Homily 20, it is clear that in this way they seek more the money of those subject to them than their salvation and this is at variance with the apostle, who says: "I seek not yours, but you," II Cor. 12 : 14. And looking ahead with prophetic vision and seeing such false apostles, he affirmed, "I know that after my departing rapacious wolves shall enter in among you, not sparing the flock," Acts 20 : 29. And because this wolfishness is clearly discerned in the robbing of temporal things and in the infliction of punishments for the very purpose of plundering temporal goods more abundantly, he declares that he had himself pursued the opposite course. No man's gold and silver, he says, or vestments have I coveted, as ye yourselves know, because for those things that were needful for me and for those that were with me these hands have ministered.

Therefore, subjects living piously in Christ ought to pay heed to the life of the apostles and see to it whether their superiors live conformably to the apostles. For, if in their spiritual ministry they are out of accord with the apostles, if they are busy in exacting money, spurn evangelical poverty and incline to the world, nay, if they evidently sow offences, then they know by their works that they have departed from the religion of Jesus Christ the Lord. Therefore, O ye who love Christ's law from the heart, first note their works and see if they [the superiors] incline to the world, second give heed to their commands, whether they savor of avarice or the gain of this world, and third consult holy Scripture whether they command in accordance with Christ's counsel. And in the light of this counsel believe them; or disbelieve them, if they command contrary to this counsel. But let not curates say to laics, 'What concern is it of yours to take note of our life or works,' for did not our Saviour say: "Do not according to their works"? Matt. 23. And afterwards he exposed the works of the prelates to the multitude that they might know them and to their advantage avoid them. Yea, much more to the prelates, who say, 'What concern is it of yours to take note of our life and works?' it is pertinent for laics to reply: 'What concern is it of yours that ye should receive our alms?' for the apostle says: "We command you in the name of Jesus Christ that ye withdraw yourselves from every brother that walketh disorderly and not after the tradition which they received of us, for ye yourselves know how ye ought to imitate us, for we behaved not ourselves disorderly among you, neither did we eat bread for naught at any man's hands, but in labor and travail, for even when we were with you, this we commanded you, If any man will not work, neither let him eat." II Thess. 3 : 6, 10.

It is clear how inferiors ought to examine and judge intelligently and reasonably in respect to the commands and works of superiors, for otherwise they would be in peril of eternal death, if they did not judge wisely about these things, how far they ought to believe their superiors, how far follow them, and in what things they ought intelligently to obey them according to the Lord's law. For that best of masters, the Lord, admonished us in advance to "beware of false prophets and the leaven of the Pharisees," Matt. 7 : 15; 16 : 11. He also said: "Believe not, go not forth and do not do their works," Matt. 24 : 26.   For he himself exhorted the priests and the multitude to examine and judge in respect to his works, saying, "Which of you convicteth me of sin?" John 8 : 46, and, "Though ye believe not me, believe the works," John 10 : 38.   And what an evil it is of Christ's church that our superiors make a larger demand that belief be given to all their approving and condemning judgments, than that belief be given to the faith of holy Scripture, which is the catholic faith.   And they punish more severely for departure from their traditions than they do those who blaspheme against that most excellent faith of Christ.   And so to them the words of the Psalm [41 : 9] may be applied: "He that ate of my bread hath lifted up his heel against me."   For as they affirm, they themselves eat up Christ's patrimony and nevertheless they put a higher value on their commandments than on the commandments of our Lord Jesus Christ himself.

CHAPTER XX

OBEDIENCE NOT ALWAYS TO BE RENDERED TO THE CHURCH OR ITS PRELATES

AGAIN, that the doctors in their double statement may be better understood, since they say that "the Roman church and the prelates are to be obeyed in all things by their inferiors," etc.,[1] and again, "Therefore ought they to be obeyed and submitted to," I take it as true from the rules of grammar that this complex statement "are to be obeyed" means as much as the complex expression, "ought to obey," and further, that this word "ought" expresses a debt of obligation to obey under pain of mortal sin. This supposition appears from the affirmation of the doctors derived from the words of the Saviour: "All things whatsoever they bid you, these do and observe," Matt. 23 : 3. For this word of the Lord is a commandment. Secondly, this supposition appears from the words of the doctors, when they say: "Certain of the clergy in the kingdom of Bohemia who do not agree, striving, so far as in their power lies, to lead the faithful people to disobedience in respect to their prelates and to irreverence for the papal, episcopal, priestly and clerical dignities." It is only noted that there would be mortal sin in disobedience, and irreverence would be mortal sin. Thirdly, this supposition appears from the assertion of St. Augustine, when he says: "If thou art not obedient to thy father (understand not thy bodily father but thy spiritual father) thou hast lost all the virtues." In this way it is plain that a virtuous man is not able to lose all the virtues except by

---

[1] In his *de sex Erroribus*, Huss has a chapter on obedience, *Mon.*, 1 : 238 *sq.*, in which he denies that it is to be rendered in all cases to ecclesiastical superiors. The terms, "inferiors" and "subjects" refer to ecclesiastical rank and orders.

committing mortal sin, and so disobedience to authority involves a serious offence. Therefore this statement, taken from the proposition of the doctors, "the Roman church and prelates are to be obeyed by inferiors in all things," etc., means this much: "that we ought to obey under pain of mortal sin."

Therefore, following this sense, they now cry out that I am disobedient to the Roman church, and for this they excommunicate me. And it is clear from God's law and from the canons that no one is to be excommunicated except for mortal sin, as I have stated in another place.

Letting this proposition stand, I lay down this conclusion, that to no apostolic seat of the Roman church, that is, to no pope with the cardinals (as these are understood by the doctors), and to no prelates do inferiors owe obedience in all things which are neither purely good nor purely evil.

It is proved that king, marquis, duke, baron, soldier, citizen or rustic is bound to obey under pain of mortal sin no Roman church and no prelates so as to be prevented from holding worldly possessions or from entering marriage. These two things, the possession of goods and the entrance upon marriage, belong, in the case of the persons mentioned, neither to the class of purely good things nor things purely evil. Hence the conclusion. The consequence has been noted and the minor premise is presented in St. Bernard's letter to the monk Adam [Migne, 182 : 96], when he says: "Truly it must be known that things intermediate often cease to be so. For marriage may be lawfully contracted or not, but when once contracted it cannot be dissolved. Therefore, what before marriage is permitted to be a thing intermediate obtains, when the parties are married, the force of a thing absolutely good. Likewise, the possession of private property is for a secular man a thing intermediate for he may or may not have property, but for a monk, because he is not permitted to hold property, it is a thing absolutely evil." So much Bernard.

The major premise is proved in this way. No Roman church is permitted to command, under pain of mortal sin, that king, marquis, duke, baron, soldier, citizen or rustic enter upon matrimony or that he may not hold private property, therefore none of the persons mentioned are bound to obey under pain of mortal sin. The consequence has been noted and the antecedent is clear, because the Roman church has no right to exalt its commandment above a counsel of Christ. In commanding, however, that a king, marquis, duke, baron or soldier may not hold property, the Roman church would exalt its commandment above Christ's counsel, for this is the first among the twelve chief evangelical counsels, namely, voluntary poverty, which consists in the renunciation of private property and is related to need. Christ counselled, he did not command, when he says to a certain young ruler: "If thou wilt be perfect, go and sell all that thou hast and give to the poor and follow me," Matt. 19 : 21. Similarly, if the Roman church commands king, marquis, duke or other secular person to enter upon marriage it would be commanding contrary to a counsel of Christ and would it, therefore, not be acting contrary to Christ? The observance of virginal chastity until death is Christ's third evangelical counsel, and of this he says: "There are eunuchs that made themselves eunuchs for the kingdom of heaven's sake," Matt. 19 : 12—because Christ does not command but counsels that what is fitting for a person, that he ought with good will to hold, and he says: "He that is able to receive it, let him receive it."

Therefore, it would be great presumption for the Roman church to bind any one, under pain of mortal sin, above what the counsels of his Lord demand. This would be to lay unbearable burdens on men's shoulders, as said the Saviour: The things which the scribes and Pharisees, sitting in Moses' seat, do not keep they lay upon others. Hence, Christ's apostle, who saw the secret things of God, which the Roman church has not seen, says that he did not dare to command any one to marry and not to remain continent, for he says: "Every one hath his own gift of God, one after this manner, one after that," I Cor. 7 : 7. The apostle did not wish to command anything except what the Lord commanded through him and so what was useful to the one obeying. For there are many counsels for others which are not counsels for us, because of our weakness or ignorance, so that one may marry in the Lord without mortal sin, when, however, it would be better to keep his virgin state, but he is ignorant, believing the opposite. Therefore, the apostle says: "Every one has his own gift from God, one after this manner, one after that." And the words follow: "But if they cannot contain, let them marry, for it is better to marry than to burn." Some things, therefore, are more useful to some which for others would be less useful. Hence, it would be a notable mistake to think that all Christ's counsels would be profitable for all men if they fulfilled them to the letter. And hence a son is not bound to obey his father under pain of mortal sin, when the father commands that the son possess nothing or that he marry. In a similar way, it is also with a daughter, who cannot lawfully be forced to remain a virgin till death or be forced to marry.

Likewise, if that statement of the doctors be true that "the apostolic seat of the Roman church is to be obeyed by inferiors in all things," etc., it follows that Wenzel, king of the Romans and king of Bohemia, and likewise Sigismund, king of Hungary, would be continually sinning mortal sins, for they have not given obedience to the commandments of the Roman church and Pope Boniface with his cardinals, and resigned their kingdoms, the former the kingdom of the Romans, the latter the kingdom of Hungary.[1] And this is

---

[1] This act of Boniface IX, 1403, referred to by the university of Prague, *Doc.*, 500, was a deposition of Wenzel in favor of Ruprecht, who had been chosen king of the Romans by three of the electors, 1400. Ruprecht threatened to pass over to the obedience of the Avignon line. See also Huss's Reply to Palecz, *Mon.*, 1 : 329.

clear because to resign their kingdoms is for the one as for
the other not a thing absolutely evil, as is seen from the statement of Bernard.   And as these kings have not yet obeyed
that mandate or been absolved by Boniface, it follows that
they are still persisting in disobedience.   But who of sound
head would want to say this, seeing that that Pope Boniface,
according to the Lord's law, ought not to have attempted to
bring this about?

Likewise, it follows that certain persons, according to the
statement of the doctors, to wit, Stanislaus, Peter of Znaim,
John Helius and yet another, are still under the ban of papal
excommunication.   This seems to be the case, because they
have not obeyed up to this day the apostolic seat of the
Roman curia, or, if on account of contentions they have
secretly obeyed, they are, however, not absolved from the
curse, as the mandate was placed upon them by the pontiff
Innocent, under the pains of excommunication, deprivation
of their benefices and disenablement, that they really should
give up and assign to Master Mauritius the place which he
wished.   And they themselves, though solemnly warned by
a notary before witnesses, do not up to this day obey that
mandate, although the turning over of a place to Master
Mauritius which was commanded is not a thing absolutely
evil, although perhaps it is an evil for Master Mauritius
that they in such an unusual degree like that place.   And
to the doctors themselves perhaps it is also an evil because,
loving the first place in the synagogues, they do not admit
Mauritius himself.[1]   Oh! that on both sides they may not
come under the heading of the salutation of that most
lowly of masters, Christ, which runs: "Woe unto you Phari-

[1] Mauritius-Marik Rwacka found favor with Innocent VII, d. 1406, who
called upon the theological faculty of Prague to make a place for him in the
university on pain of excommunication, which it neglected to do, Documenta,
pp. 53, 500.   He was one of a deputation sent to Rome, 1408, by King Wenzel.
He was then made papal inquisitor, with whom Huss had something to do, Doc.,
164, 184.   Huss also refers to the case of Mauritius and the university's disobedience to the papal mandate in Reply to Palecz, Mon., 1 : 329.

234 THE CHURCH

sees, that love the chief seats in the synagogues!" Luke
11 : 43, "and to be called of men Rabbi!" Matt. 23 : 7.

Likewise in acts good generically, as are fasting and
prayer—which are not things absolutely evil—the Roman
church and prelates are not to be obeyed except as these
acts are weighed in the balances of reason. This is plain
because an inferior must continue in prayer and fasting, so
far that the neglect to do so would mean damage to himself and the church; but this is to be avoided both by him
who commands and by the inferior; therefore, the antecedent
is true. For it is certain that it would be tempting God to
obey a prelate or for me to vow to myself that I would never
eat or drink but so much and never have but so many clothes
or wraps. And the same would be true with the other counsels, wrongly interpreted. And much more would it be folly
for a prelate to obligate a community to perform such a
singular measure of conduct as this. For one and the selfsame individual, in view of the diversity of the times, of weakness and health, of youth and old age, of heat and cold, must
vary in practices of this sort; and much more in a community made up of different persons are things that are indifferent to be adapted to individuals of different temperaments
and states of health. According to Aristotle, *Ethics*, II, that
which is a matter of indifference does not apply in the same
way to all. For in the indifferent matter of eating, the
amount proportioned to Milo, who wished to eat a whole bull
in a day, would not be the amount proportioned for every
individual whatsoever, young or decrepit, sound or weak.

Hence, the Saviour wholly excused his disciples who were
accused of not fasting, when it is said: "Then came to him
the disciples of John saying, Why do we and the Pharisees
fast oft, but thy disciples fast not?" Matt. 9 : 14. To these
calumniators who joined themselves with the Pharisees in
reproving Christ, the Saviour replied for his disciples and
said: "Can the sons of the bridegroom mourn as long as the

bridegroom is with them? But the days will come when
the bridegroom will be taken away from them and then they
will fast.   And no man putteth[1] a piece of undressed cloth
upon an old garment, for that which would fill it up, taketh
from the garment and a worse rent is made.   Neither do men
put new wine into old wine-skins, or else the wine-skins burst
and the wine is spilt and the skins perish, but they put new
wine into new skins and both are preserved," Matt. 9 : 15–17.
Here the Saviour excuses his disciples for not fasting, first for
the reason that he, the bridegroom of the church, was at that
time with his children and providing for them; secondly, because that bodily fasting did not befit them for that time, as
Lyra says: "Wherefore does the bridegroom say, 'Can the
children of the bridegroom mourn?' that is, be sad by afflict-
ing themselves with fasting?—which is as if he should say, No,
for fasting does not befit them now, 'but the days will come,'
namely, the days of the passion, 'when the bridegroom will
be taken away from them' by death, and 'then they will
fast,' that is, with the fasting of grief, as it is written: 'Ye
shall weep and lament,' John 16 : 20.   'Then shall they
fast,' namely, at a time when such fasting befits them.   And
then by a double example the Saviour proves that bodily
fasting did not befit them at that time."   Supplications are
also touched upon in Luke 5 : 33, when they said: "Why
do the disciples of John fast often and make supplications,[2]
likewise also the disciples of the Pharisees, but thine eat and
drink?   And Jesus said unto them, Can ye make the sons
of the bridegroom fast when the bridegroom is with them?"
which is as much as to say, apart from the bridegroom's will
ye cannot lawfully make his sons to fast.

Truly Christ is the good prior and abbot, who does not
burden his disciples but, laying on them an easy yoke and
a light burden, says of the Pharisees and scribes, sitting in

---

[1] *Committit.*   The Vulgate: *immittit.*
[2] *Observationes.*   The Vulgate: *obsecrationes*

Moses' seat, that they lay heavy burdens and grievous to be borne on men's shoulders, but do not move them with one of their own fingers. Even so, modern prelates and penitentiaries impose many fastings, many prayers, and other hard things upon the people, and they alone do not do the least of them.

Hence, they more often say: "Let us eat and gamble and the coarse may do our fasting." Therefore, when the Saviour calls such hard commandments as they lay upon men unbearable burdens because they are weighty beyond Christ's counsels and commands, what wise man will say that inferiors are bound in such things to obey their prelate under pain of mortal sin? Likewise to eat with unwashen hands is a neutral work, neither absolutely good nor absolutely evil, and Christ's disciples were not obligated by the command of those sitting in Moses' seat to do it. Nor are we now. The consequence has been stated, for the reasoning is the same in the case of traditions of this kind, which are not founded in the Lord's law.

The second part is manifest from Matt. 15 : 2, when the Pharisees and scribes said to Jesus, "Why do thy disciples transgress the traditions of the elders? for they wash not their hands when they eat bread," but he, rebuking them for the transgression of God's commandments, showed that his disciples did not sin in not keeping their commandments, and he said: "To eat with unwashen hands defileth not the man." What, therefore, is the reason now, that any inferior in any act whatsoever that is neutral or intermediate should be obligated to obey his prelate, if it happens that the prelate is callous, who indiscreetly and overmuch burdens an inferior with such neutral acts? Hence, as said above, Bernard well lays down the conditions of obedience, one of which is that a work commanded is judicious when neither excess nor defect attaches to it.

Hence, no human commandment or decree is valid or to

be observed except in so far as it is caused by a divine command before exemplifying it.

And hence, it is, that no obedience made to a superior profits for merit except in so far as it leans towards obedience of the counsels and commandments of the Lord Jesus Christ. This is clear, for obedience to Christ, owed or performed, is in and by itself a reason of merit which increases or diminishes with the degree of obedience or disobedience. Hence nothing is more religious than obedience unto God, as the *Decretum* 8 : 1, *Sciendum* [Friedberg, 1 : 593], teaches, where is noted what Samuel, the prophet, says, I Sam. 15 : 22: "To obey is better than sacrifice, for rebellion is as the sin of witchcraft and stubbornness as a crime."[1] "Obedience itself," says the *Decretum*, "is a virtue that possesses the merit of faith, and any one who is without it, is convicted of being an unbeliever, even though he seem to be of the faithful. The flesh of others, it says, is slaughtered in the case of sacrifices, but by obedience our own will is sacrificed." Here it appears, it is clearer than the light, that Samuel is speaking about obedience due to God, for he said to Saul: "Because thou hast rejected the word of the Lord, the Lord hath rejected thee from being king, and Saul said unto Samuel, 'I have sinned, because I have transgressed the commandment of the Lord and thy words, for I feared the people and obeyed their voice,'" I Sam. 15 : 23, 24. It is clear how much prelates of the people blaspheme who on the ground of Scripture and ecclesiastical law traffic in such obedience for themselves; secondly, from Augustine's authority, which the doctors quote for their side, Sermon 86, when he says: "If thou wilt fast, make prayer night and day, if thou wilt beg, or be in ashes, or if thou wilt do anything else but what is commanded in the Lord's law, and thou seemest wise to thyself and art not obedient to the Father [understand not the corporal Father, but the spiritual Father]—thou hast lost all the virtues. This is clear, because he who obeys

[1] The Vulgate adds: *idolatriæ*, of idolatry.

not God, as his spiritual Father, has lost all the virtues."
And hence Augustine adds: "Therefore obedience profits
more than all the other moral virtues." Far-fetched, therefore, is the proof of the doctors who seek to deduce from
this authority what they propose.

Further I lay down this conclusion and in spite of the
pretended—*prætensa*—excommunication, threatened or already issued, that the Christian ought to follow the commandments of Christ. This appears from the conclusion of
St. Peter and the other apostles: "We must obey God rather
than men," Acts 5 : 29. From this it follows logically that
Christ's priest, who lives according to his law, and has a
knowledge of the Scripture and a desire to edify the people,
ought to preach, a pretended excommunication to the contrary notwithstanding. This is clear, for to preach the Word
of God is a command to priests, as the apostle Peter bears
witness, when he says: "God charged us to preach unto the
people and to testify," Acts 10 : 42. Jesus sent out the
twelve, commanding them and saying: "Go not into any
way of the gentiles . . . and as ye go, preach, saying, The
kingdom of heaven is at hand," Matt. 10 : 5–7. The same
appears from Luke, chapters 9 and 10, and also from what
Augustine says, *Prologue* to his Sermons: "Few are the priests
who rightly preach God's Word, but many are they who
accursedly keep silence—some from ignorance, who refuse
to teach and some from neglect, because they spurn God's
Word; but neither the former nor the latter may be excused from the guilt of keeping silence, since they ought not
to have a place of authority who do not know how to preach,
nor ought they to keep silent who know how to preach, howbeit they are not in places of authority."

Likewise is this clear from what St. Jerome says on Ezek.
3 : 18: "When I say to the wicked, Thou shalt surely die, and
thou givest him not warning, nor speakest to warn the wicked
from his wicked way to save his life, the same wicked man

shall die in his iniquity, but his blood will I require of thy hand." Here Jerome says: "The priest is bound to preach, and let him see to it that fear of man does not make him to keep silence. There is a great difference in the keeping of the words of God silent for three causes—namely, out of fear, stupidity or flattery." Likewise is this clear from Gregory, *Pastoral Theology*, 15 : 43, *sit rector* [*Nic. Fathers*, 2d Ser., 12 : 27, Friedberg, 1 : 154], where he gives most solemn proof from many Scripture texts and, among other things, says: "Indeed it is written that 'the sound shall be heard when he [Aaron] enters into the holy place in the presence of the Lord . . . that he die not' [Ex. 28 : 33–35]. For the priest, going in or coming out dies if a sound is not heard from him, because he gets to himself the anger of the hidden judge, if he goes in without the sound of preaching." The same is clear from St. Isidore, who says, *de Summo Bono*, III: "Priests are condemned for the people's iniquity if they do not instruct the ignorant or convict sinners."

When, therefore, in view of what has been said, any one who has reached the priesthood has accepted as of commandment the office of preacher, it is clear that that commandment ought to be executed, a pretended excommunication to the contrary notwithstanding.

Likewise for no true catholic ought it to become a matter of doubt that a man if he be adequately trained in knowledge is more obligated to teach the ignorant, to advise the uncertain, to punish the unbridled, to remit sins to those committing injury, than he is to do any works of mercy. Since, therefore, when he is fitted for the ministry of alms for the body, he is bound to do these things under pain of damnation, as appears from Matt. 25—much more when he is fitted to administer spiritual alms [is he under obligation to do spiritual ministries]. From this it is evident that preaching for the priest and giving alms for the rich are not things intermediate but commandments.

Further, it is evident that if pope or other superior command the priest not to preach, who is disposed to do so (as has been said), or the rich not to give alms, the inferior ought not to obey. Wherefore, depending on this command of the Lord, I have not obeyed Pope Alexander's command in regard to not preaching and hence will humbly bear excommunication,[1] confident that I will secure to myself the benediction of my God. And as to God, the Psalmist says: "Let them be accursed, but do thou bless." And he also blessed, when he said: "Blessed are ye when men shall reproach you and say all manner of evil against you falsely for my sake. Rejoice and be exceeding glad, for great is your reward in heaven," Matt. 5 : 11, 12.

---

[1] This was the papal bull of Dec. 20, 1409, which forbade preaching in chapels which, like Bethlehem chapel, were not connected with a cathedral, collegiate or conventual church or their cemeteries. *Doc.*, p. 375.

CHAPTER XXI

CIRCUMSTANCES UNDER WHICH OBEDIENCE IS TO BE RENDERED TO PRELATES

Now as to the authorities which the doctors have adduced to emphasize the necessity of human obedience, the following is briefly to be said. For, in the first place, they say: "The Roman church and prelates are to be obeyed by inferiors in all things, according to the Saviour's statement, 'All things whatsoever they bid you, these do and observe,'" Matt. 23 : 2.[1] Here I wonder why the doctors openly cut off the Saviour's previous words, for they do not quote: "The scribes and Pharisees sit in Moses' seat." Nor did they add the later words, "Do not ye according to their works," but they only quote the intervening words: "All things whatsoever they bid you, these do and observe." Here it seems to me that they have so done because the pope and other prelates of the church do not wish to be compared with scribes and Pharisees, and if anything is said of their evil works they are indignant; and because also the doctors and masters are flattered by such things, and so the former heap up to themselves masters having itching ears who turn away from the truth and the masters are flattered. Therefore, the apostle's prophecy is fulfilled in both particulars, for he adjures Timothy saying: "I charge thee in the sight of God and Jesus Christ, who shall judge the living and the dead, and by his appearing and his kingdom: preach the word; be urgent in season, out of season;

[1] The exegesis of this passage, upon which so much stress is laid, Huss takes up again at length, *ad octo Doctores, Mon.,* 1 : 408.

reprove, rebuke, exhort, with all longsuffering and teaching. For the time will come, when they will not endure
sound doctrine, but having itching ears they will heap to
themselves teachers after their own lusts and will turn away
their ears from the truth and turn aside unto fables," II Tim.
4 : 1–4. It is not, therefore, to be wondered at that prelates gratefully accept the statements of the aforesaid doctors, for they anoint all those statements with the oil of
flattery and do not lay down a single word of correction with
intent to suppress their wickedness. But a Master, a Bishop,
and most just Judge will come, who will think most righteously of the flattering speaking of the doctors and the
wickedness of the prelates, even he who said: "The scribes
and Pharisees sit in Moses' seat, all things, therefore, whatsoever they bid you, these do and observe, but do not according to their works, for they say and do not."

Truly this Master never spoke fair of the wickedness of
prelates and doctors. He spoke the truth, taught his own
faithful ones and confuted the scribes, sitting in Moses' seat,
because of their evil works. He spoke truth and taught
truth, for he sat in Moses' seat, that is, the authority of
judging and teaching God's law, as has been shown above,
Chapter XVIII.

By that authority Moses said: "They come unto me,
that I may judge between them and show them the statutes
of God and his law," Ex. 18 : 16. "All things, therefore,
whatsoever they bid you," that is, pertaining to the seat of
judgment, "do," namely, from the heart, "and observe,"
namely, in deed. "But do not according to their works,"
that is, keep their doctrine, do not follow their life: "for
they say and do not." Chrysostom says: "They preach the
faith and act in unbelief, give to others peace and do not
have it themselves, cry out the truth and love a lie, denounce
avarice and love covetousness." Augustine, as above, on
Ex. 18, says: "Sitting in Moses' seat, they teach God's law;

therefore, God teaches through them, but, if they wish to teach their own things, do not hear them, do not do them."

Therefore, most true is Christ's saying and command, by which it is clear that he does not command the keeping and doing of all the precepts of those who sit in Moses' seat, for otherwise he would not have said: "They lay heavy burdens and grievous to be borne," and consequently burdens which ought not to be borne. And in the next chapter it is seen how he excused his disciples in respect to eating with unwashen hands and fasting.

Then, as for the authority of Augustine (which the doctors immediately append), the chapter preceding this, near the end, gives his statement. As for the statement of St. Jerome, on the explanation of faith, see Chapter XVI, where is set forth what he had spoken to Pope Damasus. But, after having looked at many old books, we have found that he wrote to St. Augustine, whom in his letters he often calls pope—which Augustine was a true pope—giving one significance to Peter's seat and Peter's faith, as appears near the beginning of Chapter XIII. As to St. Bernard, when he speaks of the absolutely good and the absolutely evil, and things intermediate, Chapter XIX treats of that. And it is added: "In these things which are intermediate the law of obedience is placed as—*tanquam*—in the tree of the knowledge of good and evil which was in the midst of Paradise." Certainly, in these things to prescribe our view to the judgment of the Masters is not right; and in these things neither the command nor the prohibition of prelates is in all cases to be despised. Here it is to be observed that the adverb of similitude, "as" [as it were]—*tanquam*—expresses a certain amount of likeness, not full likeness. For in the tree of the knowledge of good and evil the law was placed by God, who can neither deceive nor be deceived. This law was given under pain of mortal sin. For God said unto Adam: "Of the tree of the knowledge of good and evil, thou shalt not eat of it, for

in the day thou eatest of it, thou shalt surely die," Gen.
2 : 18. Here, then, three things are to be thought of—he
who gives the word of command, the command and the
condition of the person called upon to obey. He who commanded is God, who cannot err; the command is exceedingly useful; and man it is who heard God himself commanding. To eat, therefore, of the tree of the knowledge
of good and evil after the prohibitive command was given,
was an absolute evil. In accordance with this, let us suppose that the prelate Peter command John, his inferior, to
collect strawberries and let it be thought that it is not possible for him who commands to err in this, and let it be thought
of how much value such a work is for the person called upon
to obey, and also that the man called upon to obey is disposed to do such a work, as was Adam to do God's command,
and it is evident that in all these three, the comparison is not
the same. For a prelate may err and the work commanded
is not so useful, and the man called upon to obey is not so
disposed to do that work, as was Adam to do the command
of God.

Therefore, Bernard says that a work which is intermediate
is one which in respect of mode, time, or person may be
either good or bad; and here that saint insists upon the circumstances from the side of him who gives the command,
from the side of the work, and from the side of him called
to obey. Therefore, when he says that it is a work which is
intermediate so far as the *mode* goes, he urges a due measure
of the exercise of reason, in such a way that he who commands does not depart from the divine counsels. For, if a
prelate should command Peter, a subject, a learned priest in
God's law, to feed sows on the Lord's day and God for that
day should counsel him to do for Him a work of supererero-
gation incompatible with that act of feeding, then Peter
the priest is bound to obey God who counsels rather than
the prelate who commands. This is clear, for in this case the

superior is more to be reverenced, one whom every subject is more bound to obey; and the enjoined act also is more useful. But the act enjoined by the prelate, namely to feed sows on the Lord's day, is in respect to merit a thing indifferent, but the act enjoined by God has of and in itself the reason of merit.

Hence, I could wish that he might reply to St. Bernard in respect to this case. If St. Benedict had bid him feed sows for himself and, for the same time, God had given him a counsel to give advice to persons asking in the church with respect to the salvation of their souls, I am of the opinion that the authority of him who counsels and the greater usefulness of the counsel, as compared with the commands of St. Benedict, would have forced Bernard to hearken rather to the divine counsel than to Benedict's command, both to the honor of God and to the salvation of those asking counsel. From this it is seen to follow, that we owe more to any divine counsel whatever than to a human command which is incompatible with it. Secondly, it is seen to follow that no one is bound to obey a private command except in so far as it admonishes in accordance with the divine counsel or command; and it is clear that, as regards the mode, a due measure of reason is involved and also the quality of the command, both of which he who is called upon to obey and he who commands ought to consider. For what reason would there be for the command of a dull and fat bishop that a priest should feed sows and send away Christ's sheep without pasturing them—sheep which Christ purchased with his own blood?

Similarly must the circumstance of *place* be thought of, for, if a prelate should bid a subject to appear in a place where enemies are who are planning the subject's death, the subject is not bound to obey. Hence Pope Clement V, *de Sent. et rejud. in Clement.* [Friedberg, 2 : 1152], says: "Who would dare or by what reason would any one be held bound

to dare to submit to the judgment of such a consistory—
namely, to place oneself in the bosom of enemies and to
offer oneself voluntarily to a death from violent injury and
not by formal justice?   That, indeed, is to be feared from
the side of the law; that is to be evaded as a matter of morals;
that human sense and reason flee from; that nature abhors.
Therefore, he would be a fool who would dream of such a
citation binding the one cited." Nor ought the means of
defence to be taken away which come from the law of nature,
for the emperor himself has no right to withdraw those things
which are provided by the law of nature.

Likewise, Pope 'Nicolas wrote to the emperor Michael,
3 : 5 [Friedberg, 1 : 518]: "That suspects and enemies ought
not to be judges, reason itself dictates, and it is proved by
many examples. For what could any one give more acceptable and to be desired to an enemy than to commit a
person to him to be assailed, who might greatly wish to
hurt him?"   This thing also the Constantinopolitan synod,
Canon 6 [381 A. D.], is known to prohibit, and in the very
same chapter [Friedberg, 1 : 518] Pope Gelasius[1] a most
brave assailer of heretics, says: "I ask for the tribunal to
which they lay claim. Where can they carry their cases?
Before those who are enemies and at the same time witnesses and judges? But to such a tribunal no human business should be committed. And if to a tribunal, where enemies are the judges, no human business should be carried,
how much less ought cases of divine import, that is, ecclesiastical cases be carried! He that is wise, let him understand.
And in truth, for this reason, the good emperor Justinian
is known to have promulgated in his laws the same, when
he said: 'He who thinks a judge partial may, before the
trial begins, accuse him that the case may revert to another.
For it is just as natural to shun the assaults of judges as to
wish to flee from the sentence of enemies.' Thus St. John

---

[1] Mistake for Nicolas.

the Golden-mouthed refused to enter the college of the council assembled together against him." These things are found at the place [Friedberg, 1 : 519] where Gratian draws the following conclusion:[1] "Outside the limits of his province no man charged with guilt is under any circumstances to be summoned." Hence Pope Fabian,[2] 3 : 6 [Friedberg, 1 : 519], says: "The case is always tried there where the offence occurred, and he who does not prove his accusation should himself suffer the punishment he would inflict." Likewise Pope Stephen,[3] 3 : 6 [Friedberg, 1 : 519]: "No permission to accuse shall be proceeded with outside of the bounds of the provinces, but every charge is to be heard within the province." The same thing appears, 3 : 6 [Friedberg, 1 : 523] from the action of the Roman synod.

Therefore, what would be the nature of such obedience, or what reason would there be for it, that a person cited three hundred miles away—to the pope unknown, accused by enemies—should go with such concern to himself through enemies and come to hostile judges and witnesses and consume extravagantly the goods of the poor or (not practising extravagance) that he should go, suffering with hunger and with

---

[1] This quotation from the canon law gives only a part of the original and, as Huss's text has several mistakes, I have followed in the translation the text of the canon law. Gratian's conclusion, which Huss quotes, opens a new section of the canon law and is preceded by another statement by Gratian which it seems strange Huss did not quote as it is so apposite to what he has been saying. It runs: "Although a man's guilt be so evident, yet is he not to be condemned on the accusation of an enemy." John the Golden-mouthed, to whom Huss refers, is Chrysostom, patriarch of Constantinople, d. 407, the greatest preacher of the early church. The synod to which Huss refers was held 403 and is called the synod of the Oak. It was held under the direction of Theophilus of Alexandria, his enemy, and was made up largely of Chrysostom's enemies or disaffected members of his clergy. Chrysostom refused to attend unless his enemies were expelled. The court whom he had offended by his condemnations of extravagance in dress, etc., then deposed Chrysostom from his see.

[2] Fabian, pope, 236–250, seems to have been a vigorous administrator, in whose reign the schism of Hippolytus was completely put down and the Decian persecution vigorously resisted in Rome.

[3] Stephen I, pope, 254–257, in the dispute with Cyprian of Carthage over the baptism by heretics took ground in favor of its validity.

thirst! And what would be the fruit of such an appearance? Certainly the neglect of the work enjoined of God,
so far as his own salvation goes and the salvation of others.
Nor will he there be taught how to believe well, but how to
push litigation, which is not permitted to a servant of God.
There he will be despoiled in the consistory [curia], he will
grow cold in holy morals, he will be stirred up through op-
pression to impatience of spirit, and, if he have nothing to
give, he will be condemned, even if he have justice on his
side. And what is more serious, he will be compelled to
adore with bended knees the pope as God.[1]

Blessed, therefore, be God, who says: "I will go down
and see whether they have done altogether according to the
cry which is come unto me, and if not, I will know," Gen.
18 : 21. "Blessed be the Son of God, who came down from
heaven to seek and to save that which was lost," Luke 19 : 10.
"And he went about all the cities and the villages, teaching
in their synagogues, and preaching the Gospel of the kingdom, and healing all manner of disease and all manner of
sickness. But when he saw the multitudes, he was moved
with compassion for them because they were distressed and
scattered as sheep not having a shepherd," Matt. 9 : 35–36.
Blessed be Christ who commanded Peter, saying: "If thy
brother sin against thee, show him his fault between thee
and him alone," Matt. 18 : 15. Therefore, the pope will
not find any passages except such as prove the contrary,

---

[1] Cited by Cardinal Colonna to go to Rome, 1410, Huss, in his official replies,
his letters and at the council of Constance, constantly gave as a reason for not
complying the dangers from enemies by the way or, as he also expressed it,
from traps set by his enemies, especially the Germans whom he had offended
by his course at the university. Other reasons he gave were that he would have
to leave his work in Prague, and that the place where the offence was committed, Prague, was the proper place for the trial. Wenzel, in a letter to the
cardinal, suggested that he visit Prague, *Documenta*, p. 424, and overlook the
situation with his own eyes. In one place Huss, in urging the distance as a
reason for not going to Rome, said the distance from Prague to the holy city
was as great as the distance from Jerusalem to Tiberius, which, however, happens to be only sixty miles.

namely, that Christ answered in person citations of this kind. For, if popes would depend upon that law of Christ as stated, Matt. 7 : 12, "All things whatsoever ye would that men should do unto you, even so do ye also unto them; for this is the law and the prophets," I am of the opinion that they would not with reason desire to cite men and oblige them to make such a perilous and untried journey. Therefore, why do they urge others without a patent and reasonable cause to go to such pains and labor?

Oh that they would think of an exemplary life lived as set forth according to the authority of the pontiff, Christ, who piously went to see the erring and those oppressed by the devil, not by citing them to appear, not by excommunicating them, nor by imprisoning them, or by burning them—and who charged Peter and in him every one of his vicars, saying: "If thy brother sin against thee, go show him his fault," etc. Here Peter's vicar should take note, first, that when he wants to show a brother his fault, he ought to see first that he himself is unblamable, for love ought to begin with itself. How, then, may a prelate, full through and through with simoniacal heresy, pride, self-indulgence or avarice, lawfully show a brother his faults? To him the Lord says: "Hypocrite, first cast out the beam out of thine own eye and then shalt thou see clearly to cast out the mote out of thy brother's eye," Luke 6 : 42. Or how may he condemn any one to death, when the Saviour says: "He that is without sin among you, let him first cast a stone at her," John 8 : 7. In truth, if that law of Christ be thought of, rarely would a prelate be found in these times who could lawfully correct or condemn for heretical depravity.

Secondly, Christ's vicar should note how the Saviour commands, saying, "Go," for here he commands that judges ought in telling subjects of their faults to visit the places where the offence is said to have been committed, as even law proclaims. For so did Christ and all his apostles. And so Christ will do at the last judgment, as he alone predicts in Matt. 25. In the third place, let Peter's vicar or prelate note how in the way of telling one's fault, he ought to be prudent, diligent, and intent that he do not excommunicate before the close of the third rebuke. Fourthly, he should note the number of the faithful witnesses by whom the brother's offence is to be established. And fifthly, he ought to tell it to the church, as one greater than himself, for so the Lord bade Peter: "Tell it to the church."

From the things already said I summarize: that the proposed excommunication does not concern me or bind me because hostile judges and witnesses dwell in Rome and the case chiefly is a matter touching the judge. The distance for me is a long one and, guarded as it is all along the way by hostile Germans, I do not see any fruit of my appearance, but, on the contrary, only neglect of the people in the Word of God. I hope that Christ will guard me, as he said: "Behold, I send you forth as sheep in the midst of wolves, be ye, therefore, wise as serpents and harmless as doves. But beware of men, for they will deliver you up to councils and in their synagogues they will scourge you," Matt. 10 : 16, 17. He also said: "Behold, I have told you beforehand. If, therefore, they shall say unto you, behold, he is in the wilderness, go not forth: behold, he is in the inner chambers, believe it not," Matt. 24 : 25, 26. Therefore, I have committed myself to Christ alone that whether as a result of the false excommunication of men, or, outside that, by natural death or through violence he may bring my life to a close.

Then in respect to the circumstance of *time* [as bearing upon the duty of obedience], it is not doubtful that it is necessary for the one who gives a command as well as for the one called upon to obey to know when an act good generically, or when a neutral act, ought to be performed. For, if during the paschal festival a prelate bids a subject fast or, if he has a healthy body, on Good Friday not to fast, would it be lawful for a subject to obey contrary to the custom approved in the church and contrary to the conscience of this subject which resists, or, if he should bid him wander in the middle of the night through woods among cruel wild beasts when there was no necessity for it? And many are the commandments of this kind repugnant to reason. Nor should an argument be made in favor of obedience, if it were anywhere found in the lives of the Fathers, that subjects in the case of works which are without fitness or neutral obeyed, even as certain of the holy Fathers did obey, as Hugo of St. Victor, *Libellum Intitulatum*, speaking of these things which may not lawfully be done, said: "Just as we read that certain of the holy Fathers commanded subjects many things foreign to human reason that they might teach them the virtue of obedience, such as watering dry parts until they produced seeds or softening hard stones by pouring water over them and taming ferocious beasts by a word of command."

So far as the circumstance of the *person* is concerned, it is clear that here reason ought to direct as to a work good generically and also neutral. In a work generically good, if the prelate should command the subject to give alms by pauperizing his boys, or to take up penance by fasting which he is not capable of enduring, or to make many prayers even as confessors lay hard tasks upon men—certainly in such cases a pope is not to be hearkened to, since a parent is more bound to nourish his boys than to give alms to others; and he is not bound to bear insufferable burdens. The same is true in works neutral, for, if ever a pope should command me to play on the flute, build towers, to mend or weave garments, and to stuff sausages, ought not my reason to judge that the pope was foolish in so commanding? Why should I not prefer in this matter my common sense to the pope's sentence? Yea, if with all our doctors he should command me do these things, the reason would judge that the sentence of these persons was foolish.

Likewise, if the pope of his own motion should command that any one accept a bishopric who was incompetent on account of his inexperience of the language of the people he was to rule, would he have to obey by accepting? It is evident he would not. Similarly, it is evident that the people would not have to accept him just as they would not want the pope to put over them a shepherd of sows or goats—a pastor who would be of no account to feed those flocks.

And it is clear, that Christ's faithful disciple ought to look back to the first exemplar, Christ himself, and listen to a prelate as far as he teaches Christ's law, things reasonable, things to edification, and things lawful for the subject, for Cyprian, God's glorious martyr, says: *Decretum, Dist.* 8 [Friedberg, 1 : 15]: "If Christ alone is to be hearkened to, then we ought not to listen to what any one before us may have thought ought to be done, but what Christ, who is before all, did." This soundest of rules antichrist's satraps lay aside, who say that disobedience to papal statutes is to be punished most severely, and so Christ with his law is put aside. Hence, it being laid down that obedience is due to the pope and prelates in all things neutral, the pope, in treating the law of Christ as difficult to understand, may decree that no Christian should do any work that is neutral, except such works as he himself approves and ratifies, and consequently he may ordain that his satraps cite any persons whatsoever to appear and answer at his tribunal; and so they are able to worry the people out till they make a promise, and mulct the people as they do in absolutions, in reservations and in dispensations.

And, as is believed, they would practise this more abundantly if they did not fear that the people, perceiving their subtilty, would rebel. For now God is enlightening the people that they be not beguiled from Christ's paths. For Daniel prophesied, saying: "And arms [forces] shall stand on his part; and they shall profane the sanctuary and they shall set up the abomination that maketh for desolation, and such as do wickedly against the covenant shall he pervert by flatteries, but the people that know their God shall be strong and do exploits," Daniel 11 : 31–32. Antichrist's "arms which stand and profane God's sanctuary" are wicked prelates who are an abomination on account of their villainies, and they are the "desolation" by refusing to imitate Christ. Of this abomination Christ says, "when ye see the abomination of desolation standing in the holy place which was spoken of by Daniel the prophet," Matt. 24 : 15, and, "standing where he ought not," Mark 13 : 14. And when the prophet adds, "and such as do wickedly against the covenant," for they say they keep Christ's covenant, but will not keep it, because they obscure and gloss it for their own exaltation and to excuse their sin, "but the people that know their God," that is, know by the gift of God's grace, will obtain Christ by imitation of him and will do the commandments of the covenant of the Lord Jesus Christ. But because to those that teach these things persecution comes unto death, therefore Daniel further says: "And they that are wise among the people shall instruct many and shall fall by the sword and in the flames and in the captivity and by the fall of days. And when these shall fall, they shall be lifted up by the help of the little ones and many shall join themselves unto them with flatteries," Dan. 11 : 33–34.

The experience of the facts enables us to understand this text, for simple laymen and priests, taught by God's grace, teach very many by the example of a good life and, gainsaying publicly antichrist's lying words, perish with the sword. This is seen in the cases of the laymen, John, Martin, and Stafcon,[1] who resisted antichrist's lying disciples, and per-

[1] In the troubles arising in Prague out of the proclamation of John XXIII's bulls against Ladislaus and the sale of pardons these three men offered violent resistance and were arrested and imprisoned. As they were about to be executed, Huss, in company with others, appeared at the city hall, appealed in their behalf

ished together by the sword. And others, exposing their necks for the truth have been martyred, being seized, imprisoned, and murdered and yet did not deny Christ's truth —priests, and also laymen and women. But those who have oppressed them have gone away clandestinely for, terrified by antichrist's censures and seizures, they have turned into the opposite way. But God, up to this time, multiplies the sons of his church who suffer and are patient and publish the truth of Christ's law. Therefore, blessed be God and the Father of our Lord Jesus Christ who has hidden the way of truth from the wise and prudent and revealed it unto simple laymen and little priests who choose rather to obey God than men, who in acts generically good and acts neutral have the life of Christ before their eyes and obey prelates so far as these acts, modified by circumstances, can be reasonably put into practice for edification through the imitation of Christ. For they themselves hold that an act, in order to be virtuous, must be justified by eight circumstances, which are set forth in this line:

Who, what, where, how much, how many, why, in what manner, when.

Who, that is, the individual who ought to obey. *What*, namely, he ought to do when he is commanded. *Where*, because in one place it is fitting, in the case of an act good generically or neutral to obey, and not so in another place or in any place whatsoever. *How much*, namely, he ought to obey, in as far as the command is of something applicable to edification according to the counsel of Jesus Christ or his command. For one is not bound to obey forever his personal superior as the foolish prate, saying, that the pope's

and secured, as he thought, their immunity from death. But after he was once out of sight, the men were taken from prison and quickly beheaded. A great crowd coming together gathered up the bodies and carried them amidst the singing of sacred hymns to Bethlehem chapel, where they were buried and looked upon as martyrs. In one of his sermons, Langsdorff, p. 16, Huss refers to the death of these three men as a price for denying that the pope is the God of this world and can forgive sins as he will, and to their burial in Bethlehem.

authority extends to the right of infinite commanding, and whom individual Christians ought to obey even to that extent. *How many*, namely, acts he may lawfully do, since it matters not whether the subject, following the command of a priest binding him to penance, gives two pennies or two denarii or fasts three days weekly; and that he give as many pennies or fast as many days as the simple fellow commands or limits (unless he fill his confessor's purse), or that he give as much for the building of St. Peter as he would offer if he lived there and as much by the estimate of the pope's camera as he might consume on the journey thither; and so of other taxations invented of the devil. The faithful ought also to think of the circumstance of the end in view, namely: *why*, that is, with what end in view he ought to obey by the act which is enjoined, because, if it leads to God's honor and directly to the profit of the church, then it is a good end. But if another end is held forth, then it is against the apostle's words: "Whatsoever ye do, do in the name of Jesus Christ." For the end determines all the means—*media*—which are used with that end in view. Hence, Aristotle concludes, *de Anima*, 2, with these words: "It is right that all things should be called good by the end, so that when the end is good, the means for that end are also good." And another circumstance is also added, when it is said: *how*. For it is not enough to do a thing that is good generically, but it is demanded that it be done well, for nothing can be done well by a man except as he abides in love. Therefore, the apostle says: "Let all your things be done in love." And that nothing is well done by a man without love, the apostle proves when he says: "Though I bestow all my goods to feed the poor, and have not love, it profiteth me nothing," I Cor. 13 : 3. And this is reasonable because the branch cannot bear fruit, except it abide in the vine, as the Saviour said: "Ye cannot bear fruit, except ye abide in me," that is, by love, John 15 : 4. Hence it is said in a general way that a certain philosopher, by name Phantasma—Illusion—advanced that God is the rewarder not of nouns but adverbs [not names, but qualities], and it is clear that for obedience to be true, grace or love is needed. Then other circumstances are involved in this adverb, *how*, because one that is called upon to obey ought to perform the work commanded out of love, in humility, wisely, joyfully, bravely, and promptly. The last condition is *when*—namely, it is fitting to perform the work commanded, as has been said before, with respect to time, for without doubt there are many acts good generically and also acts neutral, which it is not expedient to command at any time whatever, and consequently it is not expedient to yield obedience to them at any time.

However, as for this [namely, that the inferior obey the superior in all things], it is argued up to this point thus: Suppose that the pope should, by the bond of holy obedience and upon the assurance of obtaining absolution from penalty and guilt or some other spiritual benefit, bind every cleric subject to him to resist the first pope obedient in all things, and that he should bind every laic by a similar formula to resist the first disobedient pope and let the injunction be made under the severest of anathemas—and suppose in addition that every cleric or laic subject to our pope was first obedient to him and that every cleric resisted every laic and vice versa. Here the contradiction would be manifest because it is allowed that Peter the cleric and Paul the laic were not at first in opposition, resisting one another, and I ask whether Peter being for the moment obedient is resisting the pope. If so, then we must say that for that moment Paul was disobedient to the pope because, inasmuch as he resists Peter who is disobedient to the pope in all things, and it was enjoined that he should resist the first disobedient pope, it follows that Paul incurs the mark of disobedience, and so also Peter for the moment being disobedient would be resisting the pope. Then we should grant that Paul is obedient and Peter also, because before they resisted one another they were both obedient, and Peter by resisting, was not disobedient but, as follows from what has been said, his obedience is confirmed. And it is not valid to deny the pertinency of this case on account of the following things, namely, (1) because only what was neutral or possible was commanded and (2) because a prelate may command what in itself is impossible and altogether unreasonable, therefore, he may command that thing, and so there remains no reply except the truth that neither more nor less on account of his commanding do the cleric and the layman incur reward or penalty. For a command must be reasonable with God if it is to be obeyed. And then it would hold good, provided no one under human authority would make that command, since otherwise a man would become disobedient to reason. And it is clear that, as in the case supposed, there would be no possibility left of looking for remission or anathema, so in a general way there would not be in the case of a papal sentence except so far as one merited them in accordance with God's will. This logical objection must be solved. And similarly suppose, that Peter the prior had a second Twelve made up of conventuals all obedient to him, and he should bid the more stable Twelve not to speak with the other unless perchance by being disobedient it might bring the other to obedience. And it is clear that the second Twelve did not talk with the rest except, by obeying Peter, to bring the other to obedience, and Paul of the former Twelve should speak with Linus of the latter Twelve both of them excelling in this that they have regard to the injunction of obedience, so that, before the talking occurred, both were lawfully obedient to Peter; and the contradiction will appear.[1]

[1] This is the most difficult passage in Huss's treatise. Wyclif, though not using the exact form above, so far as I know, uses the general method to prove

Likewise as Bernard in his letter to the monk Adam says that things which are intermediate—may equally well or equally badly be either commanded or prohibited. Therefore, when a superior commands or forbids wrongly, and when the subject knows that he has commanded or forbidden wrongly, he ought by the law of love to tell the subject his fault as a brother because when in so commanding or forbidding he sins against God and his brother. This appears by that rule of Christ: "If thy brother sin against thee, go and tell him his fault between thee and him alone," Matt. 18 : 15. Nor is there any objection to this that he who is superior in virtue should tell one inferior in his living his fault, howbeit the latter be the superior in rank, for otherwise this law of Christ would perish, which ordains that every Christian prelate, when he has sinned, should be corrected by another. For the law speaks to all men alike when it says: "If thy brother sin against thee, go and tell him his fault." But if, to make an impossible supposition, Christ had sinned, he would inasmuch as he was our brother, Heb. 2 : 17-19, have had to be corrected by the church. Hence he indicated this, when he said to the multitudes: "Which of you convicteth me of sin?" John 8 : 46.

For this reason the church in the person of our Saviour aptly sings: "O my people, what have I done to thee? or how have I comforted thee? Answer me,"—namely, by a reproach. And Isaiah, 1 : 17, says: "Cease to do evil, learn to do well. Seek justice, relieve the oppressed, judge the fatherless, plead for the widow, and come and let us reason together, saith the Lord." Therefore, it is clear that every wayfaring man ought to have his faults told him by his brother, for otherwise the law of Christ would be wanting in provid-

an utter inconsistency, as in his *de Eccles.*, p. 211. The imaginary characters, Peter, Paul, and Linus, are used somewhat in the same way as Richard Roe and John Doe. Linus is brought in as a judge, being chosen because he belonged to the second generation of presbyters or bishops. See Wyclif, *de domin. civ.*, pp. 38, 39, for a similar use of Peter, Paul, and Linus to prove the inconsistency of making natural dominion, as opposed to civil dominion, exempt from spiritual laws.

ing a remedy against the spots of his bride, and Paul contradicts the idea that it is wanting, Gal. 5, for he resisted
Peter, the pope, to his face for a light offence and also in his
writing left for those who were to come after, that in cases
of like falling away they should do the same to their brother.
Therefore, it is faithless to assert that the higher rank may
not have its fault told it in matters moral by an inferior.
Wherefore, in case of a fault, a son may lawfully tell his
father his fault, a daughter the mother, a subject the prelate, a disciple his teacher—all following the rule of love.

However, against these things the objection is made that
the pope has the place of the Lord Jesus Christ on earth.
But it is not permitted any one to tell him his fault, as appears from Matt. 16.   When, on account of Christ's rebuke,
Peter is called Satan, is it not, therefore, permitted to find
fault with him that occupies Peter's stead?   But this kind
of reasoning includes too much, for it would necessitate saying that every vicar of Christ is impeccable, just as Christ
is impeccable.   But it is a good inference that neither pope
nor other person ought to be found fault with or corrected
in so far as they follow the Head, Christ.   But, if a bishop
or confessor occupying Christ's stead attempt an act of self-
indulgence with a virgin or a chaste wife, ought he not to
be vehemently found fault with as if he were antichrist
and the faithless enemy of his own soul?   For in committing
such an illicit act, he does not occupy Christ's stead, but the
place of antichrist himself and the devil, tempting a woman
most iniquitously.   And it is clear, that that statement of
St. Bernard which the doctors adduce, namely, that in those
things, that is, 'things intermediate, it is certainly not right to
prefer our view to the sentence of the masters, and in these
neither the command nor the prohibition of prelates are altogether to be spurned'—the circumstances must be understood
fitted to the act of obedience which is owed in respect to
the mode, place, time and person, as has been said.   For often
the student with reason refuses to obey in an act intermediate

or neutral or even in an act good generically, showing the reason why it is not expedient in such a case to obey. This has frequently happened to me, when I have commanded; and being taught better and even taking gratefully information, I have obeyed the student. And the same reasoning holds in respect to a prelate, for in our times prelates often talk wildly in their commands because of ignorance, and are to be reasoned with in love, by their subjects, for the well-being of the church.

But it is objected to this that an equal has no rule over an equal. Since, therefore, the pope excels every other pilgrim and every superior his subject, it seems that it is not the business of any pilgrim to correct the pope or any subject his prelate. This means that, if the antecedent be denied, since necessarily God the Father has no rule over the Holy Spirit, and yet they are equal persons, the consequence does not follow, namely, that of necessity God the Father has rule over the Son, according to the humanity he assumed and yet necessarily they are absolutely equal. Therefore, if no equal has rule over an equal, the catholic faith is gainsaid. And again: as is the rule of a vicar, so also of the same kind is all human rule, as the apostle says: "Charge them that are rich in this present world that they be not high-minded," I Tim. 6. But such rule is either independent, derived from itself, or it is originally authorized over some creature, and so it is clear how bare this mode of reasoning is both as to its substance and form, for he understands by this principle that an equal has no authoritative rule over his equal, on the ground by which he is equal to one who rules in such a way. But what stands in the way of one who excels in virtue telling to one inferior in his living his fault, howbeit the latter be the superior in rank?

Besides, the objection is raised from the canon law, *Dist.* 21, *Nunc autem* [Friedberg, 1 : 71], where it is declared that no one of the holy bishops dared to bring a judgment against Pope Marcellinus, but they said: "By thine own mouth judge thy case. Thou shalt not subject thyself to our decision." That is to say, that this saying of the bishops is not sufficient to nullify God's law according to which in the case of Paul he reproved Peter the pope. Secondly, it means that it would be most superfluous for them to reprove him in such a case, who observed from his contrition that he was fully reproved of the Lord. Thirdly, it means that he was sufficiently reproved by them when they said, "by thine own mouth judge thy case, thou shalt not be subject to our decision." And still again, it means, Be not heard at our tribunal but gather up thy case in thy own bosom and once more thou wilt be declared righteous of thyself, they say, or be condemned out of thine own mouth. Certainly that was a great act of reproving, because those who reproved cast the duty of reproving back on the pope himself. Hence Marcellinus, when he heard these things, declared the sentence of deposition against himself.[1]

Thus it is clear that a subject following the rule of prudence and of love may correct an erring superior and lead him back to the way of truth. For, if a superior should wander away and come into a cave of thieves or into the danger of death, it would be proper for the subject to draw him back and to preserve him from danger. Therefore, this is the more allowable when a superior by a devious path of living runs into the cave of demons and into the peril of the worst death of sins. If, therefore, in the first case, the superior would

[1] Marcellinus, whom Jerome [Migne, 27 : 1111] puts among the popes, probably of the time of Diocletian, is reported to have fallen away in time of persecution and sacrificed to the gods. He acknowledged his mistake in the presence of a synod of bishops who refused to sit in judgment on him on the ground that *prima sedes a nemine judicatur*—the primal see is judged by no one. This was the theory asserted by the mediæval popes. They were subject to no tribunal but God. Higden, 5 : 104-108, reported the tradition that Marcellinus deposed himself and anathematized any one that should bury his body.

rejoice, why not much more in the second? If he employs a guardian in the first case, why not in the second?

Nor is there anything to conflict in that saying of St. Augustine, *de conflictu virtutum et vitiorum* [Migne, 40 : 1094]:[1] "What sort of men they ought to be who rule is not a question to be discussed by subjects." This is true and evident, that they ought not to discuss rashly what sort of men they ought to be, nevertheless, reason dictates to them that they who rule ought to be good, that they ought not to live in excess and, if they live badly, subjects ought to take heed and to beware of their evil works in advance. Hence Augustine says: "If human rule is to be obeyed, it is necessary that we be subject to divine government,[2] for Christ himself says, 'He who heareth you, heareth me, and he that despiseth you, despiseth me.'" And, further on, Augustine adds: "Nevertheless, because he foresees that not all will in the future be of this kind, he took all kinds of subjects into the company of his disciples and said, admonishing them in advance, 'The scribes and Pharisees sit in Moses' seat; whatsoever things they say to you, these do, but what they do, do not ye.'" And it is clear that, with the zeal of a good purpose, subjects should discuss the manner of life of their superiors or think of it, so that, if the superiors are good, the subjects may imitate them; if evil, they follow not their works, but in an humble spirit pray for them and take heed when they command good things. Otherwise, unless they discuss, they will fall with the blind leader into the hole, and easily it may happen that they will worship antichrist as God, and, like the Jewish people who followed their leaders— *prælatis*—conspire against Christ the Lord.

---

[1] The treatise was falsely ascribed to Augustine.

[2] Huss's text must be wrong or Huss is drawing an inference in his own language. The original treatise has *si obtemperandum Domini est imperio humano subdi necesse est magisterio.* If the Lord's rule is to be obeyed, subjection to human government is necessary. Romans 13 : 1–2 is quoted.

CHAPTER XXII

EXCOMMUNICATIONS, JUST AND UNJUST

FINALLY, the doctors lay down in their writing the following: "At length, because the processes [court proceedings before the curia and the archbishop of Prague] against Master John Huss have been received by the body of the clergy in Prague, and they have obeyed them, therefore these processes are to be obeyed, and especially since therein nothing absolutely good is prohibited nor is anything absolutely evil enjoined.[1] But according to the method of the church customary with the Roman curia and observed before the fathers of our fathers, only things intermediate—things between what is purely good and purely evil—are there commanded, which in respect to time, place, or mode may be either good or bad—and obedience is to be rendered in these things intermediate in accordance with the teachings of the Gospel and in accordance with St. Bernard." And they add: "And it is not the business of the clergy in Prague to pronounce judgment on the question whether the excommunication of Master John Huss is just or unjust." etc.

I will proceed to the things in the processes [court proceedings] about which for the present I chiefly consider three matters, namely, excommunication, suspension and interdict. And about these I will speak briefly, discussing first of all this, that the conclusion which the doctors draw is exceedingly bad, namely, "because the processes against John Huss

---

[1] The duty of resisting unjust excommunications Huss takes up in his *adv. Indulg.*, *Mon.*, 1 : 229–234; *de sex Erroribus*, 239 *sqq.*; *ad octo Doctores*, 383 *sqq.*, etc.

have been received by the body of the clergy in Prague, and they have obeyed them, therefore, they ought to be obeyed." It is as if we should argue in this way: because processes were received by the body of the clergy in Jerusalem against Christ, that he is a seducer, malefactor, and blasphemer excommunicate and guilty of death, therefore, those processes are to be obeyed by the doctors themselves. The conclusion from the law of similarity holds by that middle term of cause, "because the processes were received by the clergy" —and the doctors of theology ought to be ashamed for that conclusion, and especially Stanislaus, for he is the ablest logician amongst them. Perhaps they learned that conclusion from the chief priests, scribes, and Pharisees who formulated a like conclusion. For when Pilate said unto them, "What accusation bring ye against this man?" they answered and said (formulating this conclusion): "If this man were not an evil-doer we would not have delivered him up to thee," John 18 : 29–30. And again they followed the same line of argument when Pilate said, "I find no case against him," when they replied, "We have a law and according to that law he ought to die, because he made himself the Son of God," John 19 : 7. In the first conclusion, formulated by the Jews, the doctors implied that they themselves did not err when they said: "If this one were not an evil-doer, we would not have delivered him up to thee"—that is, because he is an evil-doer, therefore have we delivered him up to thee. Similarly our doctors reply in the conclusion they formulate that the body of the clergy in Prague cannot err; otherwise, if they were able to err, their conclusion would not be valid. And because that body is able to err in accepting the processes, so also it does err in securing them and wickedly executing them. Therefore, the conclusion of the doctors is not a good one.

And I wonder how this enormous conclusion—*cauda*—of the doctors, by which they wish to cover up their shame by the statement: processes to the contrary import, if received, would have to be obeyed—does not contradict this, when the conclusion is added: "Nor is it the business of the clergy in Prague to pronounce sentence whether the excommunication of Master John Huss is just or unjust." For if those processes are to be obeyed with respect to excommunication, then they are to be obeyed by them as just and not as unjust. Because the clergy together with the doctors obeys them and received them, therefore it obeys them as just and received them as just, and consequently the doctors together with the clergy passed upon them sentence that they are just. Nevertheless, their conclusion says that it is not for the clergy in Prague to pass sentence whether the excommunication of Master John Huss is just or unjust. And an evident contradiction is established, namely, the clergy in Prague cries out, affirms and asserts that the excommunication of Master John Huss is just, therefore the clergy in Prague passes the sentence that that excommunication is just; yet the conclusion of the doctors says that it is not for the clergy in Prague to pass sentence whether that judgment of excommunication is just or unjust. It is most clear that this conclusion contradicts the facts and the sentence of the clergy of Prague.

Likewise, if it is not for the clergy in Prague to pass sentence whether that excommunication is just or unjust, and the clergy approves the processes and acts in accordance with the processes; therefore the clergy in Prague does not know whether it is acting justly or unjustly, nor does it hope that it is acting justly. For hope ought to go before the sentence.

Likewise, these doctors themselves pass the sentence that the excommunication of Master John Huss is just, and this is clear because they pass the sentence that the processes are to be obeyed, and not as though they were unjust; hence, as though they were just. Consequently, the doctors pronounce the sentence that the excommunication enjoined in the processes is just.

Likewise, the doctors say that the processes [court proceedings] are to be obeyed, especially because in them nothing that is an absolute good is forbidden, nor is anything enjoined which is an absolute evil, but only things which are intermediate, in which obedience must be rendered in accordance with the teaching of the Gospel and in accordance with St. Bernard. Therefore the doctors pass sentence that the commands in the processes are just, among which is the excommunication of Master John Huss. Therefore, these doctors pass the sentence that the excommunication of Master John Huss is just. And they themselves are part of the clergy in Prague. Therefore, this very conclusion of theirs confutes these doctors.

Likewise, these doctors pronounce judgment that the excommunication which is enjoined in the processes is a thing intermediate, a thing between that which is absolutely good and that which is absolutely evil, and when it is enjoined in respect to the mode, time, place and person, then it passes over into a thing absolutely good, because it passes into an injunction of the pope and prelates. Therefore, the doctors, in pronouncing such a judgment about the excommunication, declare that it is just. Nevertheless, in view of their conclusion, they ought not to pronounce the judgment that it is just. And this they do, a thing they ought not to do; yea, they do not know what they are doing, for they say that it is not for the clergy in Prague to pronounce judgment that the excommunication of John Huss is unjust, and yet they pronounce judgment that it is just. It is certainly worthy of laughter how doctors of the law agree to this conclusion, doctors who pronounce judgment on the decrees, decretals and processes [court proceedings] whether they are just or justly given or by just men, when they ought by reasonable methods to expound the decrees and the decretals and examine the proceedings, whether they are just or un-just, and to advise others, when the emergency arises, whether processes ought to be admitted and held or whether they ought not be admitted and held; or whether it is lawful to take appeal from them. This is clear, because the doctors have irrationally shut themselves off on both sides from a reasonable judgment.

But how the processes fulminated against me are null and erroneous, the Venerable Master John de Jesenicz, doctor of canon law, showed most clearly by a public discussion and in a decision in the university of Bologna. And because, as I have said, processes of this kind chiefly enjoin excom-munication, suspension and interdict, for that reason I will say something about them briefly.

Let it be first noted that excommunication means placing outside of communication, 11 : 3, *Nihil.* and *cap. Canonica* [Friedberg, 1 : 653, 674]; 29 : 1, *Viduas* [Friedberg, 1 : 1091]; 24 : 3 [Friedberg, 1 : 988]; 11 : 3, *Omnis Christianus* [Fried-berg, 1 : 653], and the chapter following. And, because ex-communication is better understood through its opposite, namely, communication or communion—inasmuch as by the opposite of what is good everything good is understood, so also of evil and its opposite—therefore it is to be noted that communication or good communion is threefold. The first is the participation of divine grace, which makes gracious. This the apostle wishes for the Corinthians, when he says: "The grace of our Lord Jesus Christ and the love of God and the communication of the Holy Spirit be with you all," II Cor. 13 : 13. This communication is the communion of the saints, who are Christ's mystical body, the body of which Christ is the head, and this communion we believe when we say: "I believe the communion of saints." The second communication or communion is the participation in the sacraments. "There is one Lord, one faith, one baptism," Eph. 4 : 5. It is especially taken, however, for the participation in the body and blood of our Lord Jesus Christ. "The cup of blessing which we bless, is it not the communication of the blood of Christ? And the bread which we break, is it not the participation of the body of the Lord?" I Cor. 10 : 16. Because we, being many, are one bread and one body, seeing we partake of one bread and one cup. The third communication or communion is the participation in suffrages.[1] In this participation the good Lord is glorified: "I am a companion of all them that fear thee and that keep thy commandments," Ps. 119 : 63. And besides this three-fold communication is the communication which is the inter-course between all Christians, good and bad. The first three are only participated in by good men, but of this fourth men of the world think more.

Secondly, it is to be noted that in this statement I speak of excommunication, as it corresponds to the fourfold excom-munication just spoken of, namely, separation (1) from par-ticipation in divine grace which makes gracious, (2) from a worthy participation in the sacraments, (3) from participa-tion in the suffrages which prepare for the life eternal—these three being opposed to the corresponding threefold communion —and (4) from intercourse with Christians, either by the censure of the spiritual or public exclusion by the secular judge.

From these it follows: (1) that there is not and can never be an excommunication of the three first kinds except for mortal sins. This is clear, because never is any one separ-ated from the communion of the saints, which is the partic-ipation in God's grace, and the sacraments and the suffrages, preparing for the life eternal, except for mortal sin. For mortal sin alone divides or separates from communion of this kind, just as it separates from God himself. Nor can this happen except through mortal sins, because, so long as

[1] Suffrages are the prayers of the church and other benefits accruing from the acts of the church in the mass and indulgences. See Hergenröther: *K.-recht*, 567; Friedberg: *K.-recht*, 294.

a man is in grace, so long does he remain a partaker of the aforementioned threefold communion, in respect to the law of present righteousness. And as God is the most righteous judge, He cannot damn a man except for his demerit in non-participation of this kind. Therefore, the corollary is true. (2) It follows that no judge may ever excommunicate in this way unless the man himself shall before excommunicate himself by his offences. (3) It follows that no judge ought to excommunicate any one except for a criminal offence[1] or on account of mortal sin, and this is clear from 11 : 3 [41, Fried-berg, 1 : 655], where it is said: "No bishop except for the certain and evident cause of sin shall deprive any one whomsoever from ecclesiastical communion by the anathema, because the anathema is the eternal damnation of death, and only for mortal sin ought it to be imposed and only on him who may not be otherwise corrected." And it is also said, 24 : 3, *His ita respondetur* [Friedberg, 1 : 988]: "With God not the sentence of priests is sought but the life of the guilty, for no one is to be known by the sentence to whom the stain of sin does not adhere." Likewise, Lyra, Com. on Hosea, 4, at the end, says: "O Judah, send Israel away, on account of his wickedness, for their company is separated, that is, excommunicated." And also it is said by Augustine, 2 : 1, *Multi*, 5 [Friedberg, 1 : 446]: "No one ought to be excommunicated except for a criminal offence."

All, however, agree in saying that excommunication is of two kinds, major and minor, as is apparent from *de Sent. Excom. si quem de cleri excommunicat. fieri, de except. cap.* 2 [Friedberg, 2 : 912][2] where it is stated that a minor excommunication removes from the participation of the sacraments but the major separates from the communion of the faithful.

---

[1] A *crimen* or criminal offence is a violation of a natural law or a positive divine commandment, as, for example, adultery, as opposed to a violation of ecclesiastical law, *delictum*. Hergenröther, 549 *sq.*, 780 *sq.*

[2] Gregory IX's Decretals, 5 : 39, c. 59, and also 5 : 39, c. 1, make the distinction above made by Huss between major and minor excommunication, the canon law running: "If any one pronounces the words, 'I excommunicate

Minor excommunication is separation on account of mortal sin from participation in spiritual benefits by which a man makes himself unworthy through criminal offence to continue to participate in grace, and this excommunication no one may impose upon a man who persists in God's grace. Major excommunication is the separation which the prelates of the church announce against a man as an open sinner, and by which they set him off from intercourse with Christians and from participation in the sacraments.

By this excommunication they now designate me in processes and denunciations, shutting me out from all human communion. But blessed be God, who did not give such force to this [kind of] excommunication as to make it possible for it to take away from a good man virtue or righteousness, when he endures in humility, nor is it able to impose upon him sin [when he refuses to obey it]. Nay, rather when he has patiently continued to endure it helps to purify him as tools iron, and fire gold, and it helps to increase his reward of beatitude, as the Lord said: "Blessed are ye when men shall persecute you, and separate you from their company, and reproach you and cast out your name as evil for the Son of man's sake. Rejoice in that day and leap for joy, for behold, great is your reward in heaven, for in the same manner did their fathers do unto the prophets," Luke 6 : 22, 23.

But this [major] excommunication ought to be medicinal, that is, a remedy to heal a man in his soul and to lead him

him,' then he is bound not merely by the minor excommunication which separates from participation in the sacraments, but also by the major excommunication which separates from the communion of the faithful." This distinction is usually resolved into a difference in the solemnities attending the announcement. Since Martin V's decree, 1418, a distinction has been made between excommunicated persons to be tolerated and avoided—*tolerati et vitandi*. In case one of the latter is present at any meeting, the priest must interrupt the service. With those who are to be avoided are forbidden all passing of words, prayer, greetings, intercourse and fellowship at the table. See Hergenröther, 567 *sqq.;* Friedberg, *K.-recht*, pp. 293 *sqq.* Wyclif, *de Eccles.,* 153 *sqq.* and *de dom. civ.,* 300 *sq.,* gives the conditions justifying excommunication and refers to the distinction between minor and major excommunication and the solemn extinguishing of candles in the latter.

back to Christ's fold and to life eternal as a measure ordained for a final end. Therefore, St. Augustine, *Homilia, de penitentia*, also 2 : 1, *Multi*, says: "Excommunication ought not to be mortal but medicinal." Again, *Cum medicinalis. de Sent. Excom., liber* 6 : 7.[1] A notorious sinner after the third warning or public citation, when he refuses to be corrected, ought on account of his criminal offence to be kept from communication according to the Saviour's command, where he said to Peter: "If thy brother sin against thee, go show him his fault between thee and him alone. If he hear thee, thou hast gained thy brother. But if he will not hear thee, take with thee one or two more that at the mouth of two or three witnesses every word may be established. And if he refuses to hear them, tell it to the church. And if he refuses to hear the church also, let him be unto thee as the Gentile and the publican," Matt. 18 : 15-17. This exposition is given above at the beginning of Chapter XXI of this treatise, in which the conditions of a true prelate are indicated. Nevertheless, this is yet to be noted, that Christ said: "If he sin," that is, commit the sin of a criminal offence, for on that account he is deserving of correction and he is not to be excommunicated for anything whatsoever. But if he show himself incorrigible, after the third reproof, then he ought to be carefully avoided as a heathen Gentile and a publican; otherwise not. Let, therefore, prelates see to it that they act cautiously, lest they excommunicate so easily subjects for temporal gain.

Hence, St. Augustine, *Sermo de Quadragesima:* "We cannot deprive of the communion, because this prohibition is not yet mortal or medicinal, except in the case of one who has of his own accord confessed or has been named or convicted in some secular or ecclesiastical tribunal." And he also says on these words, "If any man that is named a brother be a fornicator or covetous or an idolater or a reviler or

[1] Boniface VIII's *Liber Sextus de sent. excom.*, 5 : 11; 1 Friedberg, 2 : 1093.

a drunkard or an extortioner, with such an one no not to eat,"
I Cor. 5 : 11: "Likewise it must be known that every
one sinning mortally is excommunicated of God, in accordance with that Psalm, 'Cursed are those who depart from
thy commandments,' and I Cor. 16 : 22, 'If any man love
not our Lord Jesus Christ, let him be anathema.'"   And although this excommunication is called minor because it is
not pronounced solemnly in public by a prelate, nevertheless I fear it more than the major excommunication, with
which the prelates now assail me.   But, besides, I fear the
greatest excommunication more still with which the high
priest, sitting in the sight of all the angels and men, will excommunicate the damned from participation in eternal blessedness, as he said: "Go,[1] ye cursed into the eternal fire which
is prepared for the devil and his angels," Matt. 25 : 41.   Of
this excommunication the judge ought to think and he ought
to beware lest he excommunicate unjustly.   For whoever
excommunicates another for temporal gain or chiefly for his
own honor or to revenge an injury against himself or without any known cause of criminal offence this man excommunicates himself.   For he ought to excommunicate him
whom God excommunicates, for criminal offence which he
knows [the possible offender] has committed and after the
third warning and out of love, for the honor of God and
for the salvation of the man whom he excommunicates and
also for the advantage of others that they may fear and
that he [the offender] do not infect them.   So Paul did when,
writing to the Corinthians, he charged them to cast out the
public fornicator lest he should infect others and also that
his soul might be saved, I Cor. 5 : 5.

Now, these things being considered, the faithful should
know how many prelates, clergy and laity are excommunicated of God; for all who depart from the Lord's commandments are excommunicated, and also how many excommuni-

---

[1] *Ite.* Vulgate: *discedite a me.*

cate themselves when they put excommunication on others, or publish it, and especially the clerics who, as it were, every day at prime sing: "Cursed are they who depart from thy commandments."

This much, in brief, with respect to excommunication, in regard to which that good Christian of holy memory and that great zealot of Christ's law, Master Frederick Epinge, bachelor of canon law, treating of the first article, said: "No prelate ought to excommunicate anybody unless he first knows that the person has been excommunicated by God." Of this I have written in another place. And, if thou wilt not believe it, learn it on the wall in Bethlehem,[1] and there thou wilt find how excommunication does not injure the righteous but profits and why even the righteous ought to fear unjust prelatic or Pilatic excommunication, and for these reasons, (1) that he may not be guilty at some other place or time. (2) The danger to him who unjustly excommunicates. (3) The injury to the brethren which may follow from a foolish application of censures; (4) that they may not become an occasion of stumbling by going back from the truth; (5) that they may not suffer an injury by an excommunicated person's curses; (6) that he by impatience may not fall from merit or depart from righteousness—and also for other reasons explained more fully and pertinently in another place.[2]

---

[1] Huss refers to the six inscriptions on the walls of Bethlehem chapel, *Mon.*, 1 : 237–243, which were intended to counteract six errors about the mass—namely, that the priest creates the body of Christ; faith—namely, that faith is exercised in Mary, etc., and not in God only; absolution from sin —namely, that the priest absolves whomsoever he will; obedience—namely, that subjects are bound to obey all commands issued by superiors; excommunication; and simony, which, so the inscription read, "the clergy for the most part, alas! practise." In regard to the fifth, excommunication, the inscription ran: "It is an error that every excommunication, just or unjust, binds the excommunicated person and separates him from the communion of Christ's faithful and deprives him of the sacraments." Epinge's name I do not find in Schulte or Chevalier.

[2] These six reasons for standing in fear even of an unjust sentence of excommunication, Huss quotes from memory, leaving out one which he had given in his *de sex Erroribus, Mon.*, 1 : 240. Some of these reasons he sets forth

Then, in regard to the excommunication, by which the wicked separate the good from themselves, this should be said, that the wicked excommunicated Christ and the man born blind, as appears in John 9 : 22, 34. This kind of excommunication may be distinguished also from its opposite, which is communion in evil, of which it is said: "Have no communion with the unfruitful works of darkness," Eph. 5 : 11; and, "He that giveth him greeting communes in his evil works," II John 11; and, "What communication has a saint with a dog?" Ecclesiasticus 13, as if he had said, None! Therefore, every one being in grace in respect to present righteousness is excommunicated [out of communion with] from the wicked. And this is that holy excommunication by which the righteous is said to be excommunicate, that is, placed outside of communication or participation with wickedness. Hence, John says: "And I heard another voice from heaven saying, Come forth, my people, out of her, that ye have no participation with her sins and that ye receive not of her plagues, for her sins have reached even unto heaven," Rev. 18 : 4, 5. Let us ask the Lord that He may vouchsafe to preserve us in His communion and guard us against unlawful communion.

there more clearly, for example, 3, which there reads: "The injury to neighbors which might easily arise as a result of the excommunication as, for example, the deprivation of wholesome teaching and sacraments, for he who wrongly excommunicates sometimes is the cause of the perdition of many through the withholding from the excommunicate teaching by which he would be instructed most profitably in the law of Christ." And the fifth there reads: "That the neighbors may not sin by avoiding him, cursing him, and withholding from him the works of charity." Huss's treatment of the subject of excommunication in the de sex Erroribus is more clear and practical than his treatment in this chapter. There he introduces many pertinent quotations from the Fathers and especially from the Scriptures which are not given here, as, for example, Num. 23 : 8: "How shall I curse whom God hath not cursed?" On the other hand, he leaves out there the distinction between the major and minor excommunications and the prolonged explanations of communication and excommunication. The cases of Balaam and Ananias Huss uses often, e. g., Mon., 1 : 362, 401.

CHAPTER XXIII

SUSPENSION AND THE INTERDICT

Now of suspension this is to be said that, in the statement, to suspend is an administrative act or to prohibit any good thing on account of a criminal offence. Hence, what the old decretals call suspension the new law and decretals call the interdict, and then they speak of ecclesiastical suspension from an office or from a church benefice or of an ecclesiastical interdict from executing an office of the church.

This definition of suspension, therefore, being laid down, it is to be noted that, just as it is proper in itself in the first instance for God to excommunicate a man, so also it is proper for Him in the first instance to suspend him. Hence it is impossible for a pope or bishop to suspend any one justly, except as he has been before suspended of God, just as it is impossible for the pope to think anything righteously unless the thought be before suggested of God. Hence the apostle rightly says: "Not that we are sufficient of ourselves to think anything as of ourselves, but our sufficiency is of God," II Cor. 3 : 5. And the supreme Bishop himself said: "Apart from me ye can do nothing," John 15 : 5. From this it is clear that a suspension pronounced by a prelate is only worth as much as God almighty makes it to be worth. Hence, God's efficient suspension extends itself to priests, kings and every one in authority whom He removes from office or whom He takes from life by a decree of retribution. Hence, He suspends any one from the sacerdotal dignity, as it is written: "Because thou hast rejected knowledge, I will also reject thee. Thou shalt be no priest to me," Hosea 4 : 6; "Bring no more vain oblations," Isaiah 1 : 13; and "I have no

275

pleasure in you, neither will I accept an offering at thy hand,"
Mal. 1 : 10. And Christ's apostle suspended all who were
guilty of criminal offence from the ministry of Christ's body
and blood and the Lord, as he said: "Wherefore whoso shall
eat the bread and drink the cup of the Lord in an unworthy
manner shall be guilty of the body and blood of the Lord,"
I Cor. 11 : 27. Likewise, we read of the severe suspension
of Eli and his family, in that he did not duly correct his sons,
as the Lord said to Eli: "Wherefore kick ye at my sacrifices
and my offerings which I have commanded that they should
be offered in my temple and honorest thy sons above me, to
make yourselves fat with all the chiefest of the offerings of
Israel my people? Therefore the Lord saith to Israel, I said
indeed that thy house and the house of thy father should
minister for ever before me, but now the Lord saith, Be it
far from me, for he who honoreth me, him will I honor, and
they that despise me shall be lightly esteemed. Behold the
days come that I will cut off thy arm and the arm of thy
father's house . . . and this shall be the sign unto thee that
shall come upon thy two sons, on Hophni and Phinehas; in
one day they shall die, both of them. And I will raise me
up a faithful priest, who shall do according to my heart and
my mouth," I Sam. 2 : 29–35. Likewise, of the suspension
of the king, Saul, who, in the face of God's commandments
had spared God's enemies, we read: "Because thou hast
rejected the word of the Lord, the Lord also hath rejected
thee from being king," I Sam. 15 : 23.

It is plain how suspension varies, for one is a suspension from office, one from a benefice or from some other
good from which the sinner is justly suspended on account
of open sin. Likewise, there is a suspension in fact and a
suspension by law and there are other sorts of suspension.
But, as has been said, suspension by law belongs chiefly to
God to originate and regulate, but suspension in fact occurs
when God sometimes through good, sometimes through bad,

ministers suspends by the natural order of things any offend-
ing prelate from his office and ministry when he is actually
in criminal offence.   For he sins by the very fact that he
falls into mortal sin, whatever it be that he may do, and
consequently he is forbidden of God to sin in that way, and
consequently he is suspended by God from that office.   Hence,
the prophet says: "God said unto the sinner, What hast
thou to do, to declare my statutes, and that thou hast taken
my covenant in thy mouth? seeing thou hatest instruction
and castest my words behind thee.   When thou sawest a thief
thou rannest with him, and hast been a partaker with adul-
terers.   Thy mouth abounds in evil and thy tongue blabbeth
deceit.   Thou sittest and speakest against thy brother and
thou settest up slander against thy mother's son," Psalm
50 : 16–20.   Here God enumerates the sins for which He suspends the sinner from the publication of His covenant which
is the law of truth.   The first sin is disobedience to God,
the second, rejection of His words; the third, theft; the fourth,
adultery; the fifth, wickedness of mouth, which divides itself
into lies, blasphemy, false testimony, deceit, slander, vain
speaking, malediction, base speaking, and such like; the sixth,
the sin of taking offence at Christ.

From this we gather how rare are judges, preachers and
others who publish God's covenant to the people who should
not be suspended of God from the publication of that covenant.   Therefore, let the faithful note in the matter of suspension just spoken of from the office of publishing God's
covenant and for the threefold example spoken of above
whether or not our prelates and clerics are suspended of
God.   First, if they thrust from themselves the knowledge
of Scriptures and the task of evangelization, then are they
suspended by God, as in the lesser case [that is, preaching
under the O. T.] we read in Hosea 4, for our prelates have,
on the one hand and the other, greater material for preaching and a better model and also certain reasons for preach-

ing above what the priests of the old law had, and yet they exercise this office less. Therefore, as there is a greater reason now underlying the duty to preach, and as the same Lord is present, who is not able to withhold final vengeance in view of the greater sin in not preaching, and the demands of His justice, it is clear that if our prelates are of this kind, they are under a more severe suspension. Yea, and they are under a still more severe suspension in so far as they are under more urgent obligation to fervently proclaim Christ's law in these times of antichrist.

So far as the second kind of suspension goes—that of Eli pronounced by God—the faithful should note whether our prelates either do not punish at all or punish their spiritual sons as more guilty than the natural sons of Eli, who were punished of God. And in order to discern their greater guilt, the faithful ought to note these two things: (1) that a prelate is under greater obligation to his spiritual son than any one by the law of reason is to his natural son and (2) that more detestable is the punishment meted out on account of the lack of money for which [pardon for] sin is sold than is a punishment remitted for the vindication of an injury against God out of natural affection, as Eli seems to have spared his sons. So far as the third kind of suspension goes, as it holds for prelates, kings, and other secular princes, let the faithful note that the prelates show more favor to the public enemies of God for the sake of their own comfort than Saul showed to Amalek moved by lust for his temporal goods. If this is so, then there is no doubt but that the same God who at all times must exercise the same justice punishes the delinquent more severely. Therefore, it is an evident mark of the severity of punishment that God puts off punishment till after death and does not punish them in this life in any other way but permits them to wander about in mundane prosperity as reprobates who are not reproved.

But, alas, this threefold suspension men do not think of, and especially ought those higher in worldly rank often revolve in their minds the way in which they may be suspended from office and from benefice forever. Hence, on the words, "The Lord in his anger said to Moses, Take all the chiefs of the people and hang them up before the sun on the gallows," Num. 25 : 4, Origen, *Hom.* 20, speaks thus: "The Lord said unto Moses that he should take all the chiefs and hang them up to the Lord before the sun. The people sin and the chiefs are hung up before the sun, that is, they are brought forward that they may be examined, and may be convicted by the light. Thou seest what was the condition of the chiefs of the people. Not only were they convicted for their own transgressions but they were also obliged to give a reason for the sins of the people lest perhaps the guilt was theirs that the people came short, and lest perhaps they had not taught nor moved nor been solicitous to convict those who were first in the guilt that the contagion might not be spread among many. For the leaders and doctors ought to do all these things, for, if they do not and have no concern for the common people, the people sin, and they themselves are held up and brought forth to receive sentence. Moses, that is, God's law, convicts them as neglectful and indolent, and the wrath of God is turned against them and withdrawn from the people. If men would think of these things, they would never desire the chiefs of the people or go to them. For it is sufficient for me, if I am convicted of my own sins and shortcomings, it is sufficient for me to render a reason for my own self and for my own sins. Why is it necessary for me also to be held up for the people's sins before the sun, in the face of which nothing can be hidden or kept dark or veiled?" And Origen adds, "the chiefs are held up before the sun and, if guilt is found in them, God's anger ceases towards the people." So much Origen, who shows how chiefs are heavily censured for the sin of self-indulgence which the people practise.

Woe, therefore, to the modern spiritual and secular princes who themselves practise self-indulgence, who give to their subjects a bad example and do not reprove them or, if they reprove them, do this out of avarice! Such, without doubt, are suspended from office by God, for it is written in the papal law, Decretals, 3, *de vita et honestate* [Friedberg, 2 : 455]:[1] "We command your brotherhood that, as far as the clerics of your[2] jurisdiction are concerned, who are in the subdiaconate or the orders above it, if they have mistresses, ye should studiously take care to admonish them that they remove from themselves these women who least of all ought to have been admitted. But, if they refuse to acquiesce, ye shall suspend them from their ecclesiastical benefices until they make condign satisfaction, and if they who are suspended presume to keep these women, ye shall see to it that ye remove them permanently from those benefices." Because there is no defect in the law but in the superiors who ought to practise it, therefore, the pope in the preceding chapter says that prelates who may presume to hold on in their iniquities to such persons, especially for the sake of getting money or some other temporal good, them we wish to subject to the same punishment. And it is said by the authority of St. Gregory, *Dist.* 83 [Friedberg, 1 : 293]: "If any bishop shall assent to the fornication of clerics for a price or at their petitions and not assail their authority, he ought to be suspended from his office."[3] And this suspen-

---

[1] The heading of the chapter in the Decretals is: "The cohabitation of clerics with women." The quotation is from Alexander III's letter to the archbishop of Canterbury. A part of the letter, not quoted by Huss, speaks "of the depraved and detestable custom which had prevailed in England for a long time, of clerics having mistresses in their houses." William the Conqueror did not enforce celibacy and a council at Winchester, 1076, allowed priests already married to retain their wives, prohibiting marriages thereafter. Councils under Anselm, 1102, 1108, ordered priests to dismiss their concubines, but Eadmer, Anselm's biographer, declares that few priests observed the chastity Anselm called for, and Pascal II, writing to Anselm, said most of the English priests were married. In Bohemia the law of celibacy was also late of enforcement.

[2] Huss's text wrongly has *nostræ*—our.

[3] I have restored some of the omitted words from the canon law for the sake of clearness.

sion, according to the archdeacon,[1] ought to be permanent, equivalent to deposition, because of the difficulty of assembling the bishops for the purpose of deposing such bishops or bishop who simoniacally have sold or sell righteousness. And because a metropolitan—as is the Roman pontiff—may be slow so far as his cardinals are concerned in the execution of this holy duty, therefore, in the third place, they have ordained laws intended to remedy the disorders, namely, that the mass of the priest shall not be heard from him to whom it is notorious that that priest is living in fornication, nor shall the goods of the church be administered to him to encourage the deed.   For Pope Nicolas, *Dist.* 32, *Nullus* [Friedberg, 1 : 117], says: "Let no one hear a mass said by a presbyter of whom he knows beyond a peradventure that he is keeping a concubine."[2]   Hence, Alexander II in the same place says: "We charge and command that no one hear mass said by a presbyter of whom he knows beyond a peradventure that he has a concubine."   And he goes on to say: "Therefore the holy synod [Roman synod, 1063] also decreed this under the head of excommunication, when it said: 'Whatsoever priest, deacon, or subdeacon, in view of the constitution passed by our predecessor of blessed memory, holy Pope Leo [IX] or Nicolas [II], on the chastity of the clergy, shall again take a concubine or not give up the one he already has, we in the stead of Almighty God and by the authority of the princes, Peter and Paul, charge and wholly forbid that he sing mass or read the Gospel or the Epistle in the missal service or that he remain in the presbytery with those who, in performance of divine service, have been obedient to the aforesaid constitution or that he receive anything from the church.'"   On this the archdeacon says: "That the people ought to withhold from such a one vol-

[1] One of the glossators of the *Liber Sextus*, Guido de Baysio, archdeacon of Bologna, d. 1313.

[2] The decretal adds *aut subintroductam mulierem*—a woman secretly introduced.

untary tithes, because a benefice is not given except for the
performance of duty. And inasmuch as the same sentence
or a greater one holds for spiritual fornication, which is a
greater offence, it is evident that the inferior ought to be
suspended by the superior prelate, namely, for the spiritual
sin—which is more grave—whatever it may be. And as it
is certain that Luciferian pride in a prelate, neglect of evangelizing and avarice like that of Iscariot are sins more grave
than carnal fornication, it is plain that the supreme prelate,
Christ Jesus, to whom these graver sins are chiefly known,
does not withhold suspension on any excuse proportioned
to the guilt. From these things, when the condition of the
church is inquired into, it is gathered that from pope down
to the lowest priest rarely is one exempt for a given time from
suspension unless it be he who blamelessly follows the Lord
Jesus Christ. For it has already been said how fornicators
are suspended. Likewise of simoniac clerics, *Quicumque* by
Gregory, and *Reper.* by Ambrose [1: 1 : *cap.* 2, 7; Friedberg, 1 : 358, 359]. Likewise clerics are suspended for brood-
ing over[1] base gains and lucre," *Dist.* 88 [Friedberg, 1 : 307].
And since all these persons, in view of the law of Christ, minister to the church unworthily, it is clear how manifold are
the irregularities and profanations which the clergy of the
church are involved in.

Of profanation I have treated in the tract *contra adver-
sarium occultum*,[2] showing how every wicked presbyter pro-
fanes—that is, violates, curses, and contaminates—God's spiritual temple. For, to follow the saints in their lives is un-

---

[1] Pope Gelasius uses the word *imminere* where Huss uses *incubantes*—brood-
ing.

[2] "Against the Hidden Adversary," *Mon.*, 1 : 168–179. This treatise, written 1412 in reply to an attack that Huss was destroying the law and also destroying the priesthood by his preaching, brings out: (1) That the wickedness
of the people and the priests brought about the destruction of Jerusalem, and
(2) that by driving out the hucksters from the temple and by many in-
stances in the O. T. it was taught that secular princes have the duty of pun-
ishing simoniac priests by withdrawing from them their livings.

doubtedly more honorable than all material temples, which will not last after the day of judgment. And woe is me, if I keep silence, not assailing the avarice or the evident luxury of the clergy. For it is said, *Dist.* 83 [84, 85, Friedberg, 1 : 292 *sq.*], an error not resisted is an error approved and the truth, inasmuch as it is defended least, is oppressed. Indeed, as one is able to convict[1] perverse persons, to neglect to do so is nothing else than to favor them. And there is not lacking the suspicion of a hidden fellowship in the case of him who neglects to oppose a deed evidently bad. For what does it profit him not to be polluted with another's error if he gives assent to the one who errs? For he evidently assents to him who is in error who does not help him to cut out those things that ought to be reproved.

Hence St. Gregory, *Pastoral Theology, cap.* 15 [2 : 4, *Nic. Fathers*, 2d Ser., 12 : 11], quotes Lam. 2 : 14, "Thy prophets have seen for thee false and foolish visions and they have not uncovered thy iniquity to provoke thee to repentance," and says: "Indeed in the sacred oracle the prophets are sometimes called doctors, who, while they present the present as fleeting, declare the things that are to come as evident. And the divine discourse asserts: 'They have seen false things,' for while they fear to correct guilt, they, in vain, flatter the sinning by promises of safety, because they never in any way uncover the iniquity of the sinning. For they suppress the voice of chiding. Indeed the key which opens is the word of reproof. For by chiding the voice uncovers guilt, of which often he himself is not aware who is chargeable with it." These words of St. Gregory are also found, *Dist.* 43, *sit rector* [Friedberg, 1 : 154].

Oh that our doctors would turn to these things, for then they would not speak fair of the life of prelates and they would not be slow to uncover to them their iniquity, that they might provoke them to penitence. They would see in

---

[1] *Posset arguere.* The original has *possis perturbare.*

how many ways one may consent to the open sin of another, for he consents who co-operates, who defends, who gives counsel, and sanctions, and also who neglects to threaten and rebuke.

Now, in regard to the interdict with which, on account of the sin of a single man, or of a number, the clergy vex Christ's common people—*plebs*.[1] For by the three censures, excommunication, suspension and interdict, for their own exaltation they keep the laity at their feet, increase their avarice, protect wickedness and prepare the way for antichrist. And all three censures they heap up on the ground of [as a punishment for] disobedience in this way, that every one that does not obey them and yield to their will, him they excommunicate or suspend from office, and when he continues to resist their will, they place the interdict over the people, interdicting the exercise of divine services, the display of the sacrament, burial—and these things they interdict to men altogether righteous, that they may carry out their will by the deliberate imposition of such burdens.

But this is an evident sign that these censures proceed from antichrist; and these they call in their legal proceeding fulminations when they are directed against those who preach Christ's law and who show up the wickedness of the clergy. A second sign is that these censures are multiplied on account of disobedience done to themselves rather than on account of disobedience done to God and, therefore, rather on account of the injury done to themselves than for the injury done to our God. For in this way the old enemy, skilled in wickedness, proceeds, by exalting obedience to antichrist above obedience to Christ, and so he usurps, for disobedience to himself, that excommunication which Christ instituted for disobedience to God.

[1] Luther, in his Address to the German Nobility, called for the abolition of the interdict altogether on the ground that it is a greater sin to silence God's Word and service than if we were to kill twenty popes at once, not to speak of a single priest.

And he proceeds after this fashion: He infames Christ's disciple, later accuses, and then cites him, excommunicates and suspends him, and, if he cannot bring him into prison or death, he then invokes the secular arm and, if he cannot vanquish him in this way, he superimposes by his wickedness the interdict. Chiefly, however, he proceeds in this fashion against those who lay bare the malignity of antichrist, who has monopolized the clergy in largest measure for himself. Therefore, he launches these censures for the sake of his clergy, notably those engaged in litigation out of greed for benefices and at such times as the people have not given their tithes according to promise, or in case the prince has seized or received the temporal things, or if any cleric—even though he be the most iniquitous thief or otherwise taken in crime—has been held in custody by the secular authorities, or if a priest has been wounded to the shedding of blood, or even when the people lawfully have withdrawn for a time their obedience from their prelates. But Christ, the high priest, when the prophet was imprisoned, than whom no greater has arisen born of women, did not impose the interdict, nay not even when Herod beheaded him. Yea, when he himself was stripped, beaten and blasphemed by the soldiers, scribes, Pharisees, officers, and priests, not even then did he pronounce any malediction, but he prayed, saying: "Father forgive them, for they know not what they do," Luke 23 : 34. And this doctrine he gave to his members, saying: "Love your enemies, do good to them that hate you, and pray for them that persecute you, that ye may be sons of your Father which is in heaven, for He maketh His sun to rise on the good and the evil, and sendeth rain on the just and the unjust," Matt. 5 : 44, 45.

Therefore, following this doctrine in word and work, Christ's first vicar, the Roman pontiff, also taught the faithful, saying: "Hereunto were ye called, because Christ also suffered for us, leaving us an example, that we should follow[1]

---

[1] The Vulgate has *sequamini*—ye should follow.

his steps: who did no sin, neither was guile found in his mouth: who when he was reviled, reviled not again, and when he suffered, threatened not," I Peter 2 : 21–23. And Paul traversing the same path, said: "Bless them that persecute you; bless and curse not," Romans 12 : 14. This doctrine the other saints also followed, who, in the time of persecution did not fulminate excommunication or suspension or impose the interdict, but when more serious persecution came, the more urgent were they in performing divine ministries.

But after the thousand years, when Satan was loosed and the clergy was fat with the refuse[1] of this world and lifted up in pleasure, pride, and ease, the interdict had its origin. For Pope Hadrian, who began to reign 1153, for a wound which one cardinal had received, placed all Rome under the interdict. Oh, how patient under trial was that pope—not, indeed, as Christ, Peter, or Paul, or the apostle Andrew! Later Alexander III also, who began to rule 1159, placed the interdict on the kingdom of England,[2] *de Sponsalibus*, *cap. 2, Non est vobis* [Friedberg, 2 : 665]. Pope Celestine III, who began to reign A. D. 1082, says something about the interdict in chap. *Quæsivit de majoritate et obedientia* [Friedberg, 2 : 506]. Later Innocent III, who began to rule 1199 A. D., announced the interdict in many decretals, as in chap. *in concilio Lateranensi de præbendis, lib. 3 Decretalium* [5 : 28 *sqq.*, Friedberg, 2 : 478 *sqq.*]. Still later Boniface VIII, Innocent IV and Clement V imposed interdicts of this kind, in the *Liber Sextus* and the *Clementines* [Friedberg, 2 : 937 *sqq.*]. And in this way many such interdicts have been multiplied, while the clergy were inflamed with avarice, the pomp of this world and restless ambition.

---

[1] The word used by the Vulgate, Phil. 3 : 8.

[2] Hadrian IV, the only English pope, one of whose cardinals was murdered during the excitement caused by the presence and preaching of Arnold of Brescia. Henry II of England was threatened with the interdict by Alexander III, 1173, in case he did not deliver up to his sons their wives.

Hence I always wish to know the ground or reason of the general interdict by which the righteous without demerit of their own are deprived of the sacraments, such as communion, confession, and others, and at times infants are deprived of baptism; similarly why it is that the divine ministries of God are reduced in the case of righteous men by an interdict issued on account of one single individual.[1] Exceedingly wonderful would it be if service was withdrawn from an earthly king by all good servants on account of one of the servants who was opposed to him.   And especially wonderful would this be if, on account of one that was a good and faithful servant of the king, a vassal, wishing to bend him to his own will, should interdict all the king's servants to do ministry to the king himself.   How, therefore, does a pope or bishop so inadvisedly, without support of Scripture or revelation, interdict with such extraordinary ease ministry to the king, Christ?   For when a general interdict is laid upon a city or diocese, sin does not decrease but rather increases.   For to the righteous, sepulture is denied contrary to Scripture: "Thou shalt not withhold favor from the dead," Ecclesiasticus 7 : 33.   For who doubts but that to bury the righteous dead is a work of mercy, for the angel Raphael addressed Tobias thus: "When thou didst pray with tears and bury thy dead and didst leave thy repast and hiddest the dead in thy house, and didst bury them in the night—I carried thy prayer to the Lord," Tobias 12 : 12, 13.   Who even doubts that to hear confession and consult unto salvation and to preach the Word of God are works of mercy?   Sim-

---

[1] In consequence of the interdict pronounced over Prague by John XXIII, 1411, Huss withdrew at the advice of King Wenzel from the city and remained in semi-voluntary exile for two years, until he started for Constance October, 1414.   He was in doubt whether he had done right in withdrawing, denying that he had "fled from the truth" and instancing the case of Christ, "who escaped out of the hands" of his enemies.   He insisted that he was actuated by a purpose not to prevent the ministrations of the Gospel to the innocent by his presence in Prague.   See Schaff, *Life of John Huss*, and Huss's letters written during his exile, *Doc.*, 34–66.

ilarly to present the sacrament of the eucharist to the devout
people and to baptize are works of mercy. What, therefore,
is the reason for withdrawing these things from the people
of God without any demerit on their part?

Hence St. Augustine writes to Bishop Maximus,[1] 24 : 3
[Friedberg, 1 : 987 *sqq.*]: "If thou hast a judgment about
this matter, based on sure reasoning or Scripture testimonies,
wilt thou deign to teach us how a son may be righteously
anathematized for the sins of his father, or a wife for the sin of
her husband, or a servant for the sin of his master, or how any
one in the household, yea a child not yet born—if born at
the time, when the household is held under the band of anathema—why it should not be healed by the laver of regen-
eration if it were in danger of death? For this was bodily
punishment of which we read that some despisers of God
with all their households, which had been partakers of the
same impiety, perished among the saints.[2] Then forsooth,
that the living might be struck with fear, the mortal bodies
which were destined sometime to die were destroyed. But
the spiritual punishment of which it is written, 'Whatsoever thou shalt bind on earth shall be bound in heaven,'
binds souls, and of them it is said, As the soul of the father is
mine, so is the soul of the son mine. 'The soul that sinneth
it shall die' [Ezek. 18 : 20]. Ye perhaps have heard of some
priests of great name who anathematized some sinner including his household, but if perchance they were ever asked about
it, it would be found that they did not give me a fitting
reason [for the act]. But, if any one should ask me whether
it was done rightly I do not find anything to reply to them.
I have never dared to do this thing for any deeds done against
the church, without having admonished most solemnly. But,
if God has revealed to thee that this was done righteously,

---

[1] The *Decretum* and also *Nic. Fathers*, 1 : 589 *sq.*, give it as a letter to
Auxilius, probably bishop of Murco.

[2] *Periisse inter sanctos.* The *Decretum* has *pariter interfectos:* "were likewise put to death."

I will under no circumstances despise your youth or the beginnings of your ecclesiastical honor, for I am ready to learn, an old man from a young, a bishop of so many years' experience from my colleague not yet a little year old in his office —I am ready to learn how I may give a good reason to God or men, if we punish by spiritual punishment innocent souls for another's offence which they do not derive from Adam, in whom all have sinned. For, although Clazianus, a son, drew from his parents the corruption of the first man—which is to be expiated in the sacred font of baptism—nevertheless, who doubts that some of the sin which his father, after begetting him, confessed did not belong to the child, seeing he did not actively partake of it? What shall I say of his wife? What of so many souls belonging to the whole family? Therefore, if one soul, through this severity, with which this whole household was anathematized, should, in passing out of the body, perish without baptism, the death of innumerable bodies, if innocent men are to be violently drawn from the church and put to death, is not to be compared with this damning injury. If, therefore, thou art able to give a reason for this event, would that thou wouldst honor us in writing back in order that we also may be able to give an answer; but if not, it may be possible for thee to give a reason for your acting in inconsiderate excitement of mind. Hence, if thou shouldst be asked, thou wouldst not be able to present a right reply." Thus much Augustine.

From these things Gratian draws the following conclusion: "Therefore, it is plainly shown by authority that a person is illegally excommunicated who is excommunicated for the sin of another." And back of them they have no reason whatever who, for the sin of a single person, lay the sentence of excommunication upon an entire family. An illegal excommunication, however, hurts not the person cited, but only the person who excommunicates. Hence it is to be noted that the Gloss of the *Decretum,* summarizing the chapter, says concerning these words of St. Augustine: "That that bishop had excommunicated Clazianus's whole family for Clazianus's sin, and that seemed to him the right thing to do, because one is sometimes punished with corporal punishment for the sins of another and also because some priests of great name have excommunicated certain persons for sins not their own. In the first part of the chapter Augustine asks of him [Maximus] the cause and reason of his judgment. Later he teaches that none of the reasons aforesaid suffice to confirm his sentence. Thirdly, he comes down to the specific act itself and proves that the sentence issued against the family of Clazianus was unjust. And, finally, he advises the bishop that if he is not willing to give a reason for the judgment, he ought to abandon his error and follow the truth." Thus far the Gloss.

Would, therefore, that those who excommunicate would heed the saying of St. Augustine together with the Gloss, and also they who impose a general interdict for the sake of a single man in the church or the state. Why do they afflict with excommunication and the interdict a community which is not guilty and altogether deprive the good and devoted presbyters of the exercise of the divine ministry and God's devoted people of the sacraments and God Himself, who is therein set forth, of honor, the dead of burial, and often infants of baptism, without which they pass away and are damned, according to the judgment of Augustine? Here the Gloss of the *Decretum* says on these words: "In case one soul through this severity, by which that whole household was anathematized, should perish, passing out of the body without baptism, the death of innumerable bodies, if innocent men are violently removed from the church, is not to be compared with this injury." The Gloss, *Argumentum*, says: "Greater is the sin if one soul perish through the sin of unbelief than if they should put to death the bodies of innumerable martyrs for God's sake." This seems to correspond to the very letter,

namely: "If the innocent are removed out of the church, and
the bodies of martyrs perish, it is not an injury but in popular speech it is said there has been homicide." Likewise, the
Gloss says: "More grievously does he sin, by whose guilt a
boy's soul goes out of this life without baptism, than he who
should destroy many innocent persons by violently removing
them from the church."

But, alas! all such things as these the clergy, blinded by
wickedness, do not receive, who, on account of the non-pay-
ment, now and then, of a little money, deprive by interdict,
as has been said, the people of the sacraments of the church.
Not so did Christ teach, who above all taught that the clergy
ought not to contend by resort to law, when he said: "To
him that smiteth thee on the one[1] cheek offer also the other;
and to him that taketh away thy cloak withhold not thy
coat also. Give to every one that asketh thee and of him
that taketh away thy goods ask them not again," Luke
6 : 29–30. But the clergy, at ease, hearing this most salutary teaching of Christ, ridicule it. Nor is this to be wondered at, for the Saviour says later: "Every one that heareth these words of mine and doeth them not, shall be likened
to a foolish man who built his house upon the sand," Matt.
7 : 26.

Who, I say, is a more foolish man than the cleric who
grounds himself in the refuse of this world and holds Christ's
life and teachings in derision? To such a low pitch is the
clergy come that they hate those who preach often and call
Jesus Christ Lord. And, when any one claims Christ for
himself, immediately with carping mouth and angry face they
say: Art thou the Christ? and after the manner of the Pharisees denounce and excommunicate those who confess Christ.
Hence, because I have preached Christ and his Gospel and
have uncovered antichrist, desiring that the clergy may live
in accord with Christ's law, the prelates first arranged with

[1] *Unam* is wanting in the Vulgate.

Lord Zbynek, the archbishop of Prague, to secure a bull from Pope Alexander that in the chapels the Word of God should not be preached to the people. And from this bull I have appealed and never have I been able to secure a hearing. Therefore, being cited, I have on reasonable grounds not appeared because this excommunication was secured through Michael de Causis,[1] after we had made an agreement, and now at last they have procured the interdict with which they vex Christ's common people who are without guilt.

Therefore, I could wish that the doctors, who say that in the acts of procedure nothing absolutely good is forbidden, nor anything absolutely evil enjoined but only things intermediate, would prove that these things are so, and that they would prove that an interdict so general is a thing intermediate, something between what is absolutely good and what is absolutely evil, depriving the innocent of the sacraments and sepulture, interrupting the exercise of the divine ministries and leading to no good, but to offences, distractions and hatred. And how would the doctors be able to show that it is lawful to excommunicate God's people from the sacraments and sepulture and from divine ministries? For it was about this, as has been said, that that most able doctor of the church, St. Augustine, confutes Bishop Auxilius. And the proof of the doctors, which is a combination of hypocritical excuse and the reasoning of rustics, would not satisfy Augustine as reasonable when they say: "According to the method customary with the church and the Roman curia and observed by it." See what a hypocritical excuse that is! "Before the fathers of our fathers." What a rustic method of reasoning that is! "Here only things indifferent are commanded." O doctors, of what church is this the

---

[1] Michael the Pleader, a title given to the Prague magister, Michael of Deutschbrod, by the pope. At first Huss's friend, he became one of his most bitter and persistent enemies. No sooner had Huss reached Constance than Michael posted up charges against him and went about stirring up the members of the council against him.

method? Of the apostolic church? What apostle observed this method or what saint after the apostles? Never was it the method of Christ, that head of the holy church, in whose method all truth useful for the church is contained.

But I ask where is this saying found: "Every place, city, walled town, villa, or castle, privileged or not privileged, to which the same John Huss may have gone, and how long soever he may remain and how long soever he may tarry, and for three natural days after his departure from such places, we, by these writings, do put them under such a great ecclesiastical interdict and wish that divine ministries be stopped in them"?

Perhaps that method is founded on these words: "Men ought always to pray and not to faint," Luke 18 : 2, or on these: "Praise God all ye peoples," and these: "In every place praise ye the Lord." And what will the authors of the method say, if it should happen that John Huss came to the holy city, Jerusalem, in which cherubim and seraphim cease not to cry daily with one voice, saying: "Holy, holy, holy, Lord God of Sabaoth"? Will they then stop these ministries there in obedience to the fulmination, just as if Christ, the righteous advocate, would not intercede to God the Father for his faithful members or that the angelic choir would not sing: "Holy, holy, holy, Lord God of Sabaoth"? Will that voice stop of which John says: "I heard a voice of many angels round about the throne and the living creatures and the elders, and the number of them was thousands of thousands saying with a great voice, 'Worthy is he[1] that hath been slain to receive the power, and the riches, and wisdom, and might, and honor, and glory, and blessing'; and every created thing which was in the heavens and which is on the earth, under the earth, and in the sea and all things that are in them," Rev. 5 : 11–13? And let not the doctors say that this is not pertinent, for all rational creatures, ac-

[1] The "Lamb," *Agnus*, of the Vulgate is omitted.

cording to the method practised by the Roman curia, are subject to the curia's command, for every human creature is subject to the Roman pontiff, so it is said in the *Extravagante* of Boniface VIII [the bull *Unam sanctam*], namely: "Further we declare, say and define that it is altogether necessary for salvation for every human creature to be subject to the Roman pontiff." Similarly, the angelic world is subject to the Roman pontiff, as appears in the bull of Pope Clement: "We command the angels of paradise that they lead to the glory of paradise the soul of him who has been wholly absolved from purgatory."

Since, therefore, according to this method of the curia, every rational creature—angel and man—is subject to the commands of the Roman pontiff, and since the method in the processes of the same curia states that "whatsoever place, privileged or unprivileged, to which John Huss shall go, and as long as he may be there, we do subject them to the ecclesiastical interdict"—it follows that if, by the highest possibility, John Huss, according to God's absolute power, reached by death the heavenly Jerusalem, that city would be subject to the ecclesiastical interdict. But blessed be God Almighty, who has ordered that the angels and all the saints in that heavenly Jerusalem are not subject to an interdict of this sort! Blessed also be Christ, the chief Roman pontiff, who has given grace to his faithful ones that, when there is no Roman pontiff for a given time, they may, under Christ as their leader, arrive in the heavenly country! For who would say that while the woman Agnes, to all appearances, was for two years and five months the only pope, no one then could be saved? Or again, who would say that after a pope's death and in the interval between the pope's death and the election of his successor, no man dying in that period could be saved? Blessed also be God Almighty, who ordains that His militant church shall have such life that, when a pope is dead, she is not on that account without a head or dead!

Because not upon the pope but upon the head, Christ, does her life depend. And blessed be God that, when a pope is insane or become a heretic, the church militant remains the faithful spouse of the Lord Jesus Christ![1] Blessed also be the Lord, the one living head of the church, who preserves her so effectually in unity that, even now, while there are three so-called papal heads, she remains the one spouse of the Lord Jesus Christ!

For now Balthazar, called John XXIII, is in Rome; and Angelo Correr, called Gregory XII, is in Rimini; and Peter de Luna, called Benedict, is in Aragon. Why does not one of them, called most holy father, out of the fulness of power constrain the others with their adherents to submit to his jurisdiction? By authority of which one does the Roman curia speak; which one has fulness of power over every man on earth? Therefore, the foundation is feeble enough as a foundation and proof, to wit, that anything should be held to be inviolable which is announced by the Roman curia. For the rule is laid down, *de Constitutionibus, lib.* 6, [Friedberg, 2 : 937], that, when two persons having letters from the pope in regard to the same provision given on the same day, he to whom the pope offered the canonical office has the preference, to whom he did not give it without the knowledge of the executor[2] who first besought it. But if they are equally in grace, so far as the form of the papal brief goes, he who first presents it [in the diocese concerned] will have the stronger claim over the prebend. And, thirdly, if they were equal in these three things then the canons, to whom the collation pertains, or the greater part of them, are bound to proceed to an election, the one left out being de-

---

[1] In arguing for the superiority of a general council over the pope, Gerson took the ground that a pope may be deposed who is insane or heretical. The translator must confess that in this translation he has been inconsistent in treating church now as neuter, now as feminine.

[2] The executor, usually called procurator, is the legal representative who appears before the ecclesiastical superior or puts into execution a papal or episcopal mandate. See Hergenröther, *K.-recht,* 428; Friedberg, *K.-recht,* pp. 327, 359.

prived of the fruit of grace—unless from the tenor of the papal letters it expressly appear that the pope wished to provide for both of them. But this three-membered method of the curia seems to be a principle most contrary to Christ, because, if it be laid down, as for the most part happens, that the one placed in the canonical office, either by reason of the time of the presentation or the bestowment of grace or, thirdly, the election of the chapter is, in respect to God, somewhat less worthy than the one left out, then by this greatest thing called method, a sentence ought to be pronounced contrary to Christ. From this it follows that that greatest thing called method is contrary to the conscience, and consequently contrary to Christ. What sort of a proof, therefore, is this: "The method customary with the Roman curia and observed by it grants a thing or affirms a thing; therefore, that thing is to be received as consonant with Christ's law and as catholic"?

But this rustic mode of reasoning which the doctors lay down, that "before the fathers of our fathers" such and such a thing was believed and observed, would lead to the conclusion that the doctors themselves believe and observe false customs of the Gentiles and Jews, yea, that they ought to worship Baal, as the Bohemians worshipped him when they were Gentiles. They have for their case the words of Ezek. 20 : 18: "Walk ye not in the statutes of your fathers, neither observe their ordinances." How shameless, therefore, is this argument of the doctors, "before the fathers of our fathers" such or such a thing was believed, observed or held, therefore, it ought to be believed, observed or held by us. For such insipid arguments are made by unsanctified—*insulsi*, unsalted—men, to excuse excuses for sins. Of their number is not he who said: "We have sinned, O Lord, with our fathers; we have committed iniquity; we have done wickedly. Our fathers understood not thy wonders in Egypt; they remembered not the multitude of thy lovingkindnesses," Psalm 106 : 6, 7.

And if, perchance, the doctors should say that in their statement they mean by "the fathers of the fathers" the holy prophets or the apostles or the later saints, then would they be able to give their express writings against which no one would dare to rebel. And their urgency would cease which breaks down argument and reasoning, when they say that in the proceedings, following "the method of the church customary with the Roman curia and observed by it before the fathers of our fathers," only things intermediate are enjoined, things between what are absolutely good and what are absolutely evil. For which of the holy Fathers, prophets, apostles or other saints enjoins that, wherever even the worst of men might go, there they ceased from divine ministries? For Christ, seeing that most disobedient Judas, who was also his betrayer, did not cease from divine ministry at his great supper. Yea, with Judas sitting by, he exercised the divine ministry and gave to him his most holy and divine body to eat and only the more urgently admonished the disciples to watch and pray with him lest through the violent assault of the scribes, Pharisees and priests they should fall into temptation. And that most good pontiff did not withhold the most divine prayer when he was being blasphemed and crucified, but prayed for those that crucified him, saying: "Father, forgive them, for they know not what they do," Luke 23 : 34. "Hence, praying with a loud crying and tears, he was heard for his godly submission," Heb. 5 : 7. Hence, also, his true and real vicars, the apostles and other saints, have imitated him in this, and first of all Stephen, who said: "Lord Jesus, lay not this sin to their charge," for they know not what they do, Acts 7 : 60.

And it is wonderful how, in view of the Jews, who denied Christ to be God and so his whole law, they did not impose the interdict or in view of open simoniacs who are the chief heretics, and by writings of the apostles and other saints cursed, excommunicated, suspended and interdicted and aliens from the holy priesthood. The reason is because those simoniacs buy and sell excommunications, suspensions and interdicts, and with these as their weapons they feed and defend their simony most powerfully. And a proof is not necessary, for this simoniacal trafficking is patent even to the eye of rustics, who are bound, vexed, oppressed and plundered by these selfsame simoniacs. For to such proportions has this heresy of Simon Magus and Gehazi grown that men without compunction in season and out of season, and even the unwilling, are impelled on to this sort of criminal offence. And all trafficking of this sort arises from the method in vogue with the Roman curia, which practises it in turn with the curias of the bishops after the manner of Simon Magus and Gehazi. This appears in the dimissorial letters for confirmings, pardonings, admissions, and also in other things invented to get pecuniary plunders.[1]

Now, as to the condemnation of the XLV Articles,[2] it should be said—but I speak briefly—that up to this day the

---

[1] *Literæ dimissoriales* is the name given to licenses by ecclesiastical superiors, setting aside the usual ecclesiastical practices, whatever they may be, from pope down to priest, as, for example, when a bishop grants permission to ordain a candidate of his diocese to a bishop of another diocese. Huss is referring to licenses given by popes or bishops to agents to perform acts presumably for temporal favors. See Hergenröther, *K.-recht*, 236, 239, etc.

[2] The XLV Articles of Wyclif, action upon which was first taken at Prague by the university, 1403, and more recently and drastically, 1412, forbidding any to hold or teach them, they being heretical, seditious, scandalous and erroneous, *Doc.*, 451 *sq.* At the city hall of the Old Town King Wenzel had the prohibition of the articles publicly announced, *Doc.*, 456. It seems strange that Huss has not before mentioned these XLV Articles by name, which were the first cause of his troubles in Prague. In his Reply to Stanislaus, *Mon.*, 1 : 331 *sq.*, he starts out with a prolonged reference to them and reminds Stanislaus that he was one of the doctors of the theological faculty, all of whom now condemned the articles as heretical, etc., 1412, who originally had taken most positive ground on the other side and strenuously defended them. Likewise in his Reply to Palecz, Huss brings out into prominence the discussions over the XLV Articles and makes the statement that Palecz, who was one of the eight doctors who declared the articles heretical, at one time had defended them, and in a meeting at the university, throwing down one of Wyclif's writings on the table, had said that he was ready to defend it against any one who might attack even a single word extracted from it.

doctors of the city hall—*prætorium*—have not proved that a single one of them is heretical, erroneous or scandalous. And I wonder why at the present time the doctors do not teach in the city hall that the article about the withdrawal of temporal goods should not be put into practice, the reason, presumably, being this: that temporal lords may at their own discretion take away temporal goods from ecclesiastics who are habitually delinquent [in their living and duty]. But now they are silent as were the priests and Pharisees, and do not assemble at the city hall to condemn those who put this article into practice. And certainly because, as they feared, it is being applied to them and will be applied in the future. Let them lose their temporal goods but God grant they may preserve their souls.

The doctors kept saying that when the articles were once condemned, then there would be peace and harmony. But this, their prediction, is turned into the very opposite. For they rejoiced while they were condemning, and now they lament while they have to give up their taxes [ecclesiastical incomes]. They condemned this article—namely, that tithes are pure alms and only alms, but many coming into the city hall begged that their taxes—which are alms—be not withheld.[1] But certain lords of the city hall replied and said: Behold, ye yourselves before condemned the principle that tithes are pure alms and now ye are saying that, indeed, they are alms and so ye are acting contrary to your condemnation. So much for the present, other things being left to be discussed in the future.

[1] Huss is referring here to the dismissal of certain clerics of Prague from their positions, and the sequestrations of the incomes of others by the civil authorities during the troubles between the Huss party and the party opposed to him. Tithes had been treated by Huss in a separate treatise, *Mon.*, 1 : 156–167. Huss defined an alms as "a gift to help the body made for God's sake."

INDEX